The Marvels of Lambeth

"He hunted out lost manuscripts of Bacon's works. He encouraged Bacon's eccentric disciple, Thomas Bushell, to realize 'my lord Verulam's New Atlantis' in Lambeth Marsh."
—Trevor-Roper, p.284

Publications by Allen Fisher include:
POETRY
Gravity
Entanglement
Stroll And Strut Step
Place
singularity stereo
Quietly Random
Confidence in Lack
Leans
Birds
Proposals, 1-35
A Portable Allen Fisher (forthcoming)*

Publications by Andrew Duncan include:
POETRY
Anxiety before Entering a Room. New and selected poems
Skeleton Looking at Chinese Pictures
The Imaginary in Geometry
*Savage Survivals (amid modern suavity)**
*Threads of Iron**
*In Five Eyes**

CRITICISM
Centre and Periphery in Modern British Poetry
The Failure of Conservatism in Modern British Poetry
Origins of the Underground
*The Council of Heresy**
*The Long 1950s**

AS EDITOR
Don't Stop Me Talking (with Tim Allen)

The Marvels of Lambeth

Interviews and statements by Allen Fisher, 1973-2005

edited by
Andrew Duncan

Interviewers
Eric Mottram, R.A.C. Kiss, Peter Barry, Ken Edwards,
Adrian Clarke, Scott Thurston, Victoria Sheppard, Andrew Duncan.

Shearsman Books

First published in the United Kingdom in 2013 by
Shearsman Books Ltd
50 Westons Hill Drive
Emersons Green
BRISTOL
BS16 7DF

Shearsman Books Ltd Registered Office
30–31 St. James Place, Mangotsfield, Bristol BS16 9JB
(this address not for correspondence)

www.shearsman.com

ISBN 978-1-84861-273-0

Selection and editorial matter © Andrew Duncan, 2013.
Original texts by Allen Fisher excerpted here are copyright © Allen Fisher.
All other original material in this volume remains the copyright of the individual authors and interviewers listed.

The right of Andrew Duncan to be identified as the editor of this work
has been asserted by him in accordance with the
Copyrights, Designs and Patents Act of 1988.
All rights reserved.

Contents

Prosyncel preface	7
Editor's preface	9
Fluxshoe interview with Eric Mottram at the ICA 1973	11
Interview with Dr RAC Kiss, 1974	17
Statements on early works from *Prosyncel*	20
Interview with editors of *Alembic* 1976	29
Talk for *Alembic* 1978	38
Interview with Adrian Clarke 1986	53
Interview with Scott Thurston 1999	63
Interview with Victoria Sheppard 2003	77
The Curve of Increase (lost interview), 2004	93
Interview, 'Of mutabilitie', February 2005	104
Interview, 'In One Side and Out the Other', on music, May 2005	128
Interview on sources of *Stane*, May 2005	139
Interview, 'Mirrors for Waste Heat', August 2005	167
Statements on 'Place'	186
Passages from *Long Shout to Kernewek*, 1965	192
Synopsis	196
Interviewers	198

Preface by Sir Aylmer Firebrace to original 1909 Everyman edition of *Prosyncel*

Many men without attentive schooling have written a book. Many poachers, fired with fierce bitterness against the land-owning gentry, have enjoyed the friendship of their kind. These two facts alone mark Allen Fischer (*sic passim*) as a man of common character.

Hardly less surprising, this life-long poacher who at an early age mimicked John Keats and Jack Kerouac, where a whiff of love, a spoor in the mud, or a clipping from an ill-informed review in a copy of the *Times Literary Supplement* may reveal so much, found himself the victim of a perennial conflict between the pursuits in which he delighted and that passionate concern with social justice and politics which should have absorbed so much of his time. He was a poacher—and something of a local worker for a Plumbers' Merchant and Lead manufacturer—because lack of money or originality made him so; and those who knew him well noticed that the energy which flowed from his ten stone frame seemed to be kindled and released as much by the apathy around him as by Charlie Patton singing 'Stone Pony', matching his wits against irate plumbers and a board of directors with as much interest in their employees as most car drivers have for hedgehogs. He emerges then, a suppressed member of a "progressive" and progressively reactionary society willed into submission by a public that still considers instantaneous feeding, entertainment, art and satisfaction the truest road to their own particular heavens.

How this volume comes to be published forms a typical story; stirred by the chattering in literary public houses, I received a letter from one Opal L Nations asking me to edit a retrospective book covering the work of Allen Fisher. My grandson had previously reported to me that he was experiencing difficulty coming to grips with the work of a writer and poacher he had occasion to buy beer for by the name of John Bransbody who it seemed knew Allen Fischer. Would I care to tie the two together in a visit upon him?

I shall never forget the experience. First Mr Bransbody, a retarded documentor whose youth had been spent in Surrey, introduced me to a room where jars of "objects" emerged under the static dust.

Then, with somewhat mixed feelings, I saw my host's massive hoard of nostalgic objects, carefully boxed and labelled and firmly fixed in piles of manuscripts and newspapers. I admired his fine collection of empty jars and sauce bottles that made the very light vibrate as they rattled when the door slammed. Finally, I was shown his library. We handled an old edition of Thomas Net's *Tree-Birst* with an introduction by Allen Fisher and the familiar works of poets from the same age. And then seizing a red ring-bound volume that looked like a Dictionary; he said "You might like to see this book typed up by an old friend of mine."

"He presented it to me before we left our home in London."

Loose inside the cover was a set of news cuttings. There followed a list of contents and then a photograph of a reptile I had never seen the like of before. Curious, I began to read the manuscript headed PROSYNCEL.

"Born in the year 1909 (*sic passim*) in Surrey, my father was a Joiner by Trade my Mother a Housewife in a time when to be middle-class meant you spent all you earned to feed and live."

I paused and enquired who the author might be. It was then that I heard again of Allen Fischer, a skilful poacher whose friends found him as kindly as he was industrious. Yet such was his obscurity and cunning, his Englishness, that eventually he was unknown. The anonymous artist.

It was a surprising designation, for Fischer's politics were far removed from those of the local gentry who largely governed the neighbourhood of Lambeth and Wandsworth Boroughs. Even his enemies, however, acknowledged that Fischer was an honest rogue, a man who had taken to poaching because of hunger, not laziness, who maintained his habit to the end of his days because it absorbed and thrilled his whole being.

Preface by Acoustic Dredger

These are all explanations, but they are not all the explanations.

Sound is voluble, volatile, evacuating. It just goes everywhere. It doesn't always come back. My preoccupation during the series was with acoustics—some spaces either drain the sound away or overload the diaphragm with extraneous sound. I have hours of inaudible tapes and I know I don't understand the laws of cognitive acoustics.

The series took place while a *Companion to Allen Fisher* was being prepared by other hands. This timing was not perfect, because if I'd had that book in my hands, I could have perhaps avoided overlaps, perhaps broached different subjects in interview. There is a bibliography on the Fisher website (www.allenfisher.org), which relieves me of the task of making one in duplicate.

The first interview dates from 1973. I took the decision to collect old interviews rather than make an all-new book. I am fascinated by the idea of a very long base line, records of one person's views over 30 years, change as part of the object recorded. Drawing on the creative input of Eric Mottram, Adrian Clarke, and Victoria Sheppard (among others) made the book more robust and embracing. The trackless wastes of the Mottram tape archive made an especial call. Those interviews were so hard to find that I want to make them easy to find. Of course there may be interviews I've missed. I've also included some explanations from *Prosyncel*, which is now unavailable. You can still buy *Ideas on the Culture Dreamed of*, though. One of the tapes in Mottram's archive is a 1978 talk at the Alembic workshop—not an interview, but a talk about the poetic process. I scarfed this up. Another approach to Fisher's work would be to take about 100 of the resources in the Resources lists (in each of his books) and go away and read them. I can see that notes explaining who some of the people cited here (Robert Barry, Carolee Scheemann, and so on) are would be interesting. I just focussed on recovering the texts. Try the Internet. Ask around.

All those voices make a whole universe of discourse. 1973 seems like a vanished era, an unresurrectable city, not least because of the shared project of creation and discovery and new life, which most of the stakeholders pulled out of. The gap between the poetic projects which looked at the cosmos and wanted to compete with the great modernists, and poems which aim to fit into the gaps within the columns of prose magazines, cannot be bridged. The limits of attention are self-set. If you want to switch your brain off, the switch is just by your ear.

Large-scale republications of Fisher's work took place during 2005. I have included a few pages from a 1965 work which is harder to obtain.

My thanks to all the people who made and published (in *Alembic*, *Angel Exhaust*, and *Poetry Salzburg Review*) the original interviews, and to the staff of the Eric Mottram Archive.

Snatches from Interview with Eric Mottram at the ICA, London, 1973

(The focus of the event was avant-garde magazines and self-publishing and the problems they encountered. Other people being interviewed were Doug Lang and Opal L. Nations.)

Fluxshoe

AF So far as I know, it started in New York in 1961. I think the name was first coined by George Maciunas. With George Brecht and various people in New York found that their work wasn't presentable in galleries. Or at least that gallery owners were unwilling to accept their work. It wasn't for sale. It was objects that were found, objects that weren't objects, if you like, happenings, performances, things that weren't for sale, and through some sympathy I think more than anything else, there wasn't a manifesto, there isn't a Fluxus manifesto, they came together, and they found an attic. Dick Higgins' attic or someone's. And they got together and did various performances together, various works together, and a publishing house came out of that, called Something Else press, which Dick Higgins ran.

EM When did you become aware of this?

AF Fluxus as a name? 1971.

EM Who invented the name Fluxshoe?

AF Fluxshoe is Ken Friedman. He is responsible for the West Coast of America's Fluxus. At the moment, for instance, I think it gathers something like 2 or 300 artists who are using various forms of communication between each other. Mail. They're mailing art to each other because the galleries aren't interested. Television aren't interested. You couldn't say that Dick Higgins is a poet or he is an actor. Just the same, he might be acting or he might be reading poetry.

It's very difficult to say more, because the main difficulty is that the artists are as artists separately, I mean apart from Fluxshoe. So for instance I can join in but still can do what I'm doing. And this is pretty well what happens, and has happened, and is happening. At the moment, in Oxford for instance, which is the fourth exhibition site at the moment, there are people coming to and fro with films, poems, and various performances, which haven't been at the last three. Or might not have been at the last three, and whose names might not even be in the catalogue.

EM Do you have a fixed time for this thing to start?

AF Once again that depends. If it's George Brecht then it depends. There might not be. If it's Dick Higgins quite often it's laid down. The line is not to lay it down. It seems to be more on the mail side of things. That is to say, no dogma. You hardly even give instructions.

AF Well, performance creates its own improvisory... It might even be based on two lines. For instance, George Brecht will say, *You will pick up* and it will leave a blank, and it will say, *You will do... with that*. And so you've got to fill everything in.

EM Is there an invitation to non-Fluxshoe people, like non-artists to take part?

AF It's more of an artist thing I would say. They vary. In Falmouth it was at the School of Art. In Exeter it was at a gallery, the Exe Gallery I think it's called. In Croydon it was at the School of Art. In Oxford it's the Museum of Art. But for me the actual context takes place in the post more than anything else. Then you're getting into the other side of Fluxus, the people who are speaking of non-art, who are asking for non artists. People like Walter de Maria who is into meaninglessness work, and his idea is to produce a work of art that has no meaning whatsoever. Almost so that the artist himself is not involved in the work, which is almost impossible. But amazingly enough he's pulled it off, quite frighteningly. If you actually read what he says and carry out what he suggests. And from that you can actually get, I think it's more entertainment than art. It's not art.

Well, I think it's just come to a stage now where they realise that whatever happens the gallery will pick up on it, or the buyers will pick up on it. It's anti-commercial insomuch as through the last I don't know how many years, through the twentieth century I would say, they've found that people want a commodity to buy. Whatever it is, I mean Dada was turned in fact into a commodity in the finish. So it's Neo-Dada if you like, it's anti-commodity. The idea is, they don't want to make it purchasable.

EM Where does the work of art emerge, in the kind of correspondence that goes on in the Fluxshoe group?

AF I think really as a series, as a progression, that is to say you would see a process. For me, that is it, that's all I'd need, I wouldn't hope for any more than that. Out of most of the artists involved. You have to be careful, because there's a lot of different attitudes involved.

EM If there's one governing thing, is it not political?

AF Yeah, it's a political attitude.

EM What is it, anarchist?

AF It's almost not that now. But I'm not quite sure what it is if it isn't. I'm not sure there's a label for it yet. I don't know if you've heard of Beau Geste Press, which is at the moment running down in Devon. They run on a completely community basis. Almost complete. They're run by Felipe Ehrenberg, who is the person who pays the rent, if you like, and with him is his wife and David Mayor who's the coordinator of Fluxshoe and various other people who are chopping and changing, and various visitors like myself. They produce *schmuck* magazine. Their concept there is of the craftsman, within a village if you like. Cooking a meal there is really exciting. Is it eatable? It's incredible. Apart from printing, they have letter presses they have duplicators. His experimenting with duplicators I would say is really important. It's the first extension I've seen since Bob, since Bob's work in Writers Forum.

(describes action where someone paints a wall and allows themselves to stick to it as it dries)

EM What are you doing, Allen?

AF I'm bringing a sabre to cut him down.

EM Are you reading printed text? are you improvising poems at all?

AF More prose. I'm better at improvising prose than poetry, for some reason.

EM The artist's body and voice is very much part of the action, isn't it? It's there, in the performance. When you read the poem on the page, you don't have the presence of the body and voice in that sense. The difference between the two kinds of poetry, two kinds of action that Allen's into, for example, and the one kind is very much to do with the fact that he's very much concerned in one part of his life with theatre. Isn't it?

AF Me. No. That may be what the body of it's doing, that's not what I'm doing.

EM Isn't that performance thing a kind of theatre to you?

AF Alright. Loosely. I caught that. What I picked up immediately…

EM I don't mean theatrical.

AF Lines for performance.

[…]

AF The danger with performance is that it brings in the man who will govern the performance. Sell the performance for. And that's what we're against. It's very dangerous to be against inasmuch as we don't want to become an elite. It's more dangerous to leave yourself open to that.

(Surely the material in Jimmy the Hoover and Place is very different.)

AF What I was going to say prior to that was, They're not that far apart. I think you'll find that Charles Olson was involved in dance. And that's where projection came out of, as far as I'm concerned, it came out of the body. And that's how I find the connection. At least that's one way I find it. That was a bit abstract, but really that's what we're saying. Apart from that, I'm also talking about the conceptual artists or whatever you want to call them, that I enjoy, I take an interest in. Are interested in process, are interested in progressions. And that relates back to *Place*, as far as I'm concerned.

EM Do you think it's important for the people from the non-creative area to know what those processes are?

AF I think it's more important than is realised, in fact.

(about seeing the concept rather than just seeing a woman in a banana dress [referring back to an action Doug Lang had described involving Miss Anna Banana])

AF I was going to say the opposite, actually. I believe both. Yes and no. And in fact I can't separate them. I've tried to and I can't. I find when I take part in Concept Art, in Fluxshoe, which isn't Concept Art, let's face it, I try to separate that from what I'm doing with, say, *Place*, or with my main writing. And in fact they relate and I can't stop them relating.

EM Am I right in saying it doesn't need to be read aloud at all?

AF Well to me it does. If it doesn't to you then it's OK with me. But it's not OK with me if I couldn't read it. I read it aloud to myself. I can't read it.

AF Suppose I'd arranged previously to arrange a group of words, and arrive at a group of words, by a certain system. That system is outside me. That is to say, it could be using the *I Ching*, it could be a number of things. And then I arrived at these words. I couldn't leave them like that. Because that doesn't satisfy me enough if you like. I would arrange a rhythm into them. Now I don't know how I do that, but I do. And until I do, it's not a poem as far as I'm concerned. It's something. We start, then, talking about graphics, and about whether what Dom Sylvester Houédard is doing is poetry, or whether it's graphics, it's just a…

You start getting into the field where the arrangement on the page is decorative, or pleasing to the eye, and also it enhances the poem, because it helps you read it in the rhythm intended.

It's got beyond that now. It's got to the stage where it's no longer enough to take the top of your head off and put it on a page, in that sense. It's got to the stage now where a certain amount of information has been said, and it's now to do with how that information has been arrived at.

It doesn't interest me *more*. I'm interested in Doug's poetry, but he doesn't often show me a process that he's used to arrive at to get that. I would like to visualize a poet that can show me exactly how he's got there. That's why I was interested in James Koller.

(…) I think it's one of the problems with the New York School in fact. That they've come out of John Ashbery rather than Charles Olson. And they've come to a dead end. And now they're saying, they're smacking into the dead end.

(they discuss book, Fluxus and Happenings*)*

(…) I should say, as far as Fluxshoe's concerned, that isn't what's happening now, that's what's happened.

EM You mean the next stage is to re-introduce personality somehow? beyond this systems play?

AF No, I think it's gone the other way in fact. Not as far as I'm concerned, but I would say that, now, you almost don't know whether there is an artist involved. (…) It was good, I mean we had a good game of darts the other day. We had a good game of darts, and that was it. How it relates to the poetry I'm not quite sure. It's not where I pick up from. (…) Well I am divided. I'm not disputing that. I would say, everyone is, but they might not know it. There is something out of his contradictions piece. Which says there's got to be contradictions. If there isn't, you're telling yourself a lie.

AF Well I don't know about Oxford, because that's still going, but at the Exe gallery, in Exeter, the proprietor there said there were more going in there than there's ever been, it was just amazing. The works aren't for sale, of course.

EM How much was the University of Exeter involved in this, if at all?

AF They backed the letter that went to the various councils for the grants. That's really what happened. The head of the American Arts centre there, that's Mike Weaver, and David Mayor, co-ordinated it through Ken Friedman in California. That is to say, assembled all the American works there, and catalogued them and brought them over. Apart from that, David Mayor's connected with the University of Exeter, or was, but that's the connection. I don't think it's any more than that. Who goes in there?

AF What I've produced have been books, yeah, but the people I've been related with haven't necessarily produced books. The last thing I saw at Fluxshoe was a plastic box, in fact, which contained a copy of George Brecht's *Water Yam*, which had a heap of cards in it.

Extract from interview with Dr RAC Kiss, National Poetry Centre, 28.10.74

DK Are you able to define what we are about to participate in? (i.e. *Blood Bone Brain*) Is it conceptual art?

AF No

DK Then you find that conceptual is too often a loose and usually a misleading term?

AF Yes, I find I am more often outside its terms of reference.

DK So you agree with Joseph Kosuth who said "All art (after Duchamp) is conceptual (in nature) because art only exists conceptually"?

AF —Well—

DK But a critic to comment on the work must find a framework in which to place this type of work to give a structured criticism. Would you prefer the term Dick Higgins gave, 'Intermedia'?

AF Yes.

DK Because it is dealing with several or more than one method of showing and with methodologies not necessarily in the same stage of development.

AF Well—

DK What about aesthetics, and the philosophy of beauty?

AF No, but—

DK You mean it is outside of your approach and process in art? That it only appears in terms of presentation which is again outside of what you would accept as a term for art?

AF Yes.

DK But you wouldn't refute that you are concerned with intuition and presumably sensibility?

AF No, but I would add responsibility with an emphasis on senses and responses.

DK Doesn't style quality and permanence support the notion that age is a basic consideration for the value of the art object?

AF Yes.

DK And Daniel Buren's "beware!" What d'you think of that?

AF Well—

DK —that the means becomes the end through the use of the word *concept.*

AF The better term would be process or project. But the process isn't the art itself and does not allow it the title conceptual. Documentation as Object or No-object and so on.

DK Well, what about the manner or way of approach being the art? doesn't that allow the title conceptual in some cases?

AF No, no.

DK Would a better term be *abstract*—as in reduction/selection? Something precisely describing the approach. In these terms you could not call Jackson MacLow's work conceptual just because the methodology precedes and directs the content. In fact becomes part of the content—at times all too seldom—

AF A better term would be systems. The work of Clark Coolidge and more to the point, Dan Graham's *The Conceptual Cloud*.

DK The term conceptual has been used for work that doesn't show itself, but merely verbalises itself, say by a process-showing, that is to say by verbal rather than pictorial illusion. Can you accept that?

AF No.

DK But that is beginning to indicate what you're getting at? Perhaps it might be easier if you cited works you felt could be related to the category you hint at. That is a sense that a true conceptual poem is one that does not in fact show itself and yet exists. That is not to say merely by showing a way in which it will go when written, but a way it *actually is*.

AF In particular I would cite Tom Raworth's 'Stag Skull Mounted'. Now parts of that have the feel of it. But I'll cite further. On the one hand Raworth, as I said, and Richard Miller's recent New York work. We have Robert Barry's 'Imperceptible Gas', Terry Atkinson's use of physics. On the other hand—what on the surface might appear to be unrelated works but which in fact relate on the level we first spoke of. That the work which is not yet a work or a poem but which by being presented as such indicates the poem that cannot be there. Lee Harwood's *Captain Harwood's Log of Stern Statements and Stout Sayings*; his 'Boston' pieces. Roger Cutforth's 'The Empire State Building', Lawrence Werner's statements recording a number of his words evoking a picture of the fact referred to and without metaphor. In addition there has been Jonathan Williams' *Loco Logo-Daedalist In Situ*, Tom A Clark's *Fresh water Journal*, Mel Bochner's *measurements* and Berner Vent's *Lectures*. Take this statement from Ed Ruscha: "I don't have any message about subject matter at all. They are just natural facts, that's all they are." I would add that he has made a selection of these facts which is where the problem comes in. How selected and so on. But some of these are not necessarily poetry or art.

DK But that gets us nowhere.

AF Exactly.

DK But elsewhere—you have said "Idea art is not necessarily Conceptual." The suggestion becomes obvious when we are observing a method of replacement—what is not expressible in visual/verbal—censorial terms —becomes idea art.

AF That isn't Conceptual and that isn't art! Take Carolee Scheemann's film event 'Tracking'. The films depict her cat; the trains near her house; her life with the cat and the house; nothing more. They are family, homely movies. But during their showing she hangs from a rope meditating and tracing, that is tracking, on the walls and floor around her with a crayon or chalk the energies she wishes to convey. That is—that the Act of the Tracking is the art—not whatever she may be making. Buren speaks of art as the Rupture. Not Rupture with art but with Life. Ian Tibbet's 'The feeling'.

DK So you accept Douglas Huebler's "To bring inter-relationships beyond direct perceptual experience"?

AF Yes. I find that sharp.

DK But this depends on documentation after the event.

AF The meaning of my art is the use it may have. Cage's sense of utility. A way of helping out, as well as the fact that all art, every act in life is a political act.

DK But that's not conceptual.

AF I didn't say it was.

Work Descriptions from *Prosyncel* and Elsewhere

Prosyncel
The work, described as a 'blueprint for a retrospective catalogue' is a collage of texts and pictures in the manner of the times, and contains descriptions of numerous projects past or continuing in 1975. (The 'retro' part-word is misleading.) It is also described as 'a sketch-map of heat', punning on 'work' in the sense that mechanics uses the word in, and in the sense of 'artistic work'.

The title is explained as PROcess SYNthesis, PROjects SYNopsis. 'The catalogue becomes, therefore, an artifact limited by itself and capable of its own increase as a SYNthetic Cell. In addition to this it becomes a putting of each part for sale and as a synecdochic sell (self) becomes a fiction.'...

Docking
: A set of poems worked out of 'dream sentences' in a processual and etymological manner.

The title brings in a weed with large leaves and a long root, summary of a larger writing, a place of arrival and departure, a way of cutting short, the French for bundle, a way of joining together in space, the enclosure in court for the accused, the words doctor, doctrine, documentation, dokesis, dokimasy, &c. An example has been given towards the end of *prosyncel*.

Hooks : place 32 taken out of place
Hooks uses material made ready for the work 'place 32'. This work, then, taken 'out of place', as the first chapter in the work *Convergences /in place /of the play*, where the method of composition in that work continues the work-method of *Hooks*.

Convergences describes *Hooks* as a 'preface' to *Convergences*.

Convergences, in place, of the play
During the progress of research for the work 'place forty' I accumulated data in a "Cuttings Book' which I rewrote to my own emphasis in using the limiting procedure of given word orders. This gave me 24 columns of information making syntactic sense and covered a field of as many subjects. A system was then made to juxtapose the columns so that they could read both vertically and horizontally across columns. This long

painstaking task is still incomplete and yet to be shaded by 'place forty-two'. Refer also *notes on Jackson MacLow*.

*poetry, a priority: being notes on my relationship
with the work of Jackson MacLow*
The idea of an *a priori* meaning may be found in the older mathematics. Jung cites the mathematician Jacobi's paraphrase of Schiller's poem 'Archimedes and his Pupil'.
He praises the calculation of the orbit of Uranus and closes with the lines:

"What you behold in the cosmos is only light of God's glory;
In the Olympian host Number eternally reigns."(1)

My concern here then with synchronicity and MacLow's Asymmetry. I would like to give an indication of why I feel MacLow's work *is* symmetrical conceptually and why, if I am to innovate out of it, it becomes necessary to point out the misgivings I have with his lack of PROCESS-SHOWING, and the dangers of systematic selection.

But first to continue with Jung's valuable treatise on the subject of synchronicity:

"However incomprehensible it may appear, we are finally compelled to assume that there is in the unconscious something like an a priori knowledge or immediate presence of events which lacks any causal basis. At any rate our conception of causality is incapable of explaining the facts." (*ibid.* 1)

In 1966 I started work based entirely on and limited to the letter and word order in Wordsworth's *The Prelude*. As far as I recall them, the influences I knew of, that led to the completion of the first section (*Tree-Birst* 1970), was not MacLow but Coleridge in his *Biographia Literaria* and William Burroughs in his procedure-notes and work that first appeared in Jeff Nuttall's *My Own Mag* and 'Art & Literature' published in Lausanne. In fact, the habit of crossing out letters from text books started (as some of MacLow's work did) at school, out of boredom. It remains true, however, that Jackson MacLow's work influences the procedure in my work *whether I knew it at the time or not*, in the same way that Tom Phillips was working, unknown to me, on his own *A Humument*, at the same time. (See Colin Symes' review in *Earthship* No.7.)

By 1970 I had already come up against problems that working with systems or strict procedures brings about. It is one thing to explain your procedures after composing, as MacLow does to the major works I have here, *22 Light poems* and *Stanzas for Iris Lezak*. It is quite another when you wish to incorporate those procedures in the work. This was made clearer to me in 1971 when I started work, still in progress, on the third section of *ABCD* (*Sicily*) which gave me the problem direct. I incorporated the system into the work so that without the system-showing the work would become a mere skeleton of its whole. At the same time I had commenced a different work (under the working title of *place*) which did not use these procedural techniques but what I would loosely call 'field and processual procedures' that up until that time I felt I could operate independently of my 'systems' work.

By 1973 I knew that I needed to find a method of writing processually that could incorporate process-SHOWING procedures and systems where it wished to and yet still allow me to go, to be on-going, rather than the "closed field" that systems alone inevitably would lead me into. I came at that time to two works. The first started using a methodology that I think I gathered from John Ashbery, and the second involved the extension I felt I could make out of Jackson MacLow's procedures. I completed the first (*Listen*) in 1973. It involved a series of words making sentences where the *collective* of the sentences only made sense as a concept. The process was to underline words in an already printed pile of articles, collecting them together in the order in which they appeared and making sentences out of them as I proceeded so that the sense of each became my imposition rather than the system's and that collectively the sentence made their syntaxis. So the overall syntax was casual and, I feel, synchronic. My point here with relation to MacLow's work is that in many cases this is exactly where his *Asymmetry* becomes symmetry—in its conceptualisation and in that sense where "as a whole" the work makes sense, even if it does not internally. The second work, still in progress, *(Convergences /in place/ of the play)* brings in the extensions I have been speaking of. I have taken vertical columns of phrases and sentences made by syntactical method (my own syntax as opposed to that already present) and have then made a new syntactical arrangement horizontally by spacing out the vertical-columned word-groups and placing them side by side—that is "dove-tailing" the word groups. I have reached the stage of being able to read a piece syntactically across ten columns of different informations and of course separately down them. The system is inherent in the poem so that the poem is process-showing *and* procedure-showing. It is both a process poem and a poem incorporating strict procedures.

It is noticed that my concern for synchronicity persists and as I have said I believe it does too in MacLow's work. Perhaps then this might be the point at which I should mention his often deliberate (or more often the system's) paratactic language. Such excellence of parataxis I have only elsewhere seen in the work of Paul Goodman, Clark Coolidge and many of those who contributed to Acconci's *0-9*. The use it has I believe to be twofold.

In the first place a citation from Paul Goodman:
"Deliberate literature, oral or written, is not spontaneous speech, but it has compensating advantages in providing examples for exploring language." (2)
So in the first place, my take is that much of MacLow's work provides us with just that, providing examples for exploring language, and thus, consciousness.

My second sense might be more difficult to give you. I have said that I find MacLow's work often "internally" unsynchronic, yet capable of making overall sense. The paradox will be helped if I recall, first Chomsky's generative grammar and take that with me when considering the use of the I Ching (which incidentally MacLow uses in much of *Stanzas for Iris Lezak*). What the I Ching does is to make the associations we are unable to VISUALISE. The second sense of symmetry or syntax I get then is just that. His ability to present what cannot be visualised and make, help make the associations towards it. I hasten to add that I do not suggest that his work includes religious pretension. It is, however, one of a poet's uses, if he is to give us any "wholeness", to give us an insight we might not otherwise gather. The exactness of his vision here of course becomes a matter outside of my wish to include here.

It brings me on to a danger I have sensed in my own work and thus see in MacLow's. By using systematic selection he is losing some (I don't think all) of his own invitation or imposition. Anyone concerned with politics must find this disturbing. It is easy to think that by making the initial choice of material the poet is leading the subject matter of his course. When he imposes a determinate system of selection (which he often does, e.g. Random Number Tables) where the system takes over the selection, then, because the generative is taken out of the word order, the new order might say what the poet /composer does not wish. Now it could be said that MacLow uses a rigorous selection of material to use and publish after the composing and thus rejects those works which come out as "noise"—that is as unacceptable statement. (It might well be the reason for MacLow's abandonment of his '9th Light Poem for the Algerians—27 March 1968: Their Light Poem is Their Revolution'.) If this is the case, the poet is limited to using procedure and not using process. Because, if he used process within the procedure he could allow the final rejection/ acceptance at the composition's completion to be shown and would not then be fully "process-showing". Now that might be a mere quibble, but when it really comes to it, if for instance I am saying I must incorporate both axes in the composing, both process and process-showing *and* systematic technique in a work I am involved in writing, then I must have *enough* control to make my own impositions or invitations. If we cannot use poetry to give the insights and relationships we shouldn't use it. My reasons for pursuing this, as I mentioned earlier, are that if "systematic poetry making" is continued in the present manner it needs to incorporate the processual but in so doing it needs to be aware of the aforementioned.

It is not enough to use poetry as a medium for music, for aesthetic demonstration, or as an *objet d'art*. I sense a danger in work, that because of its aesthetically pleasing procedures and/or materials, is acceptable as what we look for in poetry —especially when what it might also be is an imposition or invitation from—not from the poet, which it should be, but the system-determinations. Fortunately, Mac Low's art is such that this danger appears to be minimal, perhaps for reasons I have mentioned. But I must look to further innovation and that is where the real danger lies.

I look for the day when a poetry will rhyme with Stockhausen's intuitive *aus den sieben tagen* and I believe *that* work when it comes will be out of the work laid before us by Jackson Mac Low and some of those akin to his work.

(1) CG Jung. *Synchronicity. An Acausal Connecting Principle* (1955)
(2) Paul Goodman. *Speaking and Language: Defence of Poetry* (1971)

Blood Bone Brain

Blood Bone Brain is the most eclectic of the projects encompassing book and environmental work; process and systems; documentation; writing, sound, and graphics; printing and filming.

It is the product of earlier work & conceived as such.

The book work forms 'D' in what I called "a series of three lettered 'ABCD'". The first sets were:
A, *Ffacece*, dealing with graphics, printing, system and process;
B, *creek in the ceiling beam*, covering documentation, process, system, writing, filming, printing, graphics and conceptualising;
C, *Sicily*, covering system, process, printing and writing.
   The environmental work extended out of the live performances of the Musics made from *A&B*, and the writing out of *B&C*, and the system-concepts and processes used in *ABC* (and its Recycling).

Environmentally the concept—Blood Bone Brain—is as follows:

39 slides of local sites determined by *creek in the ceiling beam*.
39 slides of work set out for the Museum Pieces project.
39 slides of interactive and waste disposal material which changes composition as the work continues.
39 slides systematically selected from the previous 117 (including Blanks) and play simultaneously with:

39 bars of music composed for the work based on the system in *C*, titled *Blood on Rain*.
39 particles of music on loop out of the note structure in *Facece*.
39 '78 rpm' gramophone recordings of nostalgia.
39 Selections from the 117 sets (including any silences).
39 descriptions of local sites corresponding to *B*.
39 nostalgia pieces from "39 objects" out of Museum Pieces.
39 Selections from John Buchan's *The Thirty-Nine Steps*.
39 readings from the previous 117 reading sets (including silences).
39 commentaries from the medical Notes made on my Blood, Bone and Brain condition and the attendant factors such as temperature, sound, weather, foods etcetera during the Fluxshoe touring show. The systematisation of the sets is finally worked out in graphs sent to the

Fluxshoe circus during the 39 weeks of its travel (the show in fact continued after Blackburn to Hastings but this was not in the final schedule and came up at the last minute).

The work is being designed to work over a period of about 9 hours continuously with adequate provision for the easy and comfortable entry and exit of audience/participators.

The work involves the use of automatic slide projectors and tape recorders intercepted by live readings and gramophone playings; in a ratio of 3:1.

The work has yet to involve the use of 39 smells and perhaps 39 touching actions.

A more fluctuating piece is expected to work out processually from the work's completion using the Golden Section.

A 117 minute version of *Blood Bone Brain* was performed as a trial in October 1974 under inadequate audio conditions at the National Poetry Centre, London when it was suggested that the work should be made shorter. Following experiments with this suggestion the lateral concept of making it longer was finalised.

Museum Pieces

Museum Pieces encompasses four forms of assembly.
1. using Frances A. Yates' *The Art of Memory*, where a system of places and objects is collected to give a set of triggers for memories. In less useful terms this could mean an ashtray from Southend reminding the owner of a holiday there together with a set of notions connected with the place.
2. bringing together objects that would otherwise be disposed of such as empty pill cartons, broken pencils or out of date coins.
3. As pieces for the *Blood Bone Brain* project.
4. Some pieces have been extended to act as "Reversal" objects. They include sardine cans in oil, a broken purse surrounded by out of date coins and so forth.

The overall concept is to collect and document enough material for an exhibition, i.e. Museum, to clear the junk in a swoop by sale or gift.

The Art of Flight

Essentially exercises structured on the notation for JS Bach's *Die Kunst der Fuge*.

To date I have completed work on the first 3 parts of this project. The first and third have used Bach's Contrapunctus I and III as their structure. The second gives lyrics to a work by Dick Higgins which translates as "a second clear presentday language".

The words used from the onset give a consistent transformation of syntax throughout. The fourth set, in progress, incorporates Bach's Contrapunctus II (originally IV in the Berlin Autograph) and the IV Tovey gives which had not been included (or written) in the Berlin Autograph original.

The Art of Flight offers opportunities for four voices (or tapes) simultaneously and continuous readings incorporating ideas from Terry Riley, Steve Reich and George Crumb.

The lyric content is concerned formally with the uses of light and dark in science and literature (with of course religion).

The sets are prefaced with Lyric notes and sources.

The Art of Flight I, II and III was premiered in March 1975 at the Zero Event series on the Enterprise, Chalk Farm, London. The reader was Allen Fisher using four tape recorders and many pre-recorded tapes.

['Die Kunst der Fuge' translates as the art of flight if we draw *flight* from *flee*. Fuga means both 'fleeing' and 'fugue'. Fugue is a tune which runs away (from its own form? with itself?)]

[From sleeve notes to the tape *Paxton's Beacon*:]
The Art of Flight is Allen Fisher's formal treatise on the usage in ideas and in language of the terms "light and dark", where 'Flight' is fugue, folly, and fancy. The work was composed between November 1974 and July 1975.
Paxton's Beacon is comprised of extracts from 'The Art of Flight: I-XXVII (...)'

Interview for *Alembic*, January 1976
interlocutors: Peter Barry, Ken Edwards

PB I'll start by quoting what you say about *Place* in *Prosyncel*: "It appears now that the concept was to write a work primarily as an address that came out of my reading concerns at the time of writing, that would reflect upon each other in such a way as to make, as Keats, then Heisenberg and later Olson noted, Uncertainty. Or better, in Keats' terms, a balance by way of 'negative capability'." Can you say some more about the kind of balance between the various elements that you were aiming for in *Place*?

AF Yes. You put it in the past tense, in fact I haven't finished the work. I've written Books I and III. The balance I'm talking about in the first place I suppose is to do with the way the work is being structured. Book III is a partly distorted mirror of Book I, and Book II again acts as a mirror to the other two, and book IV again is a mirror, so that Book V is a composite mirror if you like. Or it might be, I don't yet know that. It's not important for me to know what Book V will be like. I mean, I have ideas of what I think will be in Books II, IV and V, in fact I've partly written books II and IV, but those ideas might change as it goes along, in other words I would allow the process of the writing to direct what will happen. But if I was to come in at any tangent and just write, the work wouldn't fully cohere, so that by "balance" again I'm implying that I'm giving the work a certain limitation, an imposed limitation, but not of a sort that I can exactly speak about it. Not of a sort, for example, that I could speak about if I was talking about other works that I've done that impose both the words and the structure because that's not the case at all with *Place*.

The word 'balance' is a bit of an awkward one. I think I've probably misused it in *Prosyncel*. I mean something else as well, though I'm not quite sure if I can express it. I mean something to do with the fact that my concerns aren't singular, and it's therefore necessary to watch that I don't overbalance one concern to such an extent that it outbalances another concern and completely overshadows it. If for instance I'm writing about the structure of buildings and the way buildings are made in the area, or generally—if I write too much about that, and I also want to write about—what can we say?—the plants in the area, I'd have to be careful that I got the right sort of balance, as far as that's concerned. I mean, that's where the uncertainty comes into it, the fact that I don't really know when I set out on the work how much information I do want to put in.

PB Yes, I was going to go on to ask about the source-books you drew on in *Place*. Thinking of things like Alfred Watkins, Michell's *View Over Atlantis*, Guy Underwood, things like that. I'm wondering what kind of interest you have in these books. Is it that they represent departures from fairly routine paradigms or ways of looking at things, or are they interesting as techniques of exploration, or are they there as facts that have to be included, that are part of the picture?

AF No, I don't think they're facts that *have* to be included. I think what you first said was right, inasmuch as they do break down archaeologists' paradigms. I don't think they do so successfully all the time, and in fact I think Michell has gone a little too far. By going over the cliff I think what Michell did was to put a strong distrust among the established archaeologists, so that if what he was saying, or what Underwood was saying, or Watkins or any of these people, did have any validity, it was never investigated by anyone whose position in the field would be respected, and I think it's only people like Professor Thom who have managed to do anything about that. As far whether or not the information is factual, I think some of it is, but to what extent is difficult to say. I've been trying to take steps to find out for myself through two friends, or rather one friend and one acquaintance, and I can't speak a lot about the acquaintance's work at the moment because of his own copyrights, but he says he's devised a machine which has proven some of the facts and disproved some other facts. His name is Herbert L. Weaver. He and David Mayor have been having long conversations concerning dowsing and lines of force and energies that aren't generally accepted by 'scientists'. I don't think it's all boloney, but I think I'm sceptical about some of what is being said. But I do find it useful as a metaphor in fairly general and broad terms. I found Underwood especially useful inasmuch as he doesn't actually finish what he wants to do, but in the last chapter of *Patterns of the Past*, he starts talking about architecture, and about how the lines of force directed how the masons have laid down the foundations for that architecture, and the entrances and all the rest of it, and I honestly don't think that's all baloney. Some of it might well be useful. That information in fact is lost to us because Underwood died before he finished his work, and I wish that somebody might continue that. The possibilities are that somebody will—either David or Herbert or somebody related to them.

KE What's the nature of this machine?

AF Its equivalent in building construction is a rod used for finding geologic content in soils, to establish whether or not a building could safely be put there, and he's inverted the machine that's being used already. He calls it 'the Revealer' after Lawrence J. Veale, who invented it, who's now dead. I found it a useful parallel for, and therefore and interaction with, Underwood's work. Although Weaver isn't working in the field Underwood was at all, I think David, having been in both fields, might be able to do something about it. There is talk of bringing about an Institute. Whether or not that will ever get off the ground—I mean that involves employing people, and that involves paying them money.

KE Moving on to another source for *Place*, I notice that you dedicate Book I to Raoul Vaneigem. Can you say a bit more about how he fits in?

AF He deeply moved me. I think I first read him in '69, '70, something like that—*The Revolution of Everyday Life*, that's really the book I'm talking about. The other material interests me, but nothing like to that extent. I haven't in fact seen other books, mainly because I don't read French, which is his language, so I read translations. They haven't been much translated if there are any. What I have read has been in anarchist publications or in Situationist manifestoes, that sort of thing. *The Revolution of Everyday Life* itself I thought had the emotional quality I feel akin with. I didn't feel akin with all of the suggestions, but I found very little to argue with, and what I did have to argue with I suppose was something to do with democracy and individuals—I think it would be wrong to say that he was anti-democratic, but that would have part of the truth in it. I would understand partly what he means by that, but I think that's just too dangerous to consider. What worries me is some of the outcome of what he's said, in terms of the movements that have been created either around him or around his group. Some of it's great, very good stuff—some of it is not, it's almost fascism in fact. He's almost a man who has not realised what he's said, in some respects. So in those respects he becomes a visionary, rather than a Marxist-type leader, if you see what I mean. The sort of direction he's given is more than one way, and so some of the ways people have taken out of him I don't necessarily agree with. But his basic principles and his sensibility I would be very akin to, and it's that sort of sensibility I was trying to put over in *Place*, certainly in Book I.

KE You quote him, 'I await the day when this book will lose & find itself in a general movement of ideas.'

AF In the Preface. You would like me to elaborate on that?

KE Yes.

AF I'm not sure I can, actually! I think that some of the ideas in *Place* are too revolutionary, inasmuch as it's very unlikely that they will come about, and if they did come about it certainly would be a revolution. But I like to think I'm an optimist, because otherwise I wouldn't write as I do. Because I've got to put a hedge up against the mainstream in English poetry, which is completely depressionist, it seems to me, and pessimistic. I was almost being romantic there, in fact, and I don't know whether or not I should say this, but I think I should. I was thinking in part about the way art was before it was called "art". This isn't a suggestion that we return to how things were, it's merely a suggestion that art now has become such that it's twofold. On the one hand it's what it should be—I'm not sure I could define what that is—but on the other hand it is a commodity, which I don't think is what it was intended for. I certainly don't write a commodity. I write for people to read. That's not quite the same thing. My sense of it is that the Egyptians, for instance, would make an art for use, as opposed to an art which is a commodity art. I might be wrong about that, which is why I think it might be romantic.

KE That comes on to one of the other things I was thinking of asking about, which is when you were talking about one of Carolee Scheemann's films, 'Tracking', you say that 'the art is the act of tracking itself, and not whatever marks she may be making'. It raises I think the problem of what exactly the role of the documentation is, and then the question of what exactly the artist is doing—there's a point where an independent figure called the 'documentator' becomes as important—

AF It becomes a commodity, you mean?

PB Well, he is producing a commodity, no matter what he tries to do to stop that—and I can see that he might try to do a lot of things to stop producing a saleable commodity simply. Is that a question that worries you?

AF It doesn't worry me in the work that I've produced, but I suppose part of that is due to the fact that I haven't had enough money to produce all I would have wanted to, or in the way I would have wanted to. But it does worry me, yes. And I think—I'm not sure how much name-dropping I ought to do!—you see, the easiest way to talk about that is to talk about instances—

PB I can think of an instance—

AF whereby people have put their art into documentation, and the documentation has become valuable, and that for me is a farce. And it's probably also a farce for them, in fact. I think we can talk about Duchamp. I think we can say that the documentation of his art isn't a farce, but the selling of that documentation is—so that it is beyond my means for instance to buy his documentation to read it. It is in fact now beyond my means—at the present day anyway, as far as I am aware—to even read them, because they're not available for reading, because collectors have purchased them and they haven't republished them. They're purely singular documents that are not available for the general public ("The Green Box" would be an exception), and that I would say goes against both Duchamp's grain and the grain of art generally. And I think that has happened to the extreme now. There are artists that in fact don't do anything except document and produce that documentation as their art-object. Whilst the philosophy behind the documentation is not outside of my thinking, the philosophy behind the livelihood aspect worries me.

It might actually cut across into something else I'd like to mention. What the question could then be is how does the artist then make any money? because I mean if he's not producing works of art for sale, how is he being paid to produce works of art? And I think it's a major question right now. I don't think he should produce art for—and it isn't to a general public, let's face it, the public is no bigger than 500—in the world—I would say. I'd be surprised if it's that big, actually. And that worries me a lot. I think it comes into this question of whether or not the artist accepts a State subsidy, a State wage, and whether or not he can do that under the present State. I mean I could find that acceptable under an acceptable State, but it's difficult to know how you would interpret that under a State you don't exactly agree with. You might on the one hand think that by taking that money you'd be screwing the State, but I would very strongly say that there is also the point of view that you're just playing their game.

PB I was thinking of a name that I wanted to drop—it's the man who walks across the country and insists that that's his art-work. That would be the equivalent to 'the act of the tracking itself'. But he also produces books of photographs of the places he goes through, which are on sale at the Tate—

AF Sounds like Richard Long.

PB Is that so?

AF Well, I don't know. He does that. His photographs are very beautiful.

PB Yes, but he insists that they are not works of art, that the work of art is really the walking—and that's a problem.

AF It really is. I wonder though how much—I mean I don't know the man, but certainly current living artists who are not producing work but are producing documentation... that brings in the question of who they are supporting.

What you have to do is to take that question out of an art context and put it in a political one. It's the pure political question of—there's enough money around to pay people for not working—why doesn't that happen? And then go on from there.

PB Can I just ask one more thing about the sources you were using in *Place*? I was enjoying a lot when I was reading Book I the use you make of the history of the lost rivers of London. Can you say something about what you were getting at?

AF I'm not sure what specifically you mean, but I'll say what I think you mean. The trouble with that question was, there's more than one aspect concerning those rivers. One aspect concerning them was that their courses were traced in the thirties and forties, and were put on the same map as a map showing pneumonia outbreaks, and the relationship was fairly positive. So to that extent they interested me, inasmuch as I was talking about the other energy lines that Watkins and other people were talking about—what exactly do those lines cause and bring about? Are they in any way related to what I would call city diseases, such as cancers, psychosomatic diseases which might be brought about—and I emphasize 'might'—by hiding these forces? For example by building over them, laying reinforced concrete over them, having rods of iron across them, and this sort of heavy building—I just wondered to what extent those influences were being turned against themselves, whether those energies which might at one time have been "good" energies, became 'bad' energies. It's not necessarily proven, but I think it was generally felt that there's more than one energy going through the system, that some of those energies are healing energies and some are non-healing energies. If architecture and roads and so forth are built without any knowledge of those, what effect must that have on us? I was interested to note that one of the dowsers, by the name of Palen, *[possibly Gustav von Pohl?]* got to the point in 1939 of almost getting the local government to appoint a dowser onto every planning committee as an adviser. That sounds totally crackpot, but I don't think it was that crackpot. Why is it, for instance, that we have to have the houses running down the straight side of the street? It's purely logistics, that's all. That isn't common sense, in fact. I think generally speaking people can feel that. You can walk down some street and think "This is just horrible." And you walk down other streets and think "This is nice". I think it's also the height of the buildings and the shapes and the colours and everything else. And that's why the problem with that question is that it's a bit more complicated than I'm able to answer just like that.

That was one of the things, anyway, I was on about. I also, I think, used the rivers as a metaphor for thought.

PB Yes, certainly the thing I was getting very strongly was what happens when certain kinds of natural energies are denied or blocked—whatever kinds of energies they may be.

AF The danger with dealing with these matters is that when you're talking about them you use the terms "natural", "Nature", and I think those terms in themselves are dangerous for the simple reason that they imply not necessarily what is meant. I mean, I don't really want to return to the homeland or return to the soil as a peasant, or any of that stuff—I mean, that's just crazy. So we have to be a bit careful about that. I haven't read much Marcuse, but Marcuse's 'Second Nature' for instance, is surely one sign to make us careful what we say. When we say 'nature', immediately what we're also saying is what we think is Nature, instinctively. And then what Marcuse would say is some of those instincts in fact aren't instincts at all, but imposed upon—they're obliged instincts actually, I mean you're obliged to carry them to live in London.

PB I wasn't meaning that there was any sort of sentimental return to Nature thing—

AF No, I thought perhaps you weren't, but I thought also that it might be good to mention it, because that might come across.

PB Yeah. Because again one of the nice things that strikes in *Place* is the idea that the man-made thing, the city, can use certain things that are already there, or can not use them, it's a matter of choice.

AF Yeah, but that choice isn't taken. It isn't even offered.

PB This again is a quotation from *Prosyncel:* "The meaning of my work is the use it may have." You then use the two phrases of 'process-showing' and 'procedure-showing'. And I take it that part of the reason why you do these two things is to make the work available for use. Can you talk about the difference between these two things, "process-showing" and "procedure-showing"?

35

AF What happened was that I came about the word "process-showing" first of all when I was working on a setting of *Place* which I've taken out of *Place*, which I've called *Convergences*. The information was in columns, which would read horizontally as well as vertically. The vertical column would tell you, it would be obvious how those notes were compiled. But the actual poem for me would be the horizontal reading. And I did think that some of what I've been doing in poetry would come across if it was possible to see how that horizontal reading was working—and I called it "process-showing" because that is exactly what it was doing, it was showing the process. Then what happened afterwards was that many months later I was asked to review the work of Jackson Mac Low for *Vort* magazine, and he's a man involved in strict procedures, in much of his older work, certainly up to the 1960s. From that I realized that the word *process* has the same Greek root as *procedure*, it means *procedure* in its Greek root, and so therefore 'process' means "procedure" to anybody reading, so I had to put the two together to show they were different.

By "procedure" I meant that the process of the work was conceptually organised before the writing. By "process-showing" I meant that that conceptual organisation took place *as* the writing. Does that answer it?

In fact the two are much easier explained by example. They really are. If I said to you, "I call that 'procedure-showing' and that 'process-showing'", the difference would be quite wide, in fact. It's got something to do with the way the brain works—the two are in fact similar, insomuch as the brain is inclined to procedurize in any case, is inclined to be consecutive.

PB Yes, the procedure type is diachronic, whereas the other kind is synchronic. Can I go on to ask about the second kind, about the use of "procedures", the use of strict systems? One of the things that comes out in *Prosyncel* is that you have certain reservations about this. You say that there are certain things about it that are politically disturbing, or that are disturbing to people that are interested in politics. Is it partly the fact that the poet is basically passive before that system that he's chosen?

AF Only partly. My main emphasis is really that what eventually happens is that somebody reads the work, and their reading from that work will be the brain reading—I'm just trying to emphasize that the work will be read as if it had been written by any method, and therefore what is said must be what the artist intends to be said—that is, if the artist is concerned that what he is saying needs to mean the same to him as he hopes it means to other people. So the danger with the procedure-showing system is that it might not say exactly what the artist would intend outside the system he's imposed. And in fact I noticed that in one of the *Light Poems* that Jackson MacLow did, he leaves the Light Poem completely out and just puts something like 'This silence is the Light Poem for the Algerian people', something like that.

PB Yes, he says that their revolution is the poem.

AF That's right. I haven't actually asked Jackson whether or not that's why he excluded it, that he found it wasn't saying exactly what should be said in terms of an Algerian war! I'm pretty sure that it would be difficult to work a procedure that could do that. No, I've got to colour that—because I do think that William Burroughs says what he means to say, although he also is using fairly strict procedures—I wouldn't say they were very rigid in fact. But I don't think many mistakes are made concerning what his stance is, in terms of government for instance.

PB Because as the poet has the right to eliminate certain things, he therefore recuperates the whole thing as his own discourse by the act of eliminating unacceptable parts. But there's a point where you say there's something inadmissible about that particular procedure, about just leaving something out.

AF Yes, right. That's where the problem starts cropping up. Once you start saying that you wish to be completely "procedure-making" or 'process-showing', what you might be saying is that you want to include the mistakes. So as soon as you start cutting out, what are you cutting out exactly if you're not cutting out the mistakes? So it's really like a paradox of some sort. I think it can be dealt with, but I don't think it's an easy one to deal with.

Procedure and Process: Talk on 'Place' at *Alembic*, 1978

What I have in front of me. I have a sheet of some key words which I'll gradually put up behind me. So we have a number of key images. I started this morning with survival. We've added to it structure and form, which I've mentioned this morning wanting to come to. I have here a number of cards, which are all quotations, from other authors and are all generally speaking authors other than poets. Scientists, philosophers, historians, that sort of thing. The cards are the sort of data cards which are used by research departments, covered with numbers and holes. The system is you decide from the numbers subject matters, extract the holes that have the subject matters on particular cards with a pair of clippers. Bang the cards up. And for instance, pick a number Four, put that through the pack, like that and you end up with those cards there and all those cards, there, are the ones with the Four on. And so you have all that you have for that particular subject matter in one hand. The advantage of the system is that you can cut many holes. So that for instance on this particular card I've cut out four one seven and 28. So that, because it raises more than one issue I was concerned with in the key words. Now what I'm doing in fact is trying to make an analogy with one method I use for working. And I think in many ways the analogy works. I think it's possible to say in some ways it doesn't, as well. Partly because I think writing, creation generally, is, at least in large part is, a private matter. That is, a matter of private experiment as opposed to social shall we say. That doesn't exclude the fact that of course it's social as well. That doesn't exclude the fact that there are many people involved in elaborations, orchestrations, and so forth. So what I've got to do immediately is first of all make a decision as to what cards I'm going to read first. The cards which if you like have my memory upon them. And I've got to find a method of first of all selecting from what amounts to a structure that's already existing. Which you won't mind me saying is the case with our own memories. I'll elaborate on that later. I believe there are at least two types of memory in any case. One which is inventive and one which we might call consistent. We'll go into that perhaps. Now, one of the interesting things someone said to me after the last time I did this—I've only done it once before—was that I threw dice and picked the numbers from the dice and therefore made the selections from the cards I was to read in whatever order. And I must agree it is an arbitrary way of making that selection. I must admit it's not a way I've ever used in a creative act.

But I'm going to do it here because I think it's a simple way to show publicly. Because I don't think private choice, if you like, is something that you can show by easy analogy. Certainly some writers have used dice. In particular I'm thinking of Jackson MacLow, who's used it to great advantage I would say. So I'll just make the selection. It's quite easy to do because the corners are cut on one side. They come out in blocks because it was done before. As you see it has many holes along the top of that particular piece. As you can see, the point I'm trying to make is that the order of the cards is in fact arbitrary. What I'm in fact trying to get at I think is that perception itself is a pattern-making procedure so that if you call that selection I've just made a perception you might begin to understand what I'm trying to get at. Something else I'm also trying to get at here is that I'm trying to cut through an awful lot of nonsense talked about intuition, inspiration, that sort of term. I'm not discounting them. I'm just trying to cut through them and find out exactly what they mean. I suppose exactly is probably too strong. That's part of the process I'm trying to go through here. The cards are showing me, in my terms, the form. And the order in which I read these cards I'll call the structure. The reading leads off from the cards. I have called that in the past the placing. I think that probably other people might prefer to call it the process. Or perhaps they would find other terms. I would hope they would, in fact. There are certainly many. I have opened on the card "existence". I think I wanted to emphasize here that what we're doing by existing is moving. That is to say we're ex-sisting, outside of standing. You could argue with that etymologically, I suppose. To sist, cause to stand, so that existing becomes to emerge. There are translators who would in fact argue with that. So I've practised what I'm doing with a couple of quotations that I have handy from recent, things that I have argument with. This from a recent book published on Raymond Roussel's *How I wrote certain of my books*. It ends:

First gramophone: But this telephone is dead.
Second gramophone: It's just because it's dead that everyone understands it.

I would express disagreement with that. But it does in fact hold within it a certain belief among very many artists, I think. Next quotation is from an interview given to Frank Stella, the painter, about a year ago, although I only found it today, and the reason I'm quoting it is to exemplify an attitude that uncreative people have towards creative people, really, I think. It's Ben Jones in fact, speaking.

"What do you get your visual stimulation from? All your vitality? Judging from this work at Oxford, you must surely be getting a lot of input, if not from other art, you must be getting around somewhere?"

And Stella says, "I get it from being alive I guess. I don't get more input than anybody else. It's just my business to make paintings, so I work at that. I don't go around being stimulated by things I see. It's usually the reverse. Usually I'm horrified at what I see. Most things are fairly ugly, I guess, in the way that everybody does things. They don't do things to make the world any more beautiful, that's for sure. You can't say the majority of people are out there trying to make things that little bit better. I can only go by what I see. If I saw the results of the opposite I probably wouldn't take such a cynical attitude. I'd probably make a more optimistic attitude."

—Which I think I would, in honesty. But that does exemplify in some ways an attitude that needs to be cut-throat. And lastly it's a quotation from a book I'm reading by Paul Feyerabend, called *Against Method*. I could almost take a random quote here, quite honestly, because he does cut through something here that is interfering with what I'm saying. "According to our present results hardly any theory is consistent with the facts. The demand to admit only those theories which are consistent with the available and accepted facts again leaves us without any theory." So I want to say that, because what I'm about to give you here is not a theory. It's much more flexible than that. I'll start with a few more word pieces. (*writes on board*) I use these very simplistic terms to give me mental pictures I think. Must be.

"Brain. Where the leaps are possible. All this, the collective of drive and organisation. Spiral. Human survival. Play. Classify possibilities.
Blood. Unconceptual. Not in anything, not in the short term.
Bone. Relates to layout structures, to layout limitations. Brain, to layout methods, methodologies. Play. Use of process."

So that might explain what I've just written up there—Blood Bone Brain. I don't mean any of these terms to be mutually exclusive, by the way. They all blur and they will all cross each other. But in very many ways one of the things that any of us will be very unlikely to want to change, let alone be able to, would be for instance our genetic structures. I certainly don't want to, and I certainly wouldn't want to see much increase in the present process of genetic engineering, for instance. So that's probably what I mean by structure: that which remains consistent. Some people might prefer to call that consistent memory. Certainly

Minkowski does. "Redundancy is protection from noise. Accepted noise loses its definition. As noise becomes music. Information without context is noise. The random distribution of energy is the domain necessity. Probability. Random information—noise—is epistemologically distinct from meta-energy." This is Anthony Wilden I'm talking. Therefore truth equals process. That's a leap. The system creates the allowance, the gap, for noise's entry. Kojève says, "For man, the adequation of being and concept is a process, and truth is a result of process." Now he says this process is logos, or discourse. And I ought to say here that my use of Logos generally throughout the afternoon is not in fact using the term to mean discourse but rather to use it to mean structure. Because coming out of a quotation Robert Kelly made, which I can't quote properly of course, language is the only genetic. Which comes back to structure, genetics, and so forth. So I'll add those terms here so I know what I'm doing here. We might then call that fate, using the old trinity of the three Norns. Fate necessity being. What I'm going to be coming to say is that, given the structure of my own nerval body, given that I have feelings and emotions, necessity, form; given that I have a method of summating or synthesizing them, making a synthesis out of my emotions and my structure, I could survive. I could exist. So I put being as opposed to becoming and I don't think I really want to get into the differences between being and becoming at this moment. But being and concept as a process, as a truth if you like, or as a result, that is interesting. "The result of process merits the name of truth." That's Kojève again. Youngblood said, "Structure and form subsumed by place." I'll put that word up. By that word place he means process, I believe. Certainly I do. And because I see process as a synthesis, a summating of form and structure, I've put it on the right hand side there. Not to categorise it too heavily. To show it would in fact cross all three. The process of dwelling in a place. The process of being. But there is no separation, only impingement, or interface. "The signal, a bite, where energy and information are one. The sign, a nip, where there is a distinction, that is, digital." This is Gregory Bateson. "Play has survival value. A nip is play but a bite isn't. The pretence of deceit, however, is essentially human, of a different order from play." "The nip denotes the bite but it does not denote what would be denoted by the bite. It is a message of a different logical type; a map for which there is no longer a simple, one-dimensional, territory." Man, people, can be classified as a survival kit. If I qualify it by saying that the people are healthy, or at least taking steps to become so. Pythagoras said, in his *Music of the Spheres*, which Butler quotes, Christopher Butler, that "the physical bodies in the heavens must be moving so rapidly that they emit sound. The spatial intervals between the seven planets and the sphere of the fixed stars would correspond to the mathematical ratios for the notes of the octave in the diatonic scale; and that the sounds emitted by them would also so correspond." The spindle of the cosmos turns on the knees of necessity. I'm taking this slowly because obviously it's not an easy thing to assimilate very quickly.

I'm trying to show various bases by which many writers have come upon aesthetic structures, whatever you like to call them, from which to work. Towards which to work. There's three more here. Pico says "Structure is that which I contemplate." Augustine, overtly literacy, "Allegorical means of interpretation, of scholarly literature, but coloured by sacred books, interest, ordained, planned, divined." Of course he has his own reasons for adding some of those words. I think in fact though that he's basing them in part at least on men like Pythagoras. The third one here, "Serious scientific hypotheses."—no name. Book of Wisdom: "Thou hast ordered all things in number and measure, and weight." That links to Augustine, and it links to Plato in *Timaeus*. If we remember Andrew Marvell, commenting on *Paradise Lost*, "By verse created, thy theme sublime, /In number weight and measure, no needs not rhyme." So there's a breakthrough there, to indicate why it might be useful. Why it might give you a security, perhaps, to have a structure. Other than rhyme.

Brain. Figuratively, the nervous makeup, the ears nose tongue, eyes, skin, brain and spinal system, acting preconsciously, subconsciously, consciously. All of which the process would have to include. Form changes. It can be organised, organised energy. It can be visible or invisible, known or unknown. But it always allows for growth. It grows. But what separates us from animals? significantly. I mean I think it could be fairly well said that structure and form is nature. I mean, Nature has structure and form. You'd have to make some very strong leaps to find out what happens next. If you take it, as Hugh MacDiarmid does, and as I do, that human consciousness is an evolution from nature, or beyond nature, then you have to start saying, there's not just structure and form taking place, but some form of summation or synthesis of those terms, which would carry those terms beyond themselves. So that whilst I might have a rigid structure to write a work like *The Art of Flight*, and whilst I have probably fairly predictable feelings, but nonetheless not predictable, in terms of translating that structure into words and so forth, before that work really becomes human, if you like, before it becomes the work by a poet, I must take into account the evolution brought about by brain. We must… This brain word here is complex, so that brain is as much here as it is there. I think I've spread that. I'll say it again. There are no compartments intended here. Each is only because of each other. There's a blur, overlap, interface, interference. Those are the kind of words that would indicate what I'm saying. Growth and structure, then, are one. Are many, if you like. But could be put inside a limitation to be called one. Whereas that cannot be the case for brain. The whole is moving in structured signatures made individual by the blood. Structured collectively in signatures. Synthesized and changed continually by the brain's wonder. You can choose between precision of organised simplicity—mechanics—and the statistical precision of the study of unorganised complexity. Which would be modern thermodynamics. But "Classical physics"—this is Anthony Wilden speaking again, "lacks an epistemology and methodology to deal with organised complexity. This is the domain of biology, communication, and human science. And possibly, more recently, of subatomic physics." So I'll just recap again. Fate being necessity, form structure place. "Time is control"—William Burroughs. "There is a need for time, and words, to think in categories." Kant. Ecstatic. Conception of time, inseparable from movement. So perhaps I ought to now add some more words there. Two. On the one side of the coin, that which is static, consistent, in terms of *The Art of Flight*, the structure from Bach's *Art of Fugue*, which didn't change, initially. So that which causes the change, call it flux. So there's a sweeping going on, probably brought about initially by what is in the middle of it here, blood. Necessity. Feelings. A sense of nausea at having the same structure, I should think. "The concept of survival must be one which considers the unit of survival to be: organism, plus environment." That is to say, it includes other organisms. It's social. "The system which disposes of its environment disposes of itself." Anthony Wilden quoting Marx. Louis Zukofsky; "Prose, chopped up into verses of alternately rhyming lines, of an equal number of syllables, is not poetry." Poetry convinces not by argument but by the form it creates to carry its content. I think that's much more useful in terms of Louis Zukofsky's work than as a general statement, in all honesty. Mainly because he's using the term form, which I would want to carry further and say, it has to be summated with structure to give a work beyond one or the other. Lévi-Strauss says, "The meaningful element was not always the one they supposed, placed where it most often is at the microscopic level. A reality revealed to us only through recent inventions—telecommunications, computers, and electron microscopes." It's this business of… It's only through the summation of feeling and structure—using those terms very freely, very widely—that you can get beyond supposition.

Because of the term feedback, which I first saw in Norbert Wiener's work on cybernetics, we've not just got that sweeping flux happening, you've got a process going the other way, changing the structure. So that's where the analogies begin to stop, because you can't start saying that is possible in poetic work, in artistic work, I'd rather it wasn't possible in genetics. I'm very happy that feedback will change the structure of the way in which I'm working. I'd be extremely unhappy if it changed the structure of my body. I mean in a very basic way. What does that lead me to? It leads me to say, whilst on the one hand I'm saying, my body has a fixed structure, I'm also saying that I want that structure to change. Because I'm not creating out of nothing. I'm creating out of my body, which is including brain and bone. I'll leave that as a question mark at the moment. The possibility of used structures, of using structures. Impossibility of not doing so. One of the—I'm not quite sure what category to put it in—one of the poetries that I have distrust of is those poetries which speak of automism, automatic writing. If the person who is the automatic writer is telling me that he's getting something which does not repeat. It is not possible to not use your structure. Your own memory bank, if you like, body makeup, your own nerval feeling, emotional complex. It is not possible to write without use of that, unconsciously or otherwise. What I would like to lead to then is to say, as that is the case, shouldn't we be making ourselves more conscious of what that structure is? which would give us more ability to move, to change, that structure.

[Martianus] Capella. Some of the cards in here are just reminding me of the concern people have had with number. Probably since the beginning of civilisation. It's almost as if it was part of the definition of civilisation. Capella gives the monad as the principle, one world one god one sun. Unity. He says that two makes a line. It makes a separation, a discord, and is capable of mediation. And he says that three is esteemed as perfect in eastern circles. Such terms keep cropping up in mediaeval literature. I'm not exactly averse to them. That mediaeval thing—I'm not going to pretend I'm a mediaeval scholar. I should say, so far as I'm aware, they certainly crop up in Chaucer, and they certainly crop up in *Gawaine and the Greene Knight*. Which I can hardly read, in honesty, because of my lack of knowledge of that older language. But both that particular time and most of Chaucer's major works are in fact composed on numeric structures which have been shown by people like Alistair Fowler, and by people whose names I don't have in my head. But for instance the *Boke of the Duchesse*, *Troilus and Cressida*, and some work at the moment for instance is being done on *The Parliament of Foules* I believe it is. Might have been *The House of Fame*. So that for instance you get into… in Sir Philip Sidney's work *Astrophel and Stella* the numerical structure is such that in the middle of the poem the sun has risen—one of the images through the poem is the celestial hemisphere—and you can follow it through day, night, and so forth, in the poem, and follow it by line number. Those are paradigms that we would change. But I think we still might find our own paradigms to do something similar with. Certainly I'm trying to. Talcott Parsons' definition of structure is, "a stable disposition of the elements of a social system", I've emphasised, "impervious to externally imposed disturbances. It leads to a theory of social equilibrium." I don't know if he means mass value there, I'm hoping not. "Order, peaceful co-existence in conditions of scarcity, is one of the very first of the fundamental functional imperatives of social systems." Thus I would suggest he's not using structure in the same way I am. Form is open to energy, open to information. Saussure says, "The change, if effected in chess, belongs not to the structure, preceding or subsequent, the change can only be explained by reference to the desire or to the goals of the chess player." The reference to patterns is not the explanation of the change. To Piaget, as a system of transformations. That would be one of his definitions of structure. "A system of transformations, preserved and enriched by the interplay of its transformalities, which never go beyond its frontiers" which is interesting, "nor employ elements that are external to it" which would lead us into what somebody like Spencer Brown would be saying. To do with boundaries. That we in fact need boundary in works of art. By that of course, I would need to add, I'd need changing boundaries. Nonetheless it is quite useful to find your own particular limitations, I mean to make use of limitations. I think it's part of the survival kit I'm talking about. One of the reasons I keep raising this matter of survival, for instance, one of the reasons, is that I often meet writers who are having blocks, mental blocks, who are unable to write at particular times. Sometimes that doesn't matter to them. That's fine, of course. But sometimes it bothers them to extreme degrees. Very extreme degrees, in fact, in some cases. And I think some of what I am saying can act towards a survival kit. That is to say, that it is possible for these people to find themselves structures to play with, to do something similar for instance to what I did with Bach's *Art of the Fugue*, in the initial stages anyway. And what that does, it seems to me, is create not open the new triggers, but create new triggers. It really does form new avenues, it changes your own structure. "In open systems"—this is Buckley—"a necessary tension which is produced of organisation." Now that's interesting. If we look upon tension, not negatively, but as something that we need as much as don't, "environmental interchange is not a random or unstructured event, because of the mapping or coding or information processing capabilities of the open, its adaptiveness." Environment is essentially an open system, OK. Perception is not. In the way which it is not possible to randomly see trees. "The ultimate conceptual poem might be the blank page. The act of writing through that." Tom Raworth. That relates back to the survival I was speaking of, in some ways, but it also impinges upon a different area. It's impossible for me to fully explain what I'm about to say but you'll just have to bear with me, disagree or otherwise. And that is that it's possible to assert that we are born with structures. Now, having said that, you can load it or unload it. You can say, that structure must include some form of innate feel for language, which Chomsky would say. He wouldn't use those words. Or it's possible to make it much heavier than that. All I'm trying to say is that there is a fixity, there is a moving. Through that interchange and that summation the leap becomes possible, the creation becomes possible. The hope. The prime task for action, for the act, is to make conscious. Therefore, if I can make as much of that process conscious as possible, I'll be in control of it. And the more I'm in control of what I'm doing, the better, presumably, the outcome is. Therefore being conscious allows for deeper conceptualization. Spenser was well up to the most technical aspects of astronomy, and well able to use them to impart a further allegorical dimension to his myth, that of course is the *Faerie Queene*. Time. Duration. Consciousness and use of the category changed. The modern novel. "Duration, not decor but an a priori, outside characters and their time." This is Anthony Wilden. "The work of writing the novel itself is the goal", Marcel Proust. In human time, the future is primary. Articulated on human desire. So if we put here perception, which has got to come across and go rattling straight across into structure, in your heads I hope, and I've got here, memory, which will do the same the other way, because of the way the brain works. It's possible to speak of hope. I don't know where to put it, really. And in that word, I would suggest, are the terms writing, creation, belief, and hop. Shakespeare's *Midsummer Night's Dream*. In fact, one of the habits I picked up last time was to continually re-read this piece, because it's a bit difficult to pick up immediately. In terms of what I'm speaking of. Things base and—he puts vile but I'll say wild, because my annotator puts a word in which I find a bit odd, vile

> Things base and wild, holding no quantity,
> Love can transpose to form and dignity.
> Love looks not with the eyes, but with the mind,
> And therefore is winged Cupid painted blind.

> Nor hath Love's mind of any judgment, taste.
> Wings and no eyes figure unheedy haste.
> And therefore is love said to be a child,
> Because in choice he's so oft beguiled.

I'll return to that. It brings me immediately to Charles Kelly's work, who I'd like to interpose. He's a post-Reichian practitioner. And from his book *Education and Feeling*—I beg your pardon, *Education in Feeling and Purpose*—What I'm working towards here—I'm using Kelly, I should add, analogically—if you like—certainly it's possible to consider I'm not doing so—that is, the intention is that I am using it analogically. "Education in feeling can profoundly deepen the emotional experience that takes place when any good conceptual approach is employed." I think that's extremely interesting. What I think he's suggesting there, or what I'm suggesting through his words, is that education in what my forms are, my form is, my emotions and so forth, takes place after I conceptualise, after I've made conscious the structure. "An individual's consciousness is a spontaneous energy-producing process and could achieve the control over itself expressed in volitional purposeful activity. Purpose and feeling, use to increase and amplify, rather than to contradict and nullify each other. Purpose is a function achieved by man alone." So by purpose he means the control by an individual of his own life over time to achieve a goal that he has selected. I don't think that is necessary to be named. That distinguishes true purpose from goal-seeking behaviour in general.

If somebody came up to me and said, What's your purpose, I wouldn't have an answer, in simple terms. "Animals must organise their behaviour around goals if they are to survive." I come back here, though, if we put that analogue through into the actual writing process. Purpose. Feeling. And summate those two terms. Creation. That is useful. "The reason voluntary attention is such an effort is that it involves a conflict of impulses. Long-range goals are attainable only when the attraction of short-range satisfactions incompatible with the goal can be successfully resisted." So for the sake of a further analogy, if in the course of writing *The Art of Flight*, in the first parts of the structure I'd noticed, that, to be mundane, three of the words rhymed, and the fourth looked much tidier, that would seem to me to be what he termed, I've lost it, a short-range satisfaction. I think I'll return to Kelly, give you one more from him. There are ten quotes I've pulled out from him. To put across my views rather than his, I ought to emphasize that. His views are much more concerned with psychiatry, and therapy and so forth. "To realise one's potential, to establish and achieve one's rational objectives, themes must not only be developed, experienced, and expressed. They must be organised and given direction." To me that's very useful. Louis Zukofsky says "Emotion is the organiser of the poetic form." Pound says "A new cadence is a new idea." Wilden equates desire with goal-seeking. Which is why this must blur. Distinguished from instinctual need and from demand. Conceptualisation thus involves knowing. Knowing what the aim is. What the goal is. "Man creates himself through labour." I heard a programme last week on Rembrandt, and I don't know whether the guy was a mathematician, but he'd calculated that in 40 years' creative work Rembrandt was producing a masterpiece every two and a half hours. Man creates himself through labour. We've all seen these bloody films of Tchaikovsky, for instance, he never sits down at his desk and puts his hand to paper, and you think, God, it must be a great life to be a composer. That comes into what I'm saying, I'm sure. "The concept of signification. It is the information which organises the work to be done." Making conscious again. "Transformations of the given is unalienated labour." The production of the artefact. Sorry, that was Anthony Wilden. We seem to have a lot of him at the moment. Another word that I would include, the processual, there. Extempore. If I recall, what I've been saying is in fact headed Procedure and process. The reason I didn't head it Survival, actually, is that I thought the wrong people would come, with the wrong idea. Herbert Read: "Perception itself is essentially a pattern-selecting and pattern-making function, a gestalt-bound formation. And that pattern is inherent in the physical structure or in the functioning of the nervous system. This organisation of parts can only be categorised as aesthetics." I don't agree with that. What he's saying there is very useful in terms of perception, I think. The word aesthetics has taken on such a load of meaning these days that it becomes difficult to use. Lancelot Law Whyte: "For many scientists the primary emphasis appears to have switched from the discovery of new fundamental laws to the progressive identification of natural structures." In many ways I equate what scientists do with what poets do. They are making a synthesis. They are also, in Feyerabend's terms, making exclusions. They are giving themselves annotations, they're also making exclusions, in order to, you wouldn't be able to see a structure if the structure was all-inclusive. So in order to see the structure, if you like, it is necessary to exclude what is not the structure. "Intuitive process is in fact taught." That's controversial, I would have said, and I agree with it. It's in fact from P. C. Scholfield: "Intuition, intuitive process, is taught." He says that in the use of systems, systems of proportion, he's talking about, "If the use of systems of proportion were the result of intuition, one would expect the same types of relationships to have appeared spontaneously in all periods of good design. In fact this is not the case, and the sorts of mathematical relationships which occur are closely related to the mathematical knowledge of the period." His works are quoted by Christopher Butler. G Spencer Brown: "In all mathematics it becomes apparent at some stage that we have for some time been following a rule without being consciously aware of the fact." This might be described as the use of a covert or convention. In many ways, by making conscious my structure, I'm making sure that I'm cutting through what Marcuse described as second nature, calling what I do natural. When I can't at all be sure that's the case. "A recognizable aspect of the advancement of mathematics consists in the advancement of the consciousness of what we are doing, whereby the covert becomes overt." And then he says, this is G. Spencer Brown, "Mathematics is in this respect psychedelic." Marvellous. For instance, 'The presence of an arrangement in the absence of an agreement. Or, procedures have been adopted without comment, even without realising they are procedures." Later on he says "One of the most beautiful facts emerging from mathematical studies is a very potent relationship between the mathematical process and ordinary language. There seems to be no mathematical idea of any importance or profundity that is not mirrored with an almost uncanny accuracy in the common use of words, and this appears especially true when we consider words in their original and sometimes lowly forgotten senses." A funny word, *lowly*, a bit odd actually. He might not have used that. I might be. "We cannot escape the fact that the world we know is constructed in order, thus in such a way as, to be able to see itself." I've picked a big pile of G Spencer Brown cards here. Some of his concepts are a bit difficult, his language I find a bit obtuse at times. "The value of a call made again is the value of the call." That's in fact quite lovely, isn't it. That the notes remain the same, if you like. If I'm using a set of notes, and call upon them again, they still remain the same. So, what's changing. It's not the structure that's changing there, but the way in which you are approaching that structure, which I might call the form. "For any name, to recall is to call."

Then he goes into this boundary business. "The value of a crossing made again is not the value of the crossing." To recross is not to cross. "Feeling does not act in the same way as structure." I feel that's a reasonable analogue to make. Although I'm approaching the same notes, each time I approach them the notes are the same, I am—I've got to be, different. "Distinction is drawn by arranging a boundary with separate sides, so that a point on one side cannot reach the other side without crossing the boundary." A circle in space. "There can be no distinction without motive, and there can be no motive unless contents are seen to differ in value." Seems clear enough. I think I mentioned it earlier in any case, in my own ways. The rest are some etymologies, from the same source—some of which I've already given from other sources, funnily enough. "Existence, stand outside." Yes, I saw much more movement there than he does. I would see not just standing outside, I would see it as moving outside, rather. So I'm not quite sure there who's. He's identifying the action with the adding. He's saying the universe—and this is presumably something that Robert Duncan has picked up on, because he no longer speaks of a universe but of a multiverse—universe, unus 1, verto turn. What is seen as the result of one turn. World. *wer*, man. He sees it as the manifest properties of the all. Its identity, the age of man. The fact that man is a primary animal with a hand. Makes manifest. hand, stuck. Not a lot of use for massaging. To explain is to lay out in a plane. Where the particulars can be readily seen. His book is called *Laws of Form*. "Structure generates language and action." Richard Grossinger, discussing Freudian slips. Signatures before language. Action before speech. I wouldn't necessarily agree with him. "A poem is the, and or a, signature of my existence. A way of making its invisibility visible." Automatic writing. "If the notion of the possibility for highly procedural"—it's a notion—it is highly procedural because of the genetic that is language. It's certainly not intuitional. It's a fake intuitional. Louis Zukofsky: the main Zukofsky quotes are coming out of a book called *The Test of Poetry*. I'm sure I'll be corrected if I'm wrong. That's not the title. It's not a book you can buy, that's the bloody nuisance of it. How someone can let these things go out of print. Somebody as important as Zukofsky. "Probably the best equivalent of the Italian sonnet form"—and he's talking now about Mark Alexander Boyd—and then he gives the details of how that's laid out mathematically. A matter of fourteen lines, set rhyme, a scheme, ten syllables to a line, ascending sentence X and so forth. "The form should involve statement of a subject, development, resolution." "It's dissociated from music, the sonnet, because it's really a poor versification of amateurs without emotion or a sense of the relation of the parts of a composition to the whole." I'm not saying I don't argue with Zukofsky. I think I might, in many ways. Although I wouldn't have the presumption to do that to his face. I mean, I have great respect for Zukofsky, it's just that I'm saying that he's not fitting into my own particular structures at this particular moment. "Although memory retains locatable information, in patterns, the information cannot be localised, because it involves a relationship between patterns." That's the blurring I was speaking about earlier. Eddington, speaking about ratios. "The ratio of particle action is to radiation action a value of 1:3:7". There's a whole list of various ratios, which I won't labour you with here at this moment. What he's doing in fact is just crossing boundaries, showing there are ratios between different structures. "Closure is control." Control isn't bad, if it's your own control over your own self. "Motive is closure." Whether about organisation of variety, independence, control, susceptibility to change. Flexibility, creativity, innate drives, repetition, entropy. "The genetic systems has been altered by the reaction of its audience." Very odd statement, that. "Changes in the level, or part of the environment result through the relation of feedback in changes in the products of the programme of the system." In Robert Kelly's *Against the Code* we seem to come to what I was looking for. "Through the manipulation and derangement of ordinary language the conditioned world is changed, weakened in its associative links, its power to hold an unconscious world-view together." "Language is the only genetics field in which a man is understood and understands, and becomes what he thinks, becomes what he says following the argument." That's in his work *Against the Code*, inside *Millinery Particulars*. Anybody wants any of these references, I'll give them gladly later. "It is not lack of organisation or lack of order, but over-organisation, over-order which threatens survival." "In language, there is a very large number of ways of saying the same thing, and an infinite number of possible messages, determined by the code or by the syntax, or over determined where the symptom is determined in several ways. But DNA is not language. The genetic code is an original system of writing, linked to natural selection, which prevents random variation." "It's not ruled by casualty, or goal-seeking, or constraint. DNA is the molecular coding of a set of instructions for the growth of a certain living system of cells, and these instructions do not cause growth. They control its possibilities, and the instructions differ because of the environment. The feedback relationship RNA—that's the messages carrying the instructions—find themselves in a feedback." I don't know what analogy one would want to pick up upon there. Certainly punctuation would come in I think. "Ezekiel's vision of the chariot has the structure of 27 verses, the number of the deity cubed. Though information is dependent on some physical base, or energy flow, the energy component is entirely subordinate to the particular form or structure of variations that the physical base or flow may manifest.", Buckley. He gets too heavy with his DNA materials there. Wilden: "The relationship between chance and necessity is directly correlative with the relationship between system and environment. Random here then is not random but necessity. What is random is only the particular form which the system decides this variation will take." That's quite interesting discussion in terms of random. Gardner's work on random numbers throws light on the fact that such doesn't exist. There's another school of thought which would throw the emphasis completely the other way. In fact Feyerabend would probably be part of that emphasis which would insist that structures are in fact random anyway. I'm not sure about that. Alberti tries to show that our aesthetic response need not be arbitrary or unpredictable. "Any attempt at randomness"—Richard Grossinger—"would be countered by the fact that no condition is random but any action or thought is instantly textural." As writers, we're talking about perception. Martin Gardner: "Most mathematicians now agree that a completely disordered series of digits is a logically contradictory concept. A series can no more be patternless than an arrangement of stars in the sky can be. The reason in both cases is that a series of digits or an arrangement of points that comes closer and closer to satisfying all tests for randomness begins to exhibit a very rare and unusual type of statistical regularity, and that in some cases even permits the prediction of missing portions. If it gets too random, a pattern of disorder, so to speak, appears." "Pythagoras: $1+2+3+4=10$." The blood. Colloquially, a lot of people would give heart, I think.

I originally got the idea Blood Bone Brain from the hieroglyphs in Egyptian art for Life, which was a jug containing the blood, presumably the heart, a bone, and an eagle, which I interpreted as brain. I'm not sure if that was correct. As a matter of interest, the highest point a bird of prey reaches in its flight is called its place. And so it would be quite appropriate to put an eagle in there.

So I'm reiterating in fact now on the cards. Blood. Changes. Is the changer. Bone in the terms I'm using here, is the structure. The shaped matter. That is possible to make visible. But there aren't any compartments and I'm not talking about three bottles on the table but a river on the table.

Interview by Adrian Clarke
for *Angel Exhaust*, 1987

Did you start writing with a sense of any sort of prevailing authority?

AF It depends how I interpret the question. I started writing in school; and part of what I was writing in school was rude rhymes for my mates—pass them round the class. Paraphrases of Keats and Kerouac and... crossing out letters in Wordsworth to create new words and sentences and so on. But if that's a response to authority, Wordsworth being an authority of some kind, then the answer would be yes to the question. But I could also interpret the question to—I mean the word "authority" to mean something more—other than literature, something outside of literature. For instance, in a response to governmental attitude or some cultural attitude that seemed to be pervading or something of that kind. Now I don't think I started writing with that in view, as far as I could say. I don't think it was politically directed in that sense.

Does that imply you had no sense of a culture within which you were writing? no sense of that culture having a weight of authority to which you had to conform or in some way respond?

AF In retrospect I could say it was cultural authority I was writing against, interfering with or even at times agreeing with. At school the most modern requirement would be to read WH Auden—or TS Eliot, whichever one thinks of as being the more modern of those two. But that was—we almost didn't touch on that. I mean that is as modern as it got. So my response was not to read Auden, but to read alternatives. I was caned at school for reading Kerouac under the desk in an English class. So that would give you some idea historically of American poetry in England. People like Kerouac were not part of the canon that was considered literature. My response to authority is that, really, it's being bored with—not necessarily with Wordsworth per se, but with the classes on Wordsworth; with the context in which Wordsworth was taught. I mean there was a period, which I'll admit was also to do with examination requirements, where I had learnt 'The Ancient Mariner' off by heart. Stupid thing to have done. But it nonetheless put me in good stead for a one hour's paper or whatever. But I was never arguing with Coleridge; I was arguing with Wordsworth, if anyone. But not with Wordsworth, rather with the way Wordsworth was being presented. The trouble with retrospection is that you're not sure what actually happened. A book like *Tree Birst* came out of what I was doing at school—doodling with Wordsworth's books: Wordsworth's *The Prelude* essentially. And it'd be too cheap of me to say it was simply an overt, realised attack on his authority, if you like. I don't think it was as self-conscious as that. What was self-conscious, in other words, after having come in this big circle, was reading literatures other than the one I was expected to be reading. Which I suppose eventually filtered through to what I was writing. So I read Kerouac, I read *The Dharma Bums*, found out this intrigue about who the characters were in *Dharma Bums*. This led on to many things like reading translations—from Chinese by Arthur Waley and Ezra Pound. That kind of thing. These people weren't on the curriculum at all.

To come to the sources of your writing, do you see them as given by your culture or chosen in spite of it?

AF Both. One of the problems is what is "the culture"? Part of the activity is involved with the creation of a sub-culture of some kind through, for instance, blues records at school. And jazz records. And snooker. Which was far more interesting than the school activity; which actually created a sub-culture. I mean, that's a task not overtly or self-consciously what it does, but that's eventually, or self-consciously, what it did. So that becomes a culture. So you work not in a culture, but in many cultures that are overlapping. So that the generalisation "culture" worries me, because I would see—especially living in London—that it's… I would agree that there could be an overview or a holistic view which says there's a culture. But that would be such a multifarious affair that it would be just as interesting to talk about the overlapping cultures occurring in London or indeed internationally through mail-art and all the rest of it. So coming back to the question, I think really it was an appreciating response to some of the Beat writers and some of what Pound was writing, had written. But I think it would be over-coy to say it was a celebration, but it was… certainly I love the work I was reading of theirs and would aspire to it at some point. What age I would be I'm not quite sure, but not very young and not that old either. I would think somewhere like the age of 18 or so.

The range of your sources seem to have increased over the past few years.

AF I missed the word source didn't I? I didn't really talk about that. So that was one kind of source then. Which is, in other words, the kind of source that I would read out of pleasure as much as anything else. But then there was this kind of feeling of being uneducated—leaving school at 17, going straight to work and—I mean the work educated me, but it was an unwritten education, if you see what I mean. And so I moved towards what's become a sort of further education. I mean what happened in school was I didn't get on in mathematics—which really amounted to I didn't get on in arithmetic, because you're not taught mathematics until they agree that you can do some arithmetic. And they didn't put me into an arts stream either, because I wasn't very good at Latin—in fact I was lousy. It was that kind of streaming technique at school. So that meant you weren't arts, because you weren't Latin and you weren't science, because you weren't mathematics, so you were technical. So I did a lot of metalwork and woodwork and so on and so forth. Technical drawing, in fact, was what I came out of school with of any substance and which I never overtly used. And so there's a recuperation occurring, I was kind of trying to generate, regenerate myself. And that inevitably becomes—whether I like it or not that would become another source-area. Because it would mean a lot of reading of—a lot of self-education involved with reading books on science, on philosophy, none of which was given at school. And that's predominantly… in the first place, an education rather than a pleasure. But there's also a pleasure involved in that, and in fact an amused fascination with the use of vocabularies. Because it was untutored, because it was self-taught, the emphasis wasn't on proving or coming out with substantial (however small) essays, for instance, to substantiate this particular area, that particular area. It was a reading and note-taking activity which—if it's centred at all, was centred around what my concerns were and at the time were to do with writing and making art performances. And so I would use the material as vocabulary rather than as, perhaps, it's intended as, in order to create this experiment or prove that this is in fact the best way to describe light. Whilst that's interesting, what was more interesting for me was the vocabulary used in order to create that description. So, so it becomes a kind of strange epistemology of some kind; it's strange because the vocabulary has more interest than the actual knowledge—the application of the vocabulary. In fact, I deliberately misapplied/misapply it quite a lot. I don't know when that started—no, I wouldn't even want to guess really, but I suppose it was in the '70s. In an early section of *Place* you write: "we are directed and ruled by material… design flows for the process … as we direct it."

Is there a shift of emphasis from directing to being directed by between much of Place *and more recent work?*

AF Yes, yes, that's right, there is. I was very much caught up in that almost idealist idea of art being processual. Although, strangely enough, it took a secondary role because of something to do with the poetry conditions in London: that is to say the response to *Place* was stronger than the response to work that was other than *Place*. Now the work that was other than *Place* is procedural as opposed to processual. I mean, clearly, you can't just separate them like that, as I've just done, but... *Tree Birst*, for instance, follows Wordsworth's *Prelude*, so in that sense it has a procedural structure which was it follows, if you like, Wordsworth as a score to be played with. Whereas *Place* used a deterministic element quite differently. It used it in an overall plan sense which was not to do with the intricacy of page or line or sentence or anything of that kind, but had to do with a requirement of, a mapping I created which was far broader than that: to do with areas that I wanted to cover. Which is, I suppose, where some of the epistemology comes in at an overt non-vocabulary level, at the same time as the vocabulary interest. Essentially what I'm trying to say is that the overview on *Place* would be that the work is very processual and seem to be almost made like some gestural painting, that is to say it's—the piece of paper is on the desk and that's that piece of paper and then we'll move on to the next piece and so on and so on. But in fact that is partly a ruse because that is not the only effective method used, because the decisions prior to the actual writings were elaborately outlined—if that's the way of saying it. So there were both elements at play in *Place*—intentionally. Whereas the processual element seemed to take—to somebody looking at it—the precedent. Now the reason for that is partly, I think, a mistake I made very early on in *Place*, which was to allude to Charles Olson. And it immediately gave this whole apparatus that was already in existence in 1950 or whenever as an overlay for the work—as *a* way of *reading* it. And I'll accept that's a way of reading the work. But in fact that isn't the—that isn't accurate, because the work was written in parallel with work that I was doing in performance ... and making art objects and making mail art objects, which has much more to do with memory. And so that fed into *Place*, but it's not apparent when taken in isolation—in other words, when *Place* is "this is the work called *Place*". The overall apparency is of a processual work, but I would suggest it's not too difficult to see that in fact there are very strongly indicated structural plans involved. I can give one brief example of that and that would be that the original plan was for five books. The idea is that, having written Book One, Book III would have—a kind of mirror to Book One. And so it's possible to relate the last page in *Stane* to the first page in *Place* and so forth—moving backward two different ways. And indicate that by using some of the same words at some point, so that at one section—in one page in *Place* Book One you get something which is called "Chorus", which in *Stane* occurs at the same place, only in reverse—which is also called "Chorus" and it's just been printed backwards. And that is just a banal indication of what I was doing. But in fact—I'm sorry to elaborate this, but in fact this might help quite a bit—if you look at that mirror structure, therefore, if we can call it a mirror structure just to simplify, you can see that quite often there's a relationship that goes to and fro like that, so that for instance when I was asked to make a selection of *Place* for Christian Bourgois in France, that's all I did: was to go through the work and say, "Where has this happened?" because what I found was it didn't always happen. There are times when—there are all sorts of reasons—I would change my mind about it. Work as dropped in as the second piece or the third piece or the fourth piece across the Books, became something else—it wasn't a mirror at all, it had almost no relationship to the other work, but I would still allow it. So that would be the processual element that disrupted the procedural—the procedural structure. But that also—and this is where it gets a bit silly, really, this also was partly intended. Not initially, but eventually—that is to say, during the course of *Place*, during the course of the writing, which I suppose was about nine years—something like that, I deliberately interfered with the work and would—do you know, I've forgotten the terminologies I once used to describe that, but they would cut in ("cut in" would be one term) and things like that… to disrupt the expectancy somewhat—for myself as much as anybody else.

To what extent does performance now affect the shape your writing takes?

AF Ah, the performance I mentioned before is actually slightly different, but it's… yes, that's a good question. In fact I think that—the problem is the word "performance". When I first mentioned what I was referring to was the kind of performance I did with Fluxus—or Fluxshoe, it was, because it was a very late development in this country. And that sometimes meant poetry, but more often than not it was a wider activity which involved sounds and objects and a lot of games, a lot of play with audience and other friends and so on. Whereas I think you're referring at the moment to the performance of the text, i.e. vis-à-vis reading of it and so on. Before I come up with a finished text I've always read it aloud. And part of my compositional procedure involves reading it aloud to myself. So to that extent there's an influence, there's a—I'm creating ways of making it better to read, so that some of the placing on the page is intended to make it better for me to read—whether that's actually affecting the work, that's something else. You see, one of the other developments I tried was to improvise the reading. Now clearly I improvise a reading in terms of speeds, in terms of tones, in terms of voices, but I don't now often add words or take words away—not intentionally. Whereas there was a period in the '70s when I was trying to actually write texts that would generate words that I hadn't yet written during the performance. That wasn't to do with *Place*, but was in fact to do with other works.

You have written of a narrative "prone to breaking up, opening, rebuilding" that becomes "an organisation of energy". I take some of the work in Brixton Fractals—*particularly 'Bel Air'—to be an exploration of this approach. Is it one you intend to pursue through the rest of* Gravity as a Consequence of Shape?

AF That's actually a question I can't answer or that I can only partially answer. Narrative is something I am pursuing at the moment—it's an area I'm having a struggle with. As to whether it's something I project will occur at a later date, I'm not sure. There is no question that it will to the extent that the work is self-referral and is self-interfering, self-critical—so it keeps going back to this or that part of this other text and disagrees with it or something of that kind. To that extent, if 'Bel Air' can be thought of as having these narrative elements, there might be a poem that latterly crops up that criticises some of those. It might, for instance, criticise continuity or it might criticise lack of it; it might criticise some of the conventionality that it creates in term of its potential reading as drama or its potential making of stereotypes or whatever—like The Burglar, for example. So there is always this self-critical framework that is going to lift narrative up again and again, but it isn't necessarily going to make narrative the centre of discussion of the work... I think the reason narrative crops up again and again is because it relates very closely to one of the areas of the work which I won't be clever enough to define at this moment. One of the problems I'm having in essay-writing is to reconcile that history and theory—certainly in this country and in France—are considered different disciplines, so if you are writing an essay which is theoretical you're not writing one which is historical. That's a problem for me because my proclivity is to do both. You see, one of the consequences of using narrative is purely temporal—an understanding of what space-time is being represented in the work or not. And I have trouble with some of that, inasmuch as I want to critique it and nonetheless have a certain consistency in my own biologic form—have breakfast every day and so on, and if I didn't I wouldn't sustain myself. So there is a consistence that is going on that is very difficult to isolate. And so to a certain extent narrative occurs because I am the same or a very similar writer over a long period. And something like my conceptual attitude disagrees with that from time to time as the parameter, because

I'm making art and not making a diary: that is to say, the emphasis in my work wouldn't be on telling anybody about myself—quite the contrary, I hope. At least, not quite the contrary, because I wouldn't want to be scientifically removed—I wouldn't want to be in the state in which I was controlling what the work was outside of who I am. So there's this kind of complex going on of the narrative of the self—because the self is always the writer at one point or another, however much the work is derived from sources—which is being interfered with by the tearing of the self—not transcending of the self, changing of the self.

Going back to work with vocabularies and so on, how concerned are you that your writing should engage non-verbal realities?

AF A slow answer. I'm slow-answering this because I haven't long finished doing some work on Kandinsky and Paul Klee and Franz Marc and clearly one of their interests was making their visual work oral—almost smellable in places—or whatever. In other words, it's very synaesthetically orientated. And that's not my project. But clearly in my work there's an interest that I have in vocabularies that change tones or ambiences—which seem to be a larger sensory area than simply sound, for instance, or words spoken, but would—yes—at times be visual and at times be smell, touch—all sorts of areas that are other.

You wrote in Spanner *Twenty-Five of cultivating a plurivocity to ensure the meaningfulness of language and the avoidance of its co-option by the State. Are you satisfied that at a time of increasing legal infringement of freedoms this is an adequate response to "self-validating" official discourse? Might it be possible to challenge such language more directly without diluting the aesthetic function?*

AF We're thinking of that conceptually, aren't we? Would it be satisfactory as a praxis?—I suppose not. What I have to say is that I feel I'm limited by my activity. That is to say I don't have some Miltonic feeling that I can stand for a wider collective action which would involve somebody painting here and somebody making music there and so on, but I see the action as being a contribution towards what I hope would change a cultural malaise. To that extent, the statement's alright, provided it's understood it's not autonomous—I don't have the ability to be as profound or Miltonic as that. I mean I'm not after all being read by Cromwell or something: I don't have that kind of direct or potentially direct exchange with the political arena—or rather my exchanges are with living, if you see what I mean.—I'm not the King's Secretary or something… These hesitations… You see, I've got an argument with

59

"plurivocity" or "pluralistic" that I don't think I had a year ago and I'm not sure that I've resolved what my alternative is. One of the arguments could be that in being pluralistic you're potentially dissipating some of your energetic capability: that is to say, by not making it extremely clear what the direction is, instead of going in any direction you might go nowhere. I don't pretend to have resolved that... except to say I'm not at all happy with singularities of direction. I could see, for instance, that a negative word that could be applied to "pluralistic" could be "spread", suggesting "thin" "lack of depth". That's what's wrong with the word, that's the kind of parlance it's reaching, but I don't know what I'd change it to yet.

Turning to your own spread of energies, what motivated you to start a press?

AF I suppose the quick answer is to publish myself, but I don't think that's a very fair answer, because I wasn't the first person to publish my work—so it clearly wasn't just that ... You see, I want to avoid the obvious answer—which is too retrospectively coy or smart—which would be to say, 'Well, I could see this cultural situation going on where I wasn't being looked after by the larger presses so I thought I'll sort this out—I'll start a press and get things moving." That's not on: it would be an exaggeration. One thing I was doing in the '60s was attending Better Books and buying material from small presses, so there was a need, therefore, to be involved in that exchange, to understand that world—and to understand it as a preference. I preferred that publishing nexus to the other. It's preference in many different ways. I don't like, for example, the way Faber present their books: there's an inclination to apply the text to the book. I think the small presses do that the other way around—or at least, that's the ideal objective. So one of my responses is to make my own work. And that's still my preference to a certain extent, though I've actually shifted on that in the last year or so. I now appreciate there's more than one angle on this... essentially, why not publish a poem in *The Times*? Maybe it's of value somewhere along the line. I hadn't felt it was, frankly. I thought it was sufficient to create a cultural condition that was being dealt with by—let's be optimistic—400 people rather than 4000.

Do you share my impression the rather more exploratory poetries have become less available over the last few years and is there more we could be doing about that?

AF I certainly share your view on that. It almost drops me into a black hole of horror, really. It seemed when Better Books was in its heyday... clearly not just through selling books, but by creating a space where you would find out about other activities going on… it was a place you'd keep bumping into people. And because of that it was not only a useful, but I felt at the time an essential nexus, almost… The question's many-layered: because you haven't got a place that people regularly go to you don't get to see people. I was struck almost by a sense of nostalgia—except it wasn't nostalgia, because it was a kind of understanding that something really ought to be done—when Bruce Andrews was reading on Wednesday and Jerry Rothenberg happens to be in town and Pierre Joris happens to be in town and Paul Brown turns up to a reading, which he doesn't often do, and Paul Green comes up, which he doesn't often do, and all of a sudden there's a whole group of people who do know one another or know of one another and it's a far more lively occasion. And when that occurs at least once a week at a centre like a bookshop that's displaying materials you create a livelier subculture. Yes, I think there's a real need and I don't know what to do about it.

To come back to the work for a final question, we're promised more Gravity as a Consequence of Shape. *What else comes next?*

AF *Gravity as a Consequence of Shape* is clearly an unfinished project. Self-interference and transformation would be two of the terms in concert with this project. Ordering and disrupting would be a second set. The work started on the conceptual understanding that I wanted to research perceptions and consciousness. There was a grouping of approaches which I summarised as direct perception, investigation, and invention. These approaches are never exclusive of each other, but overlap. My proclivity is always to have more than one project underway which is simultaneously interfered with by a shifting embodiment—my living the project and the audacities and banalities that complex that. Your question "what comes next" is therefore of necessity without complete answer and yet can be partly answered through a reading of *Brixton Fractals*. The six-part project that *Gravity* is a part of adds to this description. *Ideas of the Culture Dreamed of* offers an overall suggestion. *Stepping Out* offers some of the way this suggestion might be broken, altered through aesthetic decisions. *Amnesic Instant* adds a visual dimension to the project. I'm currently working on paintings that interface with the texts. So the complex of the work is never fully realisable and always includes a tendency to realise and defamiliarise the situation. "What comes next" is frail in that each new part to the work deconstructs and potentially damages what has been written. "What comes next" is also made possible and potentially viable through this action. The answer is unknown subject to appropriate and inappropriate expectation. The project lends itself to understanding that the processual and procedural component of composition cannot be exclusive. It's part of an effort that aspires to cure malaise inside the comprehension that such a conception remains idealist and incompatible with each new realisation.

Interview with Scott Thurston, 1999

This interview took place on the fourth of May 1999 in Fisher's office at the University of Surrey, Roehampton, South London.

ST I wanted to set up this distinction between method and technique that I've taken from Barrett Watten's book *Total Syntax* as a parameter for some of the things that I'm interested in talking to you about. His idea is that 'method is the principle of construction that begins with the finished work, with the activity of the writer as a whole, the extension of the act of writing into the world and eventually into historical self-consciousness […] technique is the principle of construction in the writing, how the writing is written prior to the finished work' [*Total Syntax*, 1985, p. 32].

AF It's difficult to quite grasp why method doesn't start until you've finished the work. Isn't the problem, or could it be a problem, that you might conceptualise some of what will happen to a work before you've finished it? Wouldn't that therefore be part of it? Particularly as quite often I'm likely to conceptualise the work with some of those views in mind before the writing takes place, or whilst during the process of, or both. What's the purpose of the distinction in other words, I'm not quite sure in that case.

ST I think of method as your general approach to writing, within the context in which you do it, and technique as your specific means of composing an individual text. For me it's separating out the questions of why do you write and how did you write this particular text.

AF I see. He might not agree with that, of course. There's another one, just to throw a spanner on that, would be process and procedure.

ST My first question! Your response to my question of 'Do you feel that you write within a specific paradigm?' was 'I write within two, maybe three paradigm clusters, that like a Venn diagram, produce new potential paradigms: Constructionist and Procedural; Improvisatory and Processual'. Could you clarify what you mean by that distinction between the procedural and the processual?

AF If I just think of examples, there's likely to be a crossover between them. A procedural example would be that there is some predetermined structure which generates the text before the text. For instance, let's go through a range, the note pattern that creates an arithmetic from Bach's

The Art of the Fugue, the order of letters in William Wordsworth's *The Prelude,* and the way in which a piece of visual collage has been laid out on a page, so the positions are already demarcated. Now, if the text is written against those parameters, against those limitations, then the work is solely procedural, effectively. But what quite often happens is that, out of that work, there's some improvisation or changes of conceptions, decision changes, which are in the process of writing the work, so I call it processual in that sense. That's really where the blur is, but the real distinction is that a work like *Place,* for instance, is processual in the sense that, whilst it's planned—this text occurs here because of this research area or it's mirroring or distorting a reflection from another text—it's not procedural in the sense that it doesn't tell me how many words, or what a word order would be, or anything of that kind, it's dealt with processually in the sense that one writes a journal, or one writes through time and doesn't go back and interfere with that writing order by a procedural means. So there's an odd distinction I'm making there which actually is clear, but whether they're the right words is another issue really.

ST Do you feel that there's a dialectic between those two things in everything you do or do you sometimes feel that one work is more processual than procedural? I suppose that's what you've said about *Place.*

AF I think *Place* is processual effectively, although it's got a planned element in it, and I think that there are procedures in it, but it's not procedural really. Whereas, *The Art of Flight* is fairly strict, and so was *Defamiliarising.* It's interesting that you use the term dialectic though. I'm not sure about that. What that's inclined to do is put it into this camp or that camp, even if that's not what you mean, and I don't think it's quite as distinct as that. When writing *Place,* a so-called processual work, under my banner, there are elements in it that deliberately restrict what I do, which one could think of as predetermined, therefore procedural. They're distinct from processual but they're not dialectical to it in a real sense, unless you think of dialectic as more than two and unless you can take it on board as a complexity that would allow more than two, which I suppose you could, but then the word becomes a bit vague. Why I'm worrying about elaborating on this is because it's not this versus that, neither is it always this compatible with that, but it's quite often one enriching the other but not wholly informing in either way, because there might be three or four other elements involved.

ST Does that depend on the way in which you're actually composing? Do you think, for it to be process, that you have to be actually doing it at the time and that's going to stand whatever happens, that you're not necessarily going to go back and cover your tracks?

AF I think that's right. I'd also say something like leave the dirt on. So that's meaningful in that regard. That, of course, also means because we're all artificers, we don't leave all the dirt on. It's very selective about that, but you're putting signifiers in which indicate lapse or change.

ST In the notes you wrote in *West Coast Line* magazine that accompanied the poem 'Mummers' Strut' [*West Coast Line*, no. 2 vol. 29 (1995); notes pp. 109-10, poem 28-37.], you were describing a three-stage compositional procedure of research, selection and presentation. Regarding the second stage you say "the selective procedure is first a choice generated by the wish to rhyme, but is also a matter of using the research to simulate an incident-set, which is then re-narrated by an 'as if this was happening' voice". Could we talk about your use of the terms rhyme, simulation, re-narration and incident-set?

AF The first one you probably get. I might have got this partly from Robert Duncan, I think, but he would rhyme "grass" on one line with "green", and then you could actually extend beyond that within your own nexus on the desk; you could have a whole complexity of ways that rhyming occurred. Simply, for instance, through sound: you could get a rhyme which then became a word that didn't actually rhyme through sound but had another meaning. So you're making it complex in a sense but you're trying to develop the vocabulary to some extent also.

ST So might it include something like rhyming 'grass' with 'chlorophyll'?

AF Yes, that's right, definitely. But also with something else. That's really rhyming through meaning, or that kind of association, but if you rhymed *orang* with *orang*, as in being orang or something like that, and then said well I don't like the word *orang*, so I'll just change that word to the word that it means—orang-utan—then it's still rhyming with *orange* because that's why it's there. So that's impossible for the reader to unravel, well, not impossible, but it's not lucrative: it would take too long to sort out. But that's not why it's there; it's there as a generator for the writer to some extent. The other supposition, however, is that eventually it's there for the reader, to help the energy in the work somehow, because there are things that don't get resolved, and you think that's interesting, that seems to link and I wonder if it does, and you never really know, and I think that's OK. I don't think you want it all resolved exactly. And, in fact, I can't remember the rhyme that orang-utan came from; it doesn't matter.

65

In terms of the other issues, first of all, one of the changes that does occur is to reify the work in the sense that some of it might have been written in a tense, in a grammar sense, different from the tense in which it eventually gets presented, because I want to all-of-a-sudden make it immediate, and it's not immediate, or, vice-versa, it's too immediate, and it needs pulling back and made reflective—that's a grammar shift of verbs. Then there's the other issue of when you're making a text, some of the time it's your voice, and it might be I, I, I, but then you say to yourself, but this isn't actually what I think, but there is an I which is thinking this that is part of the complexity that makes the other I, and so that is the moment when allegorical forms try to take new presence, I think. It's a new use of allegory. It doesn't originate with me, I'm sure. It's the twentieth century's, but it's not a baroque use; it's not a Jacobean use of allegory; it's not out of Spenser or C.S. Lewis [*The Allegory of Love: A Study in Medieval Tradition*, 1936] even. Although Lewis is twentieth century, he's talking about the medieval and late medieval, early renaissance work.

The new use of allegory, coming out of Walter Benjamin and Bertolt Brecht, and people like that, is that it's there as a collective which is not you, but which you're, so to speak, filling the voice of. Sometimes it goes as far as to name it, like it's a badger, or it's Christopher Wren who's saying it, coming out of little nips of research. Wren obviously because of Wren's biography and who he was. Badger because it's an oppressed animal in ecological terms. That in a sense, although there's all sorts of metaphorical stuff in there, the real use of it, the interesting use of it, is metonymic, because it stands for a whole complexity of oppression, rather than that oppression having to be an I, which literally isn't one I'm suffering from in the total way that I'm presenting the badger as suffering it. Although there is part of what the badger's suffering that is I, is me.

ST So that's two senses of re-narration as a term.

AF Yes. Another way in which it happens is that it's not actually my voice at all, but it's the voice of Joseph Beuys, say, who I've used on some of the texts in *Gravity as a Consequence of Shape*, and sometimes his voice is the voice of a hare, which is one of his motifs of the returning Eurasian and his idea of the mythic. So it's an I that's using the voice that's also the voice of others, so that's why, to use a pronoun as simple as I or she or he, it needs to be bounced against a metonymic use of the term first somewhere. There's a painter that keeps cropping up [in *Gravity as a Consequence of Shape*], and of course I paint, and some of the information that informs what the painter does or says is coming from me as a painter, but more often than not I'm thinking of William Blake's wife, who's not celebrated for having contributed to colouring the water-colours or his illuminated books—they're as much hers as his in some sense.

So it's quite a deep question really, because you're asking how is the composition actually coming about, using this research and text from stories about Blake or whatever somebody else said about him or what he says about himself in his notebooks and what I think about the same subject and what two other people think about it, then trying to make the statement just a single statement from somebody. And why do I want to do that rather than leave the complexity in its complexity, in its disarray rather. Well, sometimes I do leave it in disarray, which is the processual way of dealing with it, but the *Gravity* sequence has tried not to do that, it has tried to find a different way, which is synthesis, if that's the right word, but it's almost a bit cosy. I think it might just be a bit more damaged than synthesis, in some ways, because it doesn't always work, it's more open to a mixture of dismissal and misreading, really.

ST There was also this idea that the research simulates an incident-set. Do you mean that in the sense that it creates a number of possibilities that you then think about transforming in certain ways?

AF I don't know whether it's possible to demonstrate this. But one of the Situationist ideas, which we can think of as having potentially developed since '56 or '53, whatever text you're coming from, certainly since '68 or so, is that rather than confront the burden that you're experiencing as a daily social-political norm internally, instead of internalising it, the Situationist view would be to just turn it back on itself and make the situation for yourself. That's a very crude summary, but effectively what that leads to saying is that, if I'm researching in lots of little areas, many of which might be to do with troubled ecologies or something of that kind—let's take that as an example—it's quite possible to arrive at a position where you can say the way to deal with this complexity of problems is to situate it here, to actually make an incident out of these understandings, even though the incident hasn't necessarily occurred, but it has now, here it is. So it's like making the poem itself an incident in a sense.

ST Like an occasion as Samuel Beckett might say, it makes its own occasion or a new occasion.

AF That's right.

ST Something that often occurs in your work is transformations of lines between poems, I'm thinking of some things in *Civic Crime*, although it occurs in lots of places. Like in 'Camel Walk' and 'Cha Cha' in the first verses there are certain kinds of reversals.

AF I do it all the time and have for a long time.

ST Is that another kind of re-narration?

AF Yes, and transformation is one of the terms as well.

ST It's a kind of rhyme as well, isn't it?

AF Yes. Did you say "Cha Cha" [looking at *Civic Crime*]? That's interesting. So that, for instance, the last part of the stanza is "away from beginning", and, in this one, it's "towards the end". That happens a lot. There's a numerical situation where you should be able to check it, if I've done my sums correctly. These numbers should either be the same as in how many there are in a stanza, or they should be in reverse order the same. Some of the poems read up and downwards, backwards on each other, like 'Ballin' the Jack' does, in *Brixton Fractals*. There's four stanzas I think, so you read from top to bottom on the first one and then, if you then read from bottom to top on the second one, you'll see a relationship quicker than you will by reading in the normal direction, and the same happens to three and four. One of the things that's going on there is transformation.

In *Place* Book One, for example, the bishop's putting money in the collection box for soldiers in Ireland, and in *Becoming*, in Book Four or Five, there's a reggae situation, in which there's a kind of dismissal of the problem in Ireland, because I'm actually too stoned to care. So there's a kind of different attitude towards the same problem, neither of which have solutions, so that's like a rhyme in a weird sense. But they're like cluster rhymes aren't they, in a sort of odd way. So *Place* doesn't rhyme word on word as such, it's always that kind of mirroring. And probably mirror is a better word. So, by the time it becomes *Unpolished Mirrors*, it's sort of evident why that's called that to some extent.

ST I was thinking about the 'Mummers' Strut' poem because that's unusual, or at least I haven't seen other occasions, where you've got endnotes.

AF That's interesting that's happened in that way. I think what I'm inclined to do would be to take those marks out and just to put them into a resource pile, and it just so happened that I was doing that just to keep tabs with where I was going and I left it in, and Peter [Quartermain] and Ric [Richard Caddel] picked up on it.

ST I think it's quite appropriate in the sense that that poem also accompanies your statement in that issue.

AF It does, oh yes it works. I shall leave it now, but I don't remember making a conscious decision to make this an exception.

ST In the first section of 'Mummers' Strut' you've got material from some Nirvana lyrics, Helmuth Plessner, Blake, Cowper, Kropotkin. Is it in any way possible to describe the poetics that are linking those things together? Presumably they're strands from different research clusters, perhaps that are interacting. Can you nail it down to some specific location where there are these things being drawn in, that's a kind of incident-set that's formed?

AF First of all, the Blake is from Blake's notebook: it's part of the schema. I go through Blake's notebook, the Erdman version of it, page by page, poem by poem. There aren't enough notebook pages to do one for every poem, but there's an annotated way of dealing with it so I know which Blake notebook page I'm meant to be thinking about whilst I'm writing this poem. Sometimes it doesn't crop up; other times you get a direct quote from it because it's of relevance to what I'm saying. So, typically, the Blake is that. In fact, what they've done is to put the footnotes at the back, and in my text they follow the page so you can just glance up and down. This is obviously what typically happens, and eventually the numbers drop out. I might actually go back to putting it on the bottom of the page if I'm publishing it, I haven't got to that stage yet.

If I just look at what they are, first of all, let's see if I can pick out the cluster here. One of them has to do with, I've never really marked the file very clearly, but I've done a lot of work on deconstruction, not because of its affiliations to the literary industry, which is massive, and I have obviously not been able to avoid that, but I haven't looked at the way literary deconstructionists deal with literary texts, that hasn't been my interest. What I've been interested in is the architecture that comes about because of its knowledge from deconstruction. So that the new Daniel Libeskind Jewish Museum in Berlin, for instance, I think is just fantastic, it's a fantastically good idea. So that's my interest: it comes from a different mode really. I have got a folder somewhere marked deconstruction—that's my preliminary to tell you what the title on the box is—but it's not a literary allusion; it's actually to do with architecture and design. It's to do with knowing what Constructivism is, à la [Piet] Mondrian and Polish and Russian Constructivism and so on, and what then happens when you develop it. You don't take it apart and throw it away; you take it apart in order to do something else. It's still a construction in other words, effectively. And so, in that box, you would have found Cicero, he deals with it, Pliny, Vitruvius, Hegel, De Quincey, all of these people here, and even in the same box will be Anthony Kenny's work on Wittgenstein, where Wittgenstein's talking about constructivist ideas or putting language together and stuff in *The Legacy of Wittgenstein* [by Anthony Kenny, 1984].

I just quickly skated over the Dante. The Dante's just a reminder—I'm just flipping at that moment, because that's just thrown in whilst writing the poem, because I've recognised a rhyming across here. No! It's not just that, it's because, before this poem, I'd written "Horse" and "Hubble", which is partly about the architect Eva Jiricna and some of her constructivist ideas. At one time, she got a friend of mine to build her a glass staircase at Josephs in London. It's now been taken away because nobody would walk up it, but he worked for a company called Springboard, and they do a lot of her work. And I just had this feeling going up this glass staircase, and there was something about Dante's *Paradise* at the top of this staircase. And I used in that poem some direct quotations, mistranslations or translations of the end of *Paradise*, and that's where they crop up again here because I'm back into this architectural perfection, break of perfection discussion: how the new idealisation, so to speak, won't allow for a perfection, because it would be imperfect to have a perfection. So that crops up, as not part of a research set but as part of something previous in the other parts of *Gravity*.

However, what's here on the front is, so to speak, the circumstance which leads to the need for the deconstruction, because you've got Cobain standing for complexity of problems, Cowper in his 'Ode to Peace' [1782], this person talking about laughing and crying [Plessner]; they come together, they're not particularly in a box but in a reading habit at the time, which might be called a box in a research cluster, but actually is really leading into the poem, making an engine for the poem. And as the poem starts, gets underway, I'm clear to myself that there's a box over here that I need, that sorts this, that discusses this problem in a positive way and looks through the problem for a way, not to solutions as such but for ways of dealing with the situation, to transform it. So you've got there a mini-cluster which has to do with what on another occasion might be, say, the three books you're reading on the bus this week and another cluster which has been over a longer period of time to do with giving lectures for example, which you're going to and fro from on more than one occasion. Which also helps the activity in *Gravity*, because you're referring to the same box back and forth. Not in any systematic way, except that it's all in a box, in that box and not this box. The box, by the way, might be no more than that *[holding up paperfile]*. I'm calling it a box, but it might be a folder. It depends on what material we're talking about. And I have an indexing system as well, which I use on and off, so I've got a box called 'Zam-10'. I forget why. It's got something written on the side of a pair of shoes or something, and it's the tenth box, but it's Zam because I can quickly see it. And I've indexed it—alphabetically under author or something like that—in a little index I've got, so I can look up deconstruction and know the three boxes it's in. So I'm calling that the cluster, although they're in three boxes, because I know a way I can connect them.

To think of another route, there is one to do with the procedure. Some aspects of the procedure of *Gravity as a Consequence of Shape* were already present in *Place*, which as I mentioned to you, discuss this sort of mirroring business, and what I did was to make a Fibonacci set ready for *Gravity as a Consequence of Shape*, a really quite idealised natural form of complexity, and trod on it, so it broke and bent, and then took the measurement again, and then of course it's completely thrown the possibility of understanding it in any idealised sense, because the numbers don't entirely match any more. If you look at *Convergences*, it's shown in a different form in there, because, when they were experimenting with landing on the moon, they went through different ways of collapsing the objects that were going to land to see what would happen to them and presumably to see the position human beings would be in, how they would get crushed or not. So the next thing to think of as an analogy would be to think of a cigarette, and you'd be halfway through the cigarette and you'd get fed up with it and you'd stub it out on an ashtray and the cylinder would bend. And those are the two things, you put those two together and that's it really. What it's recognising is not just violence of damage, but recognising that damage actually then produces another situation. So it turns it into something you can use, in the same way that Harry Thubron, or, before him, Kurt Schwitters or Robert Rauschenberg, would use rubbish, and not say this is rubbish. They'd say no, this is something I can use.

ST I was trying to understand, if the cylinder's distorted, then perhaps in some way those relations would still be the same, but that's not necessarily so, if it bent enough, two points that were distant would become very close.

AF They'd cross each other and so forth. And, if you then put a grid on it, you'd see some of the numbers are lower than they would have normally been, and some are higher.

ST So there's also a grid that you use to measure the distortion, rather than it being just in terms of its own special form.

AF That's right. I read a poem this morning which was to do with the water board digging up the road, Palace Road, and they go down and there's layers of different activities going on over suburban civilisation. When they get to the fifth layer, however, that's not necessarily the oldest, because before them, some other guys from the gas board might have dug that out and replaced it. It's not just simple sedimentary geology, it's actually made more complex by human involvement with machinery and tools.

ST There was another layer, again from those notes in *West Coast Line*, where you also mentioned notes from living experiences and notes concerning aesthetic and political practice. Are those treated in the same way as the other kinds of research material?

AF Provided we're careful to keep the research material with a small r. What happens is, like anybody, I do pick up things off the radio, in the bus, or from conversation, and I'll jot something down, in a notebook if you like. It's more often than not, because of my habits, likely to be a little bit of paper or a bus ticket, so what I do is index it eventually, because I can't keep pace otherwise. So I have a series of books, and I'll just glue things into them at one moment. It's actually quite ephemeral in some ways as to why you put things in there, but in the front of it there's an index [picking up notebook]. Some of it's of no use so I've crossed it out, but under 'gravity' there are two pages in here that need to be referred to. So you turn to page 16 for whatever that is, which might be completely irrelevant now, and there's something I'd scribbled on a newspaper, because that's all I had at the time, and that might get used somewhere. So that's spur of the moment stuff that I feel somehow is rich because it's spur of the moment, that's where they're kept, in things like this. It's got some of my lecture notes, the shopping list, whatever it happens to be. I mean I wouldn't put shopping lists in it, but it might be a list of books I want to buy or notes I've taken from a book I'm reading. There's a lot of curriculum stuff in here.

ST The follow-up to that was whether you distinguish between this self-authored material and material you're quoting from another source; are they all just grist to the mill?

AF Think of another way of asking. Do you mean, do I distinguish between the words of Joseph Beuys and the words of Allen Fisher?

ST Yes.

AF I don't know, sometimes I do, sometimes I don't. Typically, I will change anybody's text into another text, change a tense, change all sorts of things, until the moment when I hadn't changed it and felt that it was worth acknowledging that I hadn't. The resources are about that really, but it's also about why things aren't always in quotations, because I want to acknowledge that they participated but they're not necessarily exactly their texts. It's that sort of problem. But I am in the best sense a magpie in that regard: I drop round and pick up and then use it in my own nest, not through any plagiarist view, much more like a collagist's perspective really.

ST The other thing from *West Coast Line* was the notes concerning aesthetic and political practice. Do you want to say something about what that is or is that something you might accumulate in the notebook as well as find in your reading?

AF There's likely to be a cluster called aesthetics, and there's likely to be one which is flipping in and out of discussions about it. There's likely to be one which deals with some political issues that are ongoing for me. One of these issues has been taken over by my partner, Paige Mitchell, who is the Hereford coordinator for Friends of the Earth, and therefore has taken on a lot of the issues that I would probably, if I had a moment in time, also be taking part in. So there's that side to it, the whole discussion about the genetic stuff and the whole discussion about exhaust, greenhouse gas and all the rest of it. I used to have a box marked 'Drain' that was really to do with all the real dross that I was trying to deal with, the real stuff that people are chucking.

ST I wanted to focus on the specific example of *Fish Jet*. I come to this book and read the foreword, which gives me a sense of some of the sources you've been using, and then at the back you've got another list by author of certain resources. One question which I think we've covered is how does the poem itself make use of these sources. But there's also the questions of how am I to read the poem in terms of its sources, and, indeed, am I to read the poem in terms of its sources, which I may or may not know? In this case, some I do, some I don't.

AF Well, same here. I wouldn't have known them had I not bothered to look for them, so to speak. They're not common authors particularly. They're dealing with arcane subjects and actually some of those texts are scientifically out of date. The way you deal with the text has to do with what you want from the text first, and that's very difficult to define, and whether or not you follow up elements of resources which are referential in their way, like naming people, I wouldn't want to determine in the sense that you wouldn't be required to in order to read the poem. It shouldn't be a necessity. It's not even notated very much. The less notation there is indicates really my inclination to suggest that there's not a real need to get into the actual texts of all these things, because they're quite long turgid things quite often, and really I've just pulled from them. But I didn't want to pull from them without saying I'd done so. There are two reasons for saying I've done so. One would be to do with acknowledgement, but the other is to do with ambience and context. This work is occurring in the context of me having looked at ideas of the following subjects. Once you know that, that's all you need to know in honesty, outside of the poem. Although they're extrinsic to the poem, which you could use to feed in if you wanted to, you could make an intrinsic reading of the poem. That's a way of talking about making analyses of pictures—you can make an intrinsic reading in which you don't refer to outside histories and contexts, just talk about what's in front of you in colours and shapes, or you bring in the context that it's in, in as many different ways as you want.

ST Which is very much the way Clive Bush has written about your work in his book [*Out of Dissent: A Study of Five Contemporary British Poets*, 1997], which is to go through your list of resources.

AF It comes back in part to a discussion about what is the text and which is the poem, and at what moment is the text the poem with Scott Thurston and when is it not. In other words, is this poem X for you having read it, the poem that you've made, which I wouldn't have made, and neither would anybody else except you. And, in that sense, that's always the case, but only to different degrees of course, because we all have backgrounds which have overlapping familiarity with some work and no knowledge of other things between us. So it's coming back to this reader response idea effectively: it's actually trying to make a useable tool of what Wolfgang Iser and Stanley Fish and other people made through their idea of the user-text. It's to say that the text, although these words exist in this book, doesn't actually exist until you read it: because it's not the author reading it all the time, it's other people reading it, there's all these multiple potentials. So I could decide to make those more finite or less finite I suppose, potentially at least, by the way in which I'm presenting other matter that you might feed off into or not preventing that opportunity.

Prynne quite often doesn't give you that opportunity, or, if he does, I'm not aware of it, only on occasions am I aware of it. It's interesting to note actually, if I can just sidetrack here, there's the new book *Pearls that Were*, and the fact that that's using transliterations from Chinese wasn't at all clear to me, I wouldn't have got it, but Nate [Dorward] comes across and he says I've got this translation and here it is, and here's the poem from Prynne, and you go my goodness, it's a pastiche of this poem, of this translation. That's not meant to be a criticism but it isn't anything but a translation, and I'm not demeaning it, it could be quite a magnificent difficult job, I don't know. But there's no indication to me in the text that that is what has gone on. Now that's intentional presumably, but then how does Nate get hold of it? And then one does find associations between Prynne and Chinese work in preface to this anthology, preface to that anthology, and so on and so on. So it's just a different route I guess; he's just offering different ways of dealing with the routes.

ST I've just been reading your book *Now's the Time* recently and thinking about how there's very much a change in tone, or that there's a very different lyrical aspect to these poems. Your response to my question "What is the status of the lyric voice in your writing?" included the sentence: "lyric is simply added fragment and then poised". I was wondering how perhaps these new poems are working out of that idea. I'm not sure what you mean by "added fragment and then poised".

AF I don't either! We can't always assume that if there's an I in the lyric it's me. I'm living in very close proximity to somebody who is passionate about what's going on ecologically and that's some of what's going on in that work. Because it's to do with the fact that the water meadows are under threat, and the battle's actually been won now, so we're not immediately under threat, but they were going to put a bypass through them. So they're all sorts of poems, from the end of *Dispossession and Cure* right the way through other things to do with that. I think 'lyric as poised added fragment' is difficult to talk about in relation to this because that might not be, now you've called that lyric, and I understand what you mean, I'll have to rethink what that says. What I'm thinking of here is different, it's to do with where I would move off into what I think of as a lyric, like a song, in the process of something larger than that, so it's added in a fragmentary way and poised in that sense. It's as if one were switching on and off a spraycan every so often and hitting it with a few lyrics, a few lyrical moments. It's that, it's to do with those things that really do come out of some raw experience that you want to help the poem to come quickly home to the audience every so often, even though it's over-complexed at times. You might be talking about some manipulation of gene matter, this and this, and they're putting these together and this is happening, and I'm giving you some technical detail about it and it's overload, overload, overload, technical detail of this stuff, and then all of a sudden you get something raw which is lyrical effectively, like how this feels, this is just hurting my head or something simple and that's what I mean by lyric fragment at that moment.

ST I did find moments quite strongly like that in here actually. You're talking about the Beuys sculpture here but then there's this: "There never will be autonomous moral choice | No superior dignity entitles anything | not even intelligence and the experience of pain".

AF There's that, then there's the other side of lyric which is different, which is to do with actually using lyrics, probably Dryden, who I've been playing around with. *[finds 'Jig Walk']* All of a sudden it's flipping from this supposed description to "in a garden full of blossoming bows | upon a river, in a dark green meadow | there as sweetness evermore as now", which is clearly odd for twentieth century diction and that's where it's coming out of Dryden. So, that's not quite what you mean by the lyric. Another thing to look at on lyric, which I'm still interested in pursuing a little bit, has to do with [Charles] Olson's idea of the big dream, which he calls the big traum, which he keeps coming back to, on at least three occasions in a big way, in a big text. I think it's partly coming out of him standing in front of a mirror and I use it in that proprioception discussion in *fragmente*. Olson uses it in 'Proprioception', in *The Maximus Poems* and in an unpublished letter to Maximus which was published in an Olson journal. By that dream I think he's talking about that thing that comes back as a reiteration to yourself and you don't quite know why it has come, why you've got this sudden set of words, or you've got this sudden expression in your voice, which has nothing apparently to do with the task underhand, and you choose to ignore it or not. And there are occasions when I throw it in. I showed you that notebook which is also really a lyric source in a sense because even if I didn't write it, if it came off the radio or from conversation or anywhere, it's there because it's so poignant, or poised in that sense.

About Performance
Interview with Victoria Sheppard, 2003

I interviewed Allen Fisher on the 31st October 2003, at Roehampton University, as part of a research project Southampton University and the BEPC (British Electronic Poetry Centre) are currently conducting on the history and poetics of poetry performance in the UK since 1960. The main areas of poetry readings under consideration were those surrounding issues of audience, relationship of the reading to the text, and the pragmatics of readings.

VS Starting with the issue of audience then. Do you have a clear idea of the typical audience at your own readings? How do you anticipate your audience

AF Well, I think the quick answer is yes, and the slower answer is sometimes I don't. First of all, you know the venue, so if you know the venue, more often than not, you have an anticipation of two-thirds of the audience (or even more—just be generous and say that that one third changes a bit) so an audience like SubVoicive in London, like Cambridge conferences, like the reading series associated with Cardiff and the Polytechnics down there, you pretty well know people running it, or you know of them, and you know who the audience is, or you know so many of the audience. So that's that nexus so to speak. Then you can talk about what one does because one anticipates that. There's things like Birkbeck talks which is much more indeterminate because it brings in masters and some BA students and some PhD students from Holloway and Birkbeck, who are an unknown to me essentially, because they would change not necessarily every year but quite often, and they might include some people that you might expect at SubVoicive and they might not. So you couldn't the audience to know you. Although you could expect the audience to know who you were, quite often, so that's a sort of second tier if you like, so you haven't got to introduce yourself biographically, and that also would lead to a different kind of reading as a consequence. And then there's the third kind, where you have been asked to read in the middle of Somerset somewhere and you've never been there, and you know the organiser perhaps, or they know you, and you've been invited along. And that, generally speaking I would say, is a third kind of reading. Sometimes that isn't the third kind, but generally speaking it is. There have been exceptions to that, for example Arvon Foundation might run something as a secondary event. When Andy Brown was there in Devon, he would run, because he was also interested in the kind of poetry I was interested in, as well as what Arvon was more concerned with, he would run secondary series at Exeter (or something like that or Spacex). Then you would know, actually, who was there, to some extent, so that was a bit more like the first kind of reading.

VS So it would be the dedicated few who follow you, and so you see a lot of familiar faces?

AF You do, yes, you do. And they repeat, on a sort of ad hoc basis, so I couldn't name them all, but once I'm there I could name them, but I don't know before I get there which ones will be there, but I know that they will be from a certain pool so to speak. So that's the answer to your first question. So there are certainly at least three kinds. I mean I'm going to Canada in three weeks, and I've never been to that part of Canada before, Vancouver, but there will be there people in Canada at those readings that I know. Who may never have seen me read but who have read me. So there's all sorts of interesting questions it raises.

VS So do you think all your audience are always familiar with your work?

AF No, I don't think that. No they're not. Sometimes you're at a reading where people are just turning up to a poetry reading because it's the local reading. In a small town. That happened in Hereford, it happened in Hay, it happened in Somerset at Coleridge's cottage reading. And it's happened in Oxford and Manchester and Liverpool, and I've just turned up and not known anybody.

VS And is that more intimidating?

AF Oh, it's not intimidating, it's… because I plan readings so I would have planned it differently. And I plan them with a flexibility built in so that just in case I over or underplan something. By planning, what I mean is, I have a list of what I'm going to read at a reading, a little book, so if I've read at a place before, I look at the previous list to make sure I'm not doing it again, or the same again, or if I wanted to do the same again, I'm doing it for a particular reason, in other words, it's not some accident that it's repeated. And typically if it's reading to a coterie of people that are typically listening to you or hearing you or reading you, then I try to read more recent things. And if they're not recent things they're things that are related to the recent things that they will have forgotten about, because I've re-raised… because I'm very much somebody that works out of work that I've done rather than out of nothing, and so I like to give people the connections at a reading.

So what happens then, if you're going to read somewhere where you've never read before and you don't know anybody, what I'm inclined to do is to pick things that I… treat them gently, rather than give them the hard new things all the time, which I'm not necessarily comfortable with. I give them some things that I'm comfortable with, so that they've got some area to feel relaxed in.

VS And does that stay the same—do you have a few set pieces that you've been using specifically for that purpose?

AF No, but I could have. The reason I say no is because I've got a lot of work. But I suppose the answer is yes in the sense that I do have a list of things that will within a certain time frame, so if they're less than ten minutes then they will be OK. Anything more than ten minutes would all of a sudden be in another ball park, and so I'd only use one of those in the reading or something. And so I not only make a list of everything, I time everything also, within a minute. So that that gives me a sense of how long the reading is. And then if I'm fast or slow on that particular night, I can deal with it on an improvised basis. And so if I've read too quickly and somebody says read more, I can just think of something. But more often than not, I've read too slowly because I've introduced too long, or somebody's come in and it's been disrupted, or it's started late—starting late is very typical, and so you knock something out that you thought you would include.

But having said no to something you said earlier about having set pieces, I suppose there are things I know will work better with an unfamiliar audience because they have worked before, and you don't want to alienate an audience on purpose all the time, although some of the time you might want to, just to make sure that you're not completely making the whole thing complacent. But by alienation then it's not a negative necessarily, it's a sort of… a necessary difficulty you could say, so that it makes sure that people are alert to what's going on. And so I will pick pieces that have got, albeit a broken, a narrative aspect to them, that helps anchor in every so often. And it doesn't matter if they don't get all twenty lines, if they got three of them and they've sort of got the next three, it sort of gives them connections.

VS And do you give introductions to them as well?

AF I'm inclined not to, because if I use narrative work I feel like it's self-explanatory. All I'll do—my introductions indicate what it is I'm going to do between now and the next thirty minutes or whatever it is, so this is what you're in for. And it's going to go like that and I'm going to give some bits fast and some bits slow, and that's on purpose, that sort of thing. I'm not inclined to introduce what this is about, if that would be the introduction that some people do give "this poem is going to be about…" I'm inclined never to do that…

VS "And I wrote it in such and such…"

AF Sometimes that might happen. It's very seldom I do that. And part of the reason is that the kind of work it is not autobiographically based, although that's impossible to say but it's pretty well true.

VS What about interaction with the audience then?

AF Apart from the interaction we've just talked about, which in a sense is an interaction because if I anticipate a certain kind of audience there are certain things I'll try out on them which are more risky than I would on another audience, so that's sort of interactive in a sense. Or if I don't know them at all and don't want to alienate them entirely, then that's interaction if I've picked out something that is less difficult. But in terms of… interaction is difficult to explain. Typically interaction isn't vocal. It's not like somebody shouting "oh yeah" from the audience, or the soul singer shouting back "give me a y" or something, it's not that at all, obviously, typically. It's to do with the mood of the room. For instance, let's just think of some scenarios: I've made a list, anticipated a certain group. I go to the reading and three people turn up. So you suddenly change your field of declamatoriness, you realise you're coming into yourself much more, so I might then make a radical change about what I'm going to do. That would be likely to change the pace of things. Similarly, if the audience is massive and just cramming in the door, and that's possible sometimes—very rare—you also play to that I think to some extent. Because you realise that some people are in very cramped positions and they're really very uncomfortable. And so you think, well actually, although I planned forty minutes, I'm going to do it in thirty and have two breaks, if I'm the only one doing the reading. So that's one response. The second response is to recognise musicians or certain poets of a certain kind in the audience who are interested in improvising, and I'll deliberately improvise for them from the work I'm reading. That's rarer than it should be, but it happens.

VS And they'll recognise that, that you're improvising?

AF Yes. And if I improvised it wouldn't be necessarily always as radical as changing the words. It would sometimes be the speed and lack of speed, or it would be intonations. But sometimes what I do is pick pieces that are difficult, and it sounds perverse when I say it, but they trip me up, I trip myself up in trying to read them. And out of the mistakes that occur from the trip-up I improvise. Rather than correct the trip-up I expand upon it, and develop it into "what does that now mean?" So it's hard to explain really.

VS And how far would you take that before you went back to the original?

AF Not more than what amounts to a couple of lines. Probably less actually. But I might often pronounce the wrong word, and then you know you've done it, and that split second you'd have to say I'll now re-read the word correctly, I'll say sorry and read the right word, or I'll just get on with it, or I'll actually bounce on it (so it's split second… it's very hard to explain).

VS And would you ever improvise and feel that that was somehow better than the original and then change it?

AF Oh yes, yes, sometimes I've given a reading that I've never been able to reproduce. Obviously the opposite's happened, that you'd never want to reproduce this one. And that's partly because of the way I work that it works. Because I use words on words sometimes, a lot. So that is to say I've got a list of words here which is called a poem written in 1986, and I'm writing a poem here which is linked arithmetically to a poem I'm writing in 2003, and I've said to myself, the limits on the poem I'm now writing are based on the stanza list here—I'm only allowed to make that many stanza breaks, that many line orders, that many words in a line, that kind of restriction. And I've even come to the point where I have to rhyme with the first or last word in the previous poem. So when you're reading it, say new, you don't know that this has happened—

VS Because you're not presenting them together, textually?

AF No, but at a reading I might, but I don't in the text. And so in the reading I'll open it because people can find that much more interesting than reading because they can hear it, because of the sounds and so on, and the spaces. If I did it textually, it becomes too much of a scholarly exercise, and I want to stay away from that, even though of course that is eventually what it will create I suppose. So anyway this is a very unusual explanation, a rather unusual activity, because I know many people don't do that. What's difficult to do is to take that one stage further, and then to say, I'm going tonight to go to the Camden People's Theatre and improvise this poem. That's so difficult. And in fact that's sometimes gone flat on me when I've tried to do that. Because the wrong audience response has been—response is a big word—the wrong audience ambience is there…

VS And how do you establish that, if something's gone down well (because often people are very polite anyway at poetry readings—)

AF Oh no, you can tell, yes you can. I don't know how well you tell if it's gone badly, but you can tell if it's gone well, and you know whether it's just polite… Because I'm a lecturer also so you know that very very quickly. I don't know how to say that, that's hard—

VS It's kind of like an atmosphere that you can sense?

AF But it's that, it's catching eyes, it's catching somebody doing that, one person doing that would be one thing, but a row of people doing that would be another. I'm exaggerating it but I mean it can be that kind of thing. I remember doing a lecture once when a guy wore earphones through half the lecture, and well it was up to him because in fact it didn't bother me because I don't mind whether he wanted to hear or not, I just think it's unbelievably rude… But that would be an exaggerated audience response!

VS OK. What about having question sessions afterwards—do you do that or is it something you try and avoid?

AF No, I don't avoid that, I don't offer it. The difference is I'm very open to—it depends on where it is. I don't want to avoid the question but it's difficult, it does depend on venue. If you're at the Camden People's Theatre or if you're at a SubVoicive pub venue, then people are there drinking—coffee bar or bar or both, and so you join that, and that is an interaction. A sort of passive interaction you could say. But I don't stop a reading and say any questions. That would be the opposite extreme of it. But I have been in a situation, like I've been in Robert Sheppard's class in Edge Hill College. And all the people in the room, as far as you know, maybe some aren't, are MA students doing his poetry course, so then you give a reading, and then you invite questions but that's not really what you mean is it?

VS No it was, I was interested as I have been to readings before where people do ask direct questions at the end.

AF Oh well I would be open to it, but I don't, except where the invitation's obvious, because it's an educational experience. I mean I'm going to give a reading at Simon Fraser University in November—that will be open to questions. But I'm also giving a reading at Artspeak which is a public

venue live performance place, and that won't be right for questions, so…
I haven't been there but I'm guessing that.

VS I guess it can seem a bit too lecture-like as well?

AF Well it would be something like, almost like Bob Dylan finishing and then turning around and saying well any questions. I know that would be an extreme case, but I mean somebody who was less popular doing that.

VS And do you find—because you say you have the pub venues quite often—do you find that works quite well, the alcohol-poetry mix?

AF It probably works quite well for the audience. Well, it does work quite well for the audience because it's a social occasion, it's not just a reading, it's a whole ambient social occasion, and as soon you're able to take part in that social occasion it works for you. But as reader, the alcohol doesn't work for me at all until I've read. And then it's OK. I don't have anything before the reading. As a rule really. Now you could probably speak to some others that I could name, but won't, that probably completely tank themselves up because of their adrenalin, because of their nerves before a reading. But it doesn't help me in the least to do that, it would just make me an awful reader. It actually makes some of them actual readers in fact. I mean somebody who has now passed away, Barry MacSweeney, he was absolutely appalling at that, he would be absolutely blotto before his reading, and then would read badly sometimes because of it. And you say "but Barry, if you—" you know, but you couldn't say that because there's no way he would give the reading without getting tanked up. So what can you do about it? Nothing. But I don't really think they mix well.

VS The other thing I wanted to ask about audience was with regard to listening and how you conceive of the listening experience, from your own experience of being in an audience as well as giving readings. Although it's obviously quite an individual thing—how someone actually listens, it's still somehow different from say, listening to a lecture or a speech for example…

AF Almost everything, yes it's different from anything I think. The closest it gets is to a difficult music maybe. But it doesn't get as close enough as that for me, because I don't read music in that way, I can't I mean. So let's say I'm a member of an audience at a reading of a poet who I've read—there would be two things before then that I would know. One is that I've read some of the things and second is I'd probably know why I was there, which sounds stupid, but I mean I would have gone out of my way to be there, to hear them read. So there would be an attention already given to them that they could expect and get. And I would therefore concentrate quite hard. The other case might be if I'm hearing someone for the first time, not knowing much about them. What would probably have to happen here is that they would need to surprise you. Something in their poetry was quickly attractive, or was surprising or alerted you very quickly and said I've got to listen to this. And that's very difficult to articulate actually. But it can happen quite a lot. Then there's a third case which is in between these where you have heard of them and you have sort of read them and you're at a conference and so you attend, well because everybody else is attending, but you may or may not go. And then they suddenly surprise you, because they're much better than you expected them to be. And that's happened a lot.

VS Has that happened with anyone in particular?

AF …Randolph Healy. I'd read his work and quite liked it. And I'd missed his reading… wherever it was I was at the same venue's series and I'd missed his reading at that moment. But I'd read the books and liked them and I'd come to the reading along with everybody else and he opened his mouth and I couldn't believe it, I just thought my God I can't believe how good this is, and I was almost in tears by the end of the reading—it was fantastic.

VS And what made it like that?

AF Well because it was eloquent, and eloquent means that not only was it able to say the words that were written down, that you could read, but it was able to make them clearer than you could have anticipated. Now that's a bit odd really, because that means what would happen to someone who would never ever get this chance? I don't know actually, I don't quite know. But this is all to do with… we never can know these things because time just keeps moving on, and obviously you're always in a position of—never having met W. B. Yeats I've got no idea whether or not he was completely crazy but his voice sounds like he's crazy, and I'd much rather read it than hear him read it. But I'm sure that's not necessarily the case, maybe the recordings are crummy or something. Or you hear T. S. Eliot read and you think, that's so awful, so dull, but reading his work I quite enjoy it.

VS It can actually work in a negative way for the poetry.

AF Yes, so that's interesting. Now whether that's a new discipline that's been brought about I don't know. From a series of habits that started in

America in the sixties and in Britain in the seventies, of regular poetry readings and so on. I think it probably is. People have got better at it or thought more about it. I hope that's true, I think it is. I still know some poets I read who are terrible readers. I wouldn't tell you who they were that wouldn't be fair [...] well I mean, I don't know what he's like now because I haven't been for so long, they are so difficult, is Anthony Barnett's readings. I quite enjoy his writing—it's quite sparse and internal and slow and all the rest of it, all those things. But he reads to himself. You're in the audience but you might as well not be there as far as he's concerned, and it's mumbled and you think what am I doing here? What's the point? I can't hear what he's talking about. So at that moment you say what's the point of this reading exactly? And I have mentioned this to him and he says it's not music, because he's an improvised musician as well. And with music you're composing while you're playing, and with poetry you're not. And that's the mistake, I think. I think you are composing to a certain extent, to a sort of tonal extent.

VS So you wouldn't see the reading as secondary to the text?

AF I'm not sure about whether I would want to put one on top of the other... but I'm not sure. There are many people around us now, most of the people around us now, who haven't heard Charles Olson, never will. But they could have heard recordings, and I would still recommend that they do hear those. But having said that, having saw him read live, I've never actually got over it, absolutely astonished how good it was and I never understood a blinking word he was talking about at the reading, I thought what is this? So isn't that interesting? Now I could tell you what it's about now... and I was interested before I heard it, but I'd read much more about him and read his prose and theory rather than his poetry because it wasn't available to me. It so happened at the moment that it happened... but it's very hard to explain.

VS But you don't think that as a member of the audience you have to understand everything?

AF No. You don't necessarily have to understand the words. I'm not being tricky, but I was thinking that there is another understanding possible which is to do with what it feels like, what speed it's at... you know. I heard William Empson read at the same reading as Charles Olson. He's absolutely terrible reading his own poetry, so formal, it sounds like it's an academic exercise. But before he read his poem he gave a twenty-minute introduction to a poem which is twelve lines long. Fantastic introduction, so interesting, really really interesting. So what's that about? I mean he's an older generation, obviously older older generation… so maybe things were different then.

VS So you do think things have improved?

AF I think they've improved, certainly they've changed. They've improved in Britain and they've improved in America at a faster rate, before we got there.

We could just tap back onto some histories of this because I got interested in it through some stuff I can't stand now but at the time I was intrigued by. I suppose I was a teenager—I can't really remember the dates but there was something called Poetry and Jazz. And people who were not that much older than me, like Mike Horovitz, were very young then, but he was sort of the young hippy on the block doing stuff with jazz groups… and Spike Milligan and Adrian Mitchell and people like that, other names I've now forgotten. And they did things with poetry and jazz. I was already a jazz fan. I was a blues fan and I went to folk concerts and things like that but I didn't really go to poetry readings and I came in by that route. But one of the reasons I came in by that route was that I had been reading Jack Kerouac and Allen Ginsberg and all sorts of other people. And I did know about readings. I did know that it was something they did and never heard them. There was a lag really in the history—I'd heard everything after they'd had gone so to speak. So I'd got Kerouac's recordings but not when he was alive and so on. And I suppose Olson died in 1970 so I heard him just about in time. Ginsberg I did hear, but I didn't hear him at his best I don't think, or nothing like his best.

The jazz thing does sort of overlap, and it's to do with venues probably more than anything else. There's an interesting fact here that's crops up—I've got a record of Allen Ginsberg reading, along with a couple of other things. A very early recording on Candid—red transparent record, a fantastic thing. And it was recorded in Chicago after a long journey that went wrong and he was late and he was very very tired. And he got to the reading and it's an incredibly good reading, because he's having to do something about the fact that he's almost asleep, and he's having to really pull through. And I've heard him reading fresh, later than that in the seventies, and it was awful, it just felt flat, it felt… too easy to do.

VS It needs a bit of angst or something behind it.

AF I think that's right you see, so I'm interested in that aspect of adrenalin or nerves or whatever it is. That when a work is new and fresh and therefore that's why young poets, or any poet is likely to read that more than anything else, there is a reason for that, there is an urgency about it. It's like Pound saying about literature being news (or something). It doesn't mean that you can't read old work but in order to read the old work what you have to do is prepare yourself. You have to – not psych yourself, it's too big a word, but you have to put yourself in the right frame to do it properly.

VS So would you read it as if it were new?

AF Either that, yes, or you do it as… this is part of a nexus, part of a complex thing you're going to do. So this information's going to feed into the next poem.

VS OK, and how much do you think the jazz element has been eradicated now?

AF Well I think what it's become is improvised music. Jazz became passé in a sense, maybe it always was, but at the time it didn't seem it, whereas improvised music, by the time it had become strong in Britain in the late sixties (it was probably before that but that's when I felt it) it was… a challenging situation to be in. You felt like you were going to an experience you couldn't anticipate—it could be terrible and it quite often was, sometimes it really wasn't and so I would be a staunch follower of some of the groups that were involved but not others. I flipped in and out of interests like I got interested in serious electronic music and straight quartet music as well. But that doesn't overlap in the same way somehow. Because of its formal settings quite often—Royal Festival Hall… They don't do it for poetry at all actually, hardly.

VS Do you think it's because it's just too big a venue? What about some of the Horovitz events?

AF It's a different ball park. I mean Horovitz's mode is different anyway because he's inclined to try to put it into a more popular mode, to try to get more people involved. So the Festival Hall makes sense in that regard, or the Albert Hall or something. But really it's done for a different reason somehow. I mean I've read with Michael subsequently in fact in small venues at improvised music parties and things—like they're in small venues but they've invited everybody to celebrate somebody's birthday. And he reads differently in that situation, he's less of a clown in that situation, or jester or whatever the word is, and more of the poet.

VS So you perform different roles depending on the venue.

AF Yes I think so, it does make that difference.

VS And have you been involved in many performances with music?

AF Yes, not a lot but yes. At the same time as [music] no… maybe I have, but not successfully I don't think.

VS What are the difficulties there then?

AF It's something to do with different genres or something like that. I'm quite often embarrassed by the way people put them together as if they think it works… and I don't often think it does really. I mean I think jazz and poetry is usually a disaster in fact. I mean Kerouac and jazz, you know someone goes and plays something cool and Kerouac says something cool and you go, this is so corny. And then you think well they did it then, but it still goes on. I think you're better off, if you really want to do that, to become a sound poet, and then that's a different business. Or if you do something like Bruce Andrews has done, which is to use his language and vocal expression of that language through electronics, digital electronics, so it's actually almost electronic sounds anyway. So it would probably be wrong to call it poetry in the normal sense anyway at that moment, unless you want a new genre or something. cris cheek can do that as well. There's some people can do that, but they are quite rare. Bob Cobbing was quite good at it. But they're sort of more obvious examples really, there's so many bad ones… I do quite like the idea of having music and poetry at the same event, because then you mix the audience quite a bit and you increase the audience and you also take the pressure out, it has a variety of attentions. It makes it tough on the poet sometimes… because the music's quite often loud and can take over.

VS In terms of the practical arrangements for readings – are you normally involved much in these? Do you do many readings on your own or is it more often alongside other poets?

AF I very rarely organise them, sometimes I might be asked if I would like to do something, and who I would like to do it with, that sort of question, but it's rarer than you'd expect really.

VS So do you deal with putting word around about events or anything like that? And how would you go about that?

AF Yes I do. I try to keep a network going. *Spanner* magazine I've been running since '74, and along with various books and publications I've got an address list. Then that whittles down, literally rather than up. And the more they see the stuff the less they can take of it! But more seriously, that's what happens, because I'm not a marketing person, I don't actually get into worrying about that. So there's that list and then out of that list there's some people who live in Newcastle and some people who live in London, and so depending on where an event was being held you would obviously pick from that list. And then there's a list of people who do turn up for things and so I'm inclined to keep including them on the list. But what's happened now is there's a third tier, which is e-based. There's the UK poetry list, which is run from Miami Ohio, and there's Harry Gilonis who collects together all the lists he finds and puts them out in a calendar every two months. So I take part in both of those e-mail things. And I do so in Roehampton as well. So there are three tiers really. The most successful one is probably the middle one, which is the short list of people who respond to what you're doing, so you keep sending them things. The email has improved networks in a way that you don't quite understand really, probably. That's quite interesting in the audience question isn't it? Because it does actually open up new potential unknowns in an audience

VS What about issues of funding?

AF The venue operators charge, and I demand a fee if they charge, and if they don't I don't. It varies really. SubVoicive I know will make a loss at what they're doing, so anything that they make while I read there I leave with them, so that anybody who's travelling from Newcastle gets some of their fare paid, because I don't need that. But if I go to Manchester, I hope to get my fare paid. So there's sort of minimal criteria. There used to be a poets' union in the seventies which we set up when we were at the Poetry Society. We then came up with a minimum wage of £30 per reading, and actually it hasn't got any better. It went to £40 for some poets that were better than others, and if you were Basil Bunting you got £60 or £100. But really if you get £30 at a reading today, then you've got more than you would get in many places. Some just don't pay anything like that. So obviously that's not really a wage when you think about it. That varies, but typically if it's Arts Council-funded through for instance, one of the London Arts boards, that's about where the top would be still. Unless I suppose you're somebody with a name and can make decisions about that, like I'm not going to read unless… sort of thing which I haven't yet done. I sometimes will do that in terms of having a bottom line. I was in Philadelphia a few years ago and they asked me to read in New York at the Poetry Project which is funded, quite well funded. Three of us were asked, and they offered us £20 each full stop, no fare, nothing.

So we said go to hell really just for very simple pragmatic reasons. I read in Toronto when I was at Buffalo with Charles Bernstein for a few days and that was well-paid, and Toronto invited me to read but at a venue which nobody had heard of, it was somebody's loft and they said we can get you over there, we can get people to turn up, but we don't know what the money will be and we'll just hand a hat round, and we'll give you a lift back. So I went for it. They handed a hat round and I got £200 in the hat. So you think, it's a different ball-park over there somehow, it's different feelings about it, so it was felt that that was what you did, you didn't put a dollar in you put $10. That would be difficult to happen in Britain I think, and there are all sorts of economic reasons for that as well as there are conventions. Cambridge Poetry Conference pays but it pays very little, it's funded with difficulty, it used to be funded better than it is now, but it's now relying on the equivalents of the British Council for Canada and France and Germany.

VS Difficult to make a career out of it...

AF Even career poets, even people like Ted Hughes and others, they do other things—they write children's stories, they write reviews, there are all sorts of ways that they actually make their money… or they teach. I mean Andrew Motion is creative writing professor at Royal Holloway, and he was a lecturer at East Anglia.

VS Do you use readings to sell your work; do you have your work available there?

AF Yes. I don't go overboard with that, probably do less than some do. But that's partly to do with my own efficiency really, because I don't get them ready in time.

VS Another thing I was interested in was delivery, style of delivery—is it something you practice?

AF Yes, not in front of a mirror, by having done it before. I very rarely sit down at a reading, that's a style trait. I've learnt that the energy from a reading is better for the kind of work that I make if I'm standing up. Because some of the nervous energy comes through the feet or rather comes back out of the body into the ground, so it works in a positive way usually. And it's better for the audience I think. Not necessarily for every poem and I can probably think of exceptions but I think that most poets that read well are standing up. It doesn't mean you're being declamatory necessarily. It's taking account of the audience really rather than being passive about it.

VS Some people within the audience would be likely to see the poet actually reading his or her own work as providing some sort of authority.

AF They might do, yes. I don't know if I'd use that term. I know a discussion I had with John Seed once was that one reason he didn't like his own poetry readings, was that he worked very hard at making a line have three meanings, but in saying the line he had to give it one. And I think that's a mistake, you don't know how many meanings that line has got and it's better to at least get one of those meanings than get none at all, but that's just debate I guess. There is that aspect of a reading where you hear the poet's voice when then reading the poem afterwards, and you do hear one tone rather than a tone that might be there that he or she hasn't read.

Other aspects of poetry readings—I've been a performance artist as well and done some performance work and sometimes I'll have that with a reading as well. And so that has an interactive aspect because it's using objects or furniture or space. The last one I gave here used easels, rope, charcoal, recordings, and a whole series of things as well, and that was quite deliberately set up. It's done but I don't always do that.

VS The majority of your readings then are the more straightforward ones, without performance?

AF Yes because the venues lead that way typically. Venues wouldn't really provide for the performances more often than not.

VS So to end with a very general question, do you think it's possible to define some sense of the value of poetry readings as a whole?

AF Well the first thing they did for me was to increase my interest in energy in poetry, in a way that I hadn't really anticipated. That is to say I now think it is as interesting as music, and I don't think I used to think that, even though I wrote the stuff. And there are other things, like visual art but I'm just thinking of music because it's performed, because it's in your ears. I also think that the poetry reading complex, the fact that there have been poetry readings and they continue has changed the way poetry's now written and provided. It's changed what it looks like on the page, it's changed what is on the page, it's changed what's permissible, it's changed the potential for the tones really, and the potential for non-words almost.

VS And you're very aware of that potential when you're writing?

AF Yes, most certainly. I always read the poem to myself when I've finished. My poems are never complete until I've read them to somebody. If there's any re-writing it takes place after the first reading.

VS The first public reading?

AF Yes, public might only be two people, but it would need to be public. Because it's that business of the other person hearing and their response that you somehow understand, that you then make a decision about.

VS This is the non-verbal response then?

AF Yes, well it might not be but it usually is. It has to do with your experience reading it to somebody else that informs you about something you've done, such as that line's too long, that need to break, it's that sort of discussion, it's not really whether all the words should be there, it's much more to do with layout and things like that.

VS That's great, thank you very much.

The Curve of Increase or, On Growth and Form
An Attempt to Reconstruct a Lost Interview

Andrew Duncan

Based on plans, contemporaneous notes, and memory impressions.

I interviewed Allen in June 2004, in a café area at the Royal Festival Hall. That interior is like a marquee, noise blowing in from all over the place. When I played the tape back, there was simply too much ambient noise on it for the words to be made out. But it did begin with this question:

I want to question the idea of numerical form. Any shape is a geometrical shape, and any number of words is numerical. Could we modify the idea to say that *Place* has large-scale preset procedures, and that the preset form refers to some shape outside the poem? Roy Strong's *The Renaissance Garden in England* is about gardens which have a strict form because they have to conform to an allegory embodied in that form. You mentioned *Astrophel and Stella* as an example of numerical form. Maybe the Spiral in *Place* is like a signature in Renaissance Neoplatonism. Neoplatonism talks about influences coming down from the stars in a spiral motion—*heiligden*. The maths is the relationship between two symbolic objects but we also have to ask what the objects are.

Notes say "ARK magazine 1965 issue. IO magazine doctrine of signatures. Bard University College. psychotectonics. image pattern. sinuses. point to define is a visualiser dominated by shape."

The interview was distracted by mutual misunderstanding about the word Neoplatonism, AF seeing it simply as "late Platonism (since Plotinus)" and AD seeing it as "the application of geometrical magic", as described in Frances Yates' book *Giordano Bruno and the Hermetic Tradition*.

One similarity between *Place* and *Gravity* is that both have a spiral close to their centre—as a repeated motif in the first work and, in the specific form of the Fibonacci series, as the directing principle of *Gravity*. (One could represent the Fibonacci series in many, many different ways, but a visual realisation of the numbers would be a spiral.) This allows some reflections on someone who is a visualiser, and whose writing stems from that. It also invites us to think about D'Arcy Thompson, as the probable source of this geometrical approach, and about some peripheral examples of spiral imagery. The Spiral appears in *Place* 7, 8, 27, 32, 36, 45, 74.

We could describe *Place* simply as a follow-up to Thompson's *Of Growth and Form* (originally published 1917) with the morphology which the latter applies to biological forms transferred to the forms of buildings, urban aggregations, river courses, and social phenomena. The spirals in *Place* should, then, be compared to the sixth chapter of Thompson's book, *The Equi-angular Spiral*. Let us pause for a moment to consider a phrase of Kepler's, quoted by Thompson: *gnara totius geometriae, et in ea exercita*. This is a description of the Godhead: expert in all geometry, and practised in the same. Thompson says "In general terms, the Spiral is a curve which, starting from a point of origin, continually diminishes in curvature as it recedes from the point; or, in other words, whose *radius of curvature* continually increases." Further, that "we can recognise typical though transitory spirals in a lock of hair, in a staple of wool, in the coil of an elephant's trunk, in the 'circling spires' of a snake, in the coil of a cuttle-fish's arm, or of a monkey's or a chamaeleon's tail." It may be true that someone who does not find this pair of statements interesting will also not be interested in Fisher's work.

In looking at books based on spirals, we need to consider the rate at which information is added to a book as it progresses. The information added by a new page of text is not equal to the number of words on it. Both are incremental series which can be visualised as curves. We can think of the addition of any new page to a volume of poetry as $I + i$, where the large I is the information already available and the little i is the amount added by the new page. Where i constitutes a genuine extension of the information base displayed in the text, it can validly be called a segment of a spiral. A spiral is as we have seen a series representing a curve whose radius *expands* with each term of the series. The spiral is not an arbitrary image for the serial design of a long book. If we visualise the design of a successful book as a series we will always see a spiral. To put this the other way around, the page whose i is zero is the page you delete. The spiral is simply your guide through a mass of data awaiting determination. Any text where the information available increases in a proper relationship to the increase of bulk can be visualised as a spiral.

One has to ask whether other long poems have an adequately reflexive design. Because they constitute books, we should ask the same question about collections of poems and indeed collected poems. We can speak of *flatlining* for books where each new page adds nothing but a sense of weariness. Putting poems into books can offer a fatal proximity, where an inconveniently persistent memory means that the texts become utterly predictable. The problem of i is one which no poet can ever escape.

A spiral is a curve of increase. A poet who does not stop writing is faced with a constantly increasing bulk of work. There are definite costs to this increase. If the separate statements are confined in a static area, for example that defined as the poet's style or personality, then each new statement makes it more difficult to generate a new next statement which does not repeat one already made. As the notebooks fill up, the area within that limit becomes progressively more devastated—one can speak of an ecological disaster here, as the using-up of resources leads to an ever more monotonous and frustrating diet. Not only facts, but also gestures, sound sequences, all devices, become irritating when repeated. One can speak of a negative spiral: as a text grows longer, the information it uses up increases as a spiral, and the information it needs in order to sustain attention increases as a spiral. Designing a similar increase into the ordering of the text is almost a defensive measure, to fight off the awesomely increasing arithmetic of damage of information which is out of action because it has been used up. The shape of a text is not the same as its extent. Visualising this shape may be a basic literary skill. The proposal of a work which occupies four volumes and several hundred pages is a recognition that the poet will go on living for the next ten years; it simultaneously proposes a replacement for the notion of personality or tradition as the generator of continuing variations, and for the rules of genre which once told the poet how to assort themes together, and which have now withered and become unusable.

An essential difference between language and number is that the latter is complete and malleable in every direction, whereas the former is finite, constrained by pre-existing sets, both of lexicon and of representation. Words are surrounded by non-words whereas numbers are not surrounded by non-numbers. One of the possibilities haunting poetry, therefore, is of sounds becoming as free as numbers, with infinite availability and unlimited transformability. *Becoming* is the most direct realisation of this dream. Another path towards this is to link words to a set of data so large that the constraints are not apparent. One of these might be the stars, and in fact we find that a text which Fisher frequently refers to is Alistair Fowler's *Edmund Spenser and the Numbers of Time*, which relates *The Faerie Queene* to the movement of the stars. That is, as a development of the calendrical pattern of *The Shephearde's Calendar* into a larger and more intricate set of periodicities. There is a recognisable relationship between the programmed variation over time of the stars and the ineluctable curves along which context and used information grow within a large text. Both ride along the curves of an unconscious mathematics which the visualiser can gain a conscious knowledge of.

What do I find beautiful in poetry? I think, most often, that it should point, constantly and as a principal intent, to larger and more permanent beauties around it. With the spiral, we are looking at the concept of a harmonic, Neoplatonist universe, with its forms arranged by a cosmic music, and at a transcendental state of knowledge—as in an acid trip, maybe—where this pattern becomes, fleetingly, visible, and we can watch the play of forms without the constraints of ignorance or, apparently, of more banal considerations interrupting. Part of section VIII of *Place* goes:

> who are the dodmen the snails   the surveyors
>   no longer with horns   or dowsing wands
> no longer tracing the earth in lung-mei & ley
> stretching the globe
>   or as Manzoni   encircling the earth
> who are you now that would draw the St. Michael line
>
>   from Avebury circle to the extreme southwest

The passage which follows this is a direct quote from John Michell's book *The View over Atlantis* (p.61 of the 1973 edition). (I think the artist Piero Manzoni encircled the earth simply by jumping in the air.) *Lung-mei* is a Chinese version of the "dragon power" which Michell identifies as the principle forming the landscape. *Dodman* means 'snail' but was interpreted by the brewer Alfred Watkins, in a strange kind of breakdown, with Neolithic surveyors carrying sighting-staves like snails' horns. Guy Underwood writes about a spiral force (which he finds governing the behaviour of water on hills with Neolithic sites). John Michell writes about a serpent force and 'paths of the dragon', both representing spiral shapes. His thesis is summarised as "The entire surface of the earth is marked with the traces of a gigantic work of prehistoric engineering, the remains of a once universal system of natural magic, involving the use of polar magnetism together with another positive force related to solar energy." This is still somewhat more rational than Underwood. Michell sees the shapes of paths running round hills as the marks of the coils of dragons, cf. "the way hill serpents slept/ on religious spins of force" (*Place* VII), and sees spirals everywhere, always as signs of a Dragon power. The *Alembic* interviewers were concerned by this, because Michell departs from the norms of sanity in interpreting or inventing evidence. Someone who reads a crackpot is under suspicion of being a crackpot. I find it logical for Fisher to bring the set of proposals linked to sacred geometry within the semantic field of *Place*. In a 'pop' crack, one could say that 19th C English poets were failing to write like Shakespeare and 20th C English poets were failing to write like Blake. One could also say that Blake went "behind" the physical theory of the universe, as a field whose forces affect our bodies and the objects we perceive, in order to produce a unified account of the spiritual and material cosmos expressed in the form of myth. It seems possible to me that the 1960s saw a collective attempt to carry out this blakean pattern, and that *Place* is the climax of this attempt. If you set out with the firm blakean precept of rejecting Locke and Newton and projecting marvellous powers into British antiquity, it was natural to pick up on Paul Screeton and John Michell, because they had developed that precept into a whole world view, with hundreds of moving parts, and because they were, in that blissful moment of roughly 1968-70, politically compatible and uncontaminated. All the same, the ideas which achieved circulation in the '70s, under the aegis of Blake, LSD, and the rejection of all authority, (amongst other factors), included an amount of catastrophic rubbish.

My interpretation of the quoted passage about ley lines goes via Neoplatonism. Michell claims that all hills in Britain are artificial, having been built by means of a force-field which they also served to channel. (The dragon energy, etc.) A scientific view does not propose that the count of artificial hills is zero—but one, since Silbury Hill apparently was piled up by human hands. The use of the term Natural Magic takes us to Neoplatonism. This notion of shape acting to channel cosmic forces is fundamental to Neoplatonism. The Neoplatonist ideas entered Europe partly through the book *Picatrix*, a Latin translation of an Arabic original written around AD 1048 by the moon-worshipping pagans of Harran, in northern Syria. (*Picatrix* from *Bucratis* from *Harpocrates*.) This is based on a physics in which shape is the lens through which energies are directed; the cosmos is pervaded by a vast force-field, so that power is virtually free once you have developed the right geometric lens. *Place* is open to the sacred geometry line because it is already in love with Spenserian allegory and star symbolism, and via Neoplatonism the ley-hunters are a contemporary equivalent of these starry harmonies.

The Neoplatonic idea proposes the universe as a visualiser who displays the rules of the universe in visible form, as the stars and planets. This is an almost unbearably beautiful idea, and it is hard to realise that there were ever people who believed in it, and not just poets who wanted to imagine it.

The Renaissance idea of allegory based on shape was probably greatly influenced by Neoplatonist ideas. The idea of shapes embodying truths was not wholly separate from a notion about physics which saw shape as channelling energies. The rise of science saw the decline of allegory as an artistic device, as educated people began to expect explanations of events on earth, rather than fanciful depictions of them. In early times, there was no way of saying that plants and animals produced hormones in response to luminosity levels, so it was possible to imagine Spring happening as the direct result of a command from the stars. This era of roughly the 15th to 17th centuries is very significant to Fisher's major works, and to their basis in geometry. A key source for Fisher, as we have said, is Alistair Fowler's *Edmund Spenser and the Numbers of Time* (1964).

Frances Yates has recovered Tommaso Campanella's *City of the Sun* as an adaptation of the magical ideas of *Picatrix*, sometimes drawing on these in great detail. At one stage, Campanella and Bruno were in prison in Rome at the same time. After these heretical flights, Campanella was released to engage in royal propaganda, for the French king, something which has not been taken on by the modern tradition which recuperates him as a pioneer Socialist. But the propaganda genre had thoroughly absorbed the imagery of Astraea, whose name means "starry" and who is the symbol of returning justice in Virgil's Eclogues, as a way of linking royal justice and reliability to the march of the stars. Yates also recovered the natural magical ideas of Giordano Bruno, by no means the scientist-martyr of post-Enlightenment mythology. Astraea is of course the central figure in Spenser's royalist allegory; Elizabeth was allocated cosmic status as the source of calmness which quelled rebellion and dissent and granted the realm peace.

Roy Strong's *The Renaissance Garden in England* describes allegorical gardens, which had strict patterns reflecting, typically, shapes in the stars. The key concept of signature connects these with Neoplatonism, at its most popular in the form of astrology. The difference between Michell and Strong is partly one of scale: for Michell, "The entire landscape of Britain has been laid out to a celestial pattern."

Of the cast of characters in *Place*, Underwood, Michell, Screeton and Watkins belong to the area of sacred geometry: a collective description for a very wide range of psychotic ideas connected with the geometry of churches, pyramids, lost knowledge, etc., which are a development of *Picatrix*, through whatever underground channels. The para-mathematics of Charles Piazzi Smyth and his successors treats the Great Pyramid as an allegory—a map of the cosmos. In fact, one of the intellectual sources of these ideas is diffusionism, another school which placed Egypt at the centre of everything. Like Perry and Elliot Smith, H J Massingham thought that all civilisation had diffused from Egypt, and, in his 1926 book *Downland Man,* looked at the artificial hill, 130 feet high, at Silbury, and declared that it was "a perfect replica in earth" of the Pyramids of Egypt, and further that the whole landscape of the Downs was the product of deliberate engineering by Neolithic peoples. The political urge behind his attribution of supernatural power to Neolithic peasants was to exalt the village and make out that everything wrong in history derived from urbanisation. The ley line/ hippy/ New Age contingent lapsed snugly into the worship of the Imagined Village which had been one of the major projects of conservative literati in 20th century England. For Screeton, "Neolithic man's efforts went not into making things, but into making himself more perfect. He built his stone circles not simply to make astronomical calculations, but created places where ritual was harmonised with mathematical skill and terrestrial power manipulation techniques so as to link himself to the infinity of the cosmos where he played no small part. Metal-working brought a radical change to society, and the spiritual age ended." We may wonder how, if these people left no artefacts (not being into making things), and no writings, Screeton knows what they thought. In fact, they are just projections of 1975-style hippies.

More recently, Andrew Jordan has used the idea of artificial hills in his vast cycle of satires on Charles Mintern and the Equi-Phallic Alliance, promoting the nonist idea that prehistory is wholly the projection of modern archaeologists and so that nothing has any real foundations—consequently, that all hills are artificial. The development of hills was a long-term project, driven by the competitive display of land-owning elites. Jordan has pointed out that early pictures of hills show few details—the elaboration of details was the creation of later, more expensive artists working for wealthy people, while featureless landscapes belong with the folk tradition, free from foreign influence or pretensions. Jordan's claim that the simplest hills were essentially squares of green canvas supported by wooden poles has not found much resonance within the archaeological profession. It challenges the very basis of their social power.

Geoffrey Ashe, the para-archaeologist, also promoted, in *Avalonian Quest* (1982), the idea that the design of a hill was artificial and imbued with symbolism. The ridges of Glastonbury Tor are for him low-tech equivalents of the stepped sides of ziggurats. He develops a modified diffusionism (partly based on A.M. Hocart) in this book, and also claims that the sides of the Tor form a maze. Although the moon's gravity is exerted continuously, waves of the sea are clearly discontinuous and rhythmic. I believe the explanation of this has to do with quantum phenomena. Many hills have ridges along their sides—the lines attributed by Michell to the coils of dragons, who once clenched them while coiled up in sleep. That is—a hill is a wave. As such, it would have to be the product of a flow of energy—just as sea waves are the product of gravitational pull by the moon and the sun. Unfortunately—there are other explanations for the periodic ridginess of hills. Take the *Oxford Companion to the Earth*, for example, at p. 502, "Terracettes affecting a chalkland hillslope in Wiltshire, southern England. Although the flights of narrow steps have been attributed to preferential trampling by animals, they are widely viewed as the expression of discontinuous downslope creep of the soil." Further, "Expansion and contraction generally occur through the action of freeze-thaw, where the expansion of water, present as soil moisture, upon freezing causes a consequent increase in soil volume, and, in turn, the bulging of the soil surface perpendicularly outwards from the slope. On thawing, the regolith material sinks vertically downwards under the direction of gravity." The action of expansion and contraction creep, he says, "is commonly considered to be manifest as flights of narrow steps, called 'terracettes', on steep, grass-covered slopes." Good heavens! could this mean that hills are not the product of a universal cosmic force-field after all? (Regolith essentially means the mobile zone, i.e. the part of a slope which is soil rather than rock.)

The geometric style of garden was all swept away by the Romantic landscape movement of the eighteenth century, so that Strong could not find one single surviving instance in the British Isles; he reconstructed the genre from early pictures and documents. Symbolic architecture is also a rare genre; the triangular lodge at Rushton in Northamptonshire, which symbolises the Trinity, is an example of reasoning through shape which can still be visited today. The design includes some very elaborate conceits illustrating the same idea, as a kind of stone emblem. The pagans of Harran built a temple, of which ruins are still in existence, at Sumatar Harabesi, consisting of seven buildings, of which each one was dedicated to one of the seven planets and each had a shape, in its ground plan, appropriate to that planet. The habit of seeing allegorical truths in the shapes of buildings hung around, reaching modern times in a sub-genre of archaeology.

The symbolic buildings, of which very few are known, were sometimes the investment of Roman Catholic nobles, who could not aspire to public office. The greatest Catholic family was that of the Earls of Arundel, of whom Philip Howard, the second earl, is known as the inventor of the collection (around 1630). (That is, in England.) He travelled to Prague to see the Emperor Rudolf's collections, and thus became England's closest link with the fonts of Mannerism. He also played a key role in the development of the Folly. (I have to point out that he first became a Protestant, perhaps to avoid spending his life in jail like his father.) There was a genre of entertainment, more in the Low Countries than in England, which involved masques outdoors in a landscape transformed by temporary buildings into a scene from a romance. The most ambitious Mannerist gardens had devices, clearly linked to the "romance" architecture of these costly performances, with giants, hermits in grottoes, fountains, and so on. The Folly as we know it, from roughly the 17th to 19th centuries, can plausibly be seen as a translation of flimsy scenographic architecture into permanent form. Several of Arundel's grandchildren played key roles in its early stages. We can see the Folly as a realm of subjective space which by its permanence and containing qualities offers a home space for subjective moods. As a game which produces spatial experiences unpredicted by its builder, it is peculiarly relevant to Fisher's work—and can be related to Constructivism and to conceptual art.

The link of this romantic architecture—in some part—to Roman Catholic nobles, disqualified from taking part in the government of the country, offers a suggestive analogy to the Underground of the 1970s. The English Heritage leaflet on Rushton Lodge says that some of the emblems or puzzles in its decoration have not been deciphered. An avant-garde—in the 17th century? Just as perception can be seen as a damper on spontaneous brain patterns which would otherwise run out of control, so the removal of political responsibility permits the florescence of cultural ideas in a pure form.

If we look at the continuation of that passage from *Place* VIII:

> from Avebury Circle to the extreme southwest
> Mont St. Michel in Normandy, the chapel of St. Michel L'Aiguille,
> the hilltop church of St. Michel facing the stones of Carnac,
> the Celtic church on Skellig Michael,
> the chapel on the crag near Torre Abbey, Roche rock hermitage,
> Brentor church, Gare Hill in Wiltshire, St Michael's Mount

—we see that this Michael alignment is romantic architecture; a dazzling line drawn through perfect space; a scenographic realm; the view from a near star; a Prospect Tower.

The theme of *Of Growth and Form* is the possibility of the forms of living things deriving from the play of physical forces as well as simply from the action of genes in, as it were, a sealed vessel. Thompson is interested in dead substances which imitate the forms of living ones, as for example in the forms which droplets assume in various contexts. Cells are droplets—with special properties. This campaign is carried out in multiple directions; Thompson is as interested in the fitness of body forms to the environment as in the effect of mechanical forces, surface tension, etc. on the growth of cells. The theme of physical constraints—the reasons why, for example, animals cannot grow beyond a certain size within a given physical design—is not anti-Darwinian, but proposes a considerable addition to the theory of evolution. Natural selection cannot choose from all forms, but only from the ones which physics allows cells (along with the inorganic props such as *spicules*) to build. We read about the *tourbillons cellulaires*, or cellular vortices, which Benard observed in films of heated liquids, hear that they form cells, symmetrically packed and with apparent walls—and wonder if the distribution of cells in certain living tissues is simply the result of *convection*. The book is exhausting because it addresses all aspects of the subject. Thus, when he is writing about the distribution of radiolarian shapes, he relates them to bubbles:

> the symmetry which the organism displays seems identical with that symmetry of forces which results from the play and interplay of surface-tensions in the whole system: this symmetry being displayed, in one class of cases, in a more or less spherical mass of froth, and in another class in a simpler aggregation of a few, otherwise isolated, vesicles. In either case skeletons are formed, in great variety, by one and the same kind of surface-action, namely by the adsorptive deposition of silica in walls and edges, corresponding to the manifold surfaces and interfaces of the system. But… there are certain forms… which display a no less remarkable symmetry, the origin of which is by no means clear, though surface-tensions may play a part in its causation. (p.167)

The fully-grown organism owes its shape to the packing of the droplets on which its young form was accreted. The space of variations of radiolarian shapes is seen to correspond to the area of possible tesselations of fluid droplets. But—there are so many radiolaria, and they do not all obey this pattern.

Thompson, one of the great visualizers of the 20th century, is truly looking for the origin of forms. His conceptual vocabulary, looking for the key to variation, for generalisations which explain many forms, for the 'break points' where form is decided, for the microscopic origins of gross anatomy, for the action of physical forces on biological systems, for the limits of lethality which eliminated the forms we do not see—supplies the vital preoccupations of *Gravity* (and, to a lesser extent, *Place*). It is possible to see metaphor as a realisation of an underlying type of mental jump which Thompson is developing, in an extensive and systematic way, in thinking about biological form.

Let us just consider one site, the graphic on the cover of *Stane*, book III of *Place*, published by Allen Fisher's own Aloes Books in 1977, price £1.50. The main image is a map of part of South London, showing many of the features mentioned in *Place*. But it is interrupted, at three points, by an image which (the inner cover tells us) is taken from *Scientific American*. It shows an anonymous structure, perhaps part of a building or cells in an organism, visibly giving way; and the note tells us that all the sources show "photos and drawings of environments giving way under stresses it was assumed they could bear". It assumes a grammar of stress moving through structures irrespective of scale. The boldness of the graphic is startling. It points to the way the mind does its business with different cognitive frames, constantly linking them to produce unique paths and sequences. It also focuses one of the abiding themes of the work, that the urban environment is overloaded and damaged, and that this puts unnatural stresses on the people living there. The montage reminds us, once we have read the book, of the material inside which relates the action of fire on buildings, via the extension of fire insurance as an early financial industry, to the rick-burning which spread through the starving Southern counties in the depression years after 1815 in a movement known as Captain Swing. Swing was the subject of a book by George Rudé, who also wrote a history of the crowd—an analogy for fire, as something which grows, which has a flash point, which expands by convection, which transforms its own substance, which abruptly vanishes. The rick-burning was precisely a symptom of a social fabric giving way under stress. The map of South London (with Brixton ripped out and replaced by a picture of stress!) mainly shows roads. Their width and trend must, however, show some of the density of traffic, the continuous faring of human subjects who are somehow traced by this built environment. The pattern of interconnecting, slender, long strips distinctly resembles the lines we see in the "pictures of damage". We can see cracks as a kind of map, a tracing of where energies run; a visualisation.

This is not a record of what Allen was saying, but a reconstruction of a space I went into during the conversation. My father was a historian of astronomy, so when I think about the past it tends to have stars in it.

Of Mutabilitie
Interview at Roehampton University, February 2005

Andrew Duncan

AD The question most on my mind had to do with something Rob Holloway was telling me about in the pub, which is to do with mutation of texts, and individual poems in *Gravity* being at least partly mutations of other poems.

AF That is explicitly one of the methods in the work. I can see why you would use the word *mutation* because of the introduction at times of biotechnology, some vocabulary from DNA science and so on. I'm more inclined to use words like transformation because they lead me in terms of vocabulary to something more positive, whereas mutation, because of science fiction movies and various other agendas always seem to lead to a worse period of time and so on. So that's not the… the intention isn't to mutate towards something sinister, but to something that leads to discussion of improvements perhaps. So let's just be more explicit about what's meant here. There are a range of different kinds of transformation within the work, and the work is planned in the sense of, it had an alphabetical basis in *Ideas of a Culture Dreamed of*, which explicitly lists a series of jazz dances from A to Z which are then interleaved with descriptions of some scientific terms I was interested in at the time and which are then followed. Transformations as such aren't written out as methods intimately for each transformation. They are partly derived from improvisatory debates with myself, and they're partly derived from previous practice. One of the most obvious examples perhaps is 'Banda' which is the first poem you come across in the Collected *Gravity*. It's not the first poem I wrote in that sequence, but if you take 'Banda'. There's a motive in 'Banda' which includes cycling on a bike in Brixton and there are 2 or 3 other motives in there which you could pick up at different moments throughout the work as seeming to link back to cycling and/or Brixton. So that's one kind of transformation, that is to say a narrative transformation, a narrative continuity. But then much more difficult to recognise but nevertheless apparent to anybody reading through is that some things start to rhyme in the sense of sound or repetition or reconfigured repetition, that is to say not quite repetition but using the same words perhaps in a different order or perhaps with a different purpose. Let's just think of some examples of that. The word *orang-utang* crops up, I'm trying to think of the line that crops up in. It's not going to work like that, because I'm not going to remember in time. I've got some unusual lines in 'Banda', in the sense that they don't seem to explicitly record typical documentary phenomena. For instance, *birds/ over the rail bridge, seem purple*, which is actually my perception. Nonetheless it's not necessarily documentary in the normal sense. And then I might then in a poem latterly after 'Banda' use the same line sequence, and so you would find another poem with the same number of lines, with the same stanza breaks. And that would therefore ring an alarm bell, make an explicit alarm bell, because you'd go, oh hold on, there are parallels going on, there are some transformations going on. And generally speaking this would be the case. But line by line there might be a different concept or criteria for the change. So the transformations aren't from that poem to that poem, the transformations are from that line to that line, or that stanza to that stanza. And sometimes they involve going backwards through the stanza. You've got the same numbers of lines and the same number of words. Word count is also involved, knowing how many words in the line. There are a whole set of elaborations, which I probably need to come back to. To give you explicit examples rather than keep remembering examples. Every so often you come across a really unusual line. Let's just talk about the ones that are in the English vocabulary. And you go, That's not a perception. What on earth's going on. And then you realise that what it is is a word for word transformation into a sentence that doesn't really make, it almost makes a, surrealist kind of sense. Although I'm not a surrealist. I'm just trying to think of a shorthand way of saying it. What happens then is that eventually I start to improvise, through the experience of performing some of the work, so that you actually get words that aren't in the English vocabulary, or in the typical dictionary vocabulary. And you get words that become invented as a consequence, because they sound like another word, or they're tonally like another word. Or they had some other reason for linking. I was interested in Robert Duncan's earlier idea of rhyming *grass* with *cream*. That's not fair, but if you could rhyme *concrete* with *grains*, and that would be a rhyme. So one wouldn't necessarily just look for sound in a rhyme. So there's that kind of transformation going on. We need to stop there to think if that's all we need to talk about, those terms. There's a whole numeracy involved here, which has to do with setting up ideas that I wanted to critique, which are ideas derived from my weak understanding of the Golden Section and Fibonacci, which I took to be, which is, a Renaissance elaboration which doesn't really fully get elaborated until the 17th century, people have a sort of romantic notion of this. Which derives initially from Euclid and

Greek architecture, so far as I know. And I wanted to critique that in 20th century ideas. One of the ways I first did it was to make a diagrammatic range of numbers in a way that I'd already produced or understood in a book called *Art of Flight* in the '70s. Which strictly used music, formulations and notations, in Bach's *Art of the Fugue*. It developed from that, from a late Beethoven quartet and also from a Ferneyhough work for bass clarinet. So this gradually elaborated so that in 1982 I was ready to apply it without the same almost rigid ideas, but actually to try to open those ideas out or to change them. We will eventually understand this as transformation. So I made this diagrammatic, geometrical diagram which used the arithmetic of Fibonacci and the Golden Section, which are directly linked, and crushed it, in the way that you almost put out a cigarette in an ashtray. Bent the cylinder. So that it becomes a squashed cylinder. To the point where some parts of the top half of the cylinder impinge on the lower part of the cylinder. And that diagram moved the numbers with it. Numbers crunched into numbers. I'm not expecting the reader to understand this, I'm just trying to explain the method. And what that did was to disturb my sense of, rather the romantic sense of order, that Fibonacci and the Golden Section provides. It undermines it in a way that leads to a positive transformation, because it means that the artist in the 20th century, or subsequently, has to then tackle the situation of the damage, and transform that damage into part of a creative activity, part of an aesthetic act. So that's leading on to tell you that although there's a direct numerical correlation between 'Banda' and some other poems, in *Gravity as a consequence of Shape*, what there is also is a damage of 'Banda'. Such that you wouldn't need as a reader to understand it geometrically or numerically. What would happen is… what I would hope could happen is that there would be an understanding of damaged vocabulary, of damaged vocabulary and syntax, that bring about that complexity, in the reader. That the reader feels every so often referred to a previous reading of the texts, texts that they've previously read in the same sequence. That's a very long-winded way of saying it. I couldn't really think of another way of getting round to it. So that's one kind of transformation that goes on in the work.

AD Just to clarify. The point of the Fibonacci, for example, is that it's a series, so that wherever you are you can generate the next term in the series.

AF Yes, that's right. What it is also is exponential, or rather it's logarithmic, and so it's always an increase, or a decrease depending on how you look at it. It's always larger steps. They're quantum steps, almost, in a sense. And the geometric form of these steps, the logarithmic form, leads into the same forms that the Golden Section ratios and proportions provide, and that's how they are brought together by, for instance, Pacioli around 1500. He and Leonardo, or probably Leonardo, put together that book called *Divine Proportions*, I suppose you'd translate it as. Now that was not I think particularly known to Alberti, or Masaccio, or some of those artists of the 15th C who get labelled with this material. I think it's much more intuitive and incidental then, and that the articulation of this sequence, this series, takes a monk mathematician, like Pacioli, with Leonardo's help, to sort it out. It's actually much later that European society understands it and uses it rather explicitly. So by the time you've got through to the 18th C it's used explicitly as a kind of, a way of describing beauty, visually and in music. So you could then start searching for it in baroque music, you could look for it in late baroque painting, and I'm only guessing, I presume I should think also in Romantic poetry. I'm, to be tangential for a moment, I got interested in numeracy and numbers in poetry, by looking at Christopher Butler, by looking at Alistair Fowler, in their analyses of Milton, Philip Sidney's *Astrophel and Stella*, Shakespeare's 'Venus and Adonis', works like those. Which on the surface, even on a very straightforward view of the surface, in one of the poems, for instance they're looking at the sunrise and the sunset, there's a sort of curve, with a high point, i.e. noon, in the middle of the poem. The stanzas would actually follow that visual sequence, you might call it visual sequence. That daily sequence. The numeracy would follow it, as well. And then someone like Milton would come along, and be much more difficult and tricky about it, much more complex, in his mathematical system. If we're to believe Fowler's understanding of the poem. There's a sense in which we needn't worry whether we do or not, because there's a sense in which aesthetic products lend themselves to this kind of analyses, because inherently there are elements in them which are geometrically or arithmetically repetitive, and so, like rhythm in verse or rhyming structures, and so on and so forth have that propensity anyway. I think I took it on board that they actually did know what they were doing, these guys, and by these guys I certainly mean the 17th century and later. And I think it strongly influenced the way in which I then thought about how I read Jackson Mac Low or somebody from that generation and after, that started to provide arithmetic formulas for writing. Which I then subsequently disagreed with. Or I'd rather make work which implicitly disagrees with them, which still prefers, as I continue to prefer, still prefers meaning. That is to say, some kind of syntax however agrammatical it is.

AD I'm curious about the historical hiatus there. I suspect we can't really go into that now. But I suspect that Neoplatonism is involved in there somewhere.

AF I'm sure it is. I'm certain it is. (Thomas) Taylor and people. Blake was reading Taylor, I don't know who Taylor was reading, presumably Dionysus of… (the Areopagite) somewhere else. And so on and so forth. Plato's quite late in the scene in terms of Renaissance Italy. He's translated for Cosimo, so that's late 15th century. Unless you were a particularly Greek scholar which most of those painters wouldn't have been, I don't think, I don't know. People like Ficino were before the 15th C. It's interesting. Before Ficino was asked to translate aspects of the Bible, he translated Plato, for Cosimo. So that was thought of as as important, or more important, than Christian and other scriptures at that time. Or you could read it that way. Certainly you could read it as a parallel.

AD The stars provided a set of numbers sufficiently complex to reach a state of freedom, perhaps. Which is why astrology inspired so much of this. But perhaps not really dependent on astrology.

AF No. I suppose one of the questions we would need to come to, whether or not it's quickly answerable, would be why do that anyway, why generate systems, or damage to the systems, within a poem.

AD A lot of writers haven't done that. But perhaps they had another competing principle which didn't allow it to happen. Which might be something like realism, or a theological, didactic programme.

AF I've had a couple of reasons for doing it. One is to make more interesting and complex the meaning that is being conveyed. By not just allowing one poem to do it, but by allowing connections between poems that therefore improve the experience of the poem. That's the first one. By reading the second poem it improves the experience of the first. Because there's a connection between them. Simple. Then when you go back to the first poem it's enriched by having read the second. That kind of circularity I'm interested in. I don't mean circular—jagged circular. But I'm also interested in recognising that, if you're reading Donne or someone like that, who is particularly strong on, keen on, particular rhythms, particular expectation of line endings or something of that kind, what that does for them is, it draws from them, it puts them on their mettle, it makes them have to very strongly search, or research, how to produce line 2 having written line 1, or line 10 having written lines 1 to 9. And I think I've understood from that that those kinds of restriction are in fact liberating. And so I didn't want to then say, in which case I'll adopt what the 17th or 18th centuries have already put in place, I want to think, well, where are we now? What is the basis, numerically, geometrically, for arriving at some of these parameters, some of these patterns? And I quickly recognised that the patterns basis that we'd experienced in the 20th century has quite clearly changed, radically changed, through the process of the 20th century, but particularly through the latter process of the 19th. From Faraday and Maxwell onwards. And I felt that our understanding of physics, and eventually through cellular and DNA understanding, that pattern is not quite what it was idealised as, by Newton and by Harvey or by Hooke or whoever we want to talk about. So that complex is the reasons for it to some extent. It complexes them but it also opens them, it makes clear why I'm interested. And in fact that overlaps not surprisingly through an interest in those assumptions anyway. Those subjects, what are our criteria for truth, for certainty, for lacks of truth, for lacks of certainty. What our criteria is for experience. Sometimes I find that quite interesting and difficult. I was looking at—this is tangential—at Christopher Ricks on Milton and the grand style, the pamphlet, they're really quite good. His tackling Leavis and Eliot's complaint about Milton not being consistent, how, there are a number of examples he quotes, one of them, within the same sentence group, this group of people are sitting down and standing up at apparently the same time. And Ricks completely opens it up and makes it clear that this isn't the case. It's completely consistent because, and then he elaborates. I'm still very very intrigued by the ability of vocabulary to be inventive in that way. I'm much more criminal about it than that. Much more disestablished, if that's the way of saying it. So that I'm open to invent words, but I'm also open to misusing them, deliberately. I will leave mistakes in sometimes. I'll create mistakes sometimes. I'll put words in that clearly are grammatically in the wrong place, or they're plural when they should be singular, or seem to be gender-based but all of a sudden aren't, they appear to refer to the I when it's not me at all. This whole playful use of vocabularies has come out of those worries about consistency, because I have the reverse feeling, I don't have the worry about consistency in the sense of being. I think we need inconsistency to some extent, it's a mistake to keep thinking we should cohere all the time, and make sense of it. So I was delighted to find that quantum mechanics used that term decoherence, I was just blessed to get it. I can't believe how lucky I am to get this sent down to me from some high physicist. But it's that idea that just because it's not coherent doesn't mean it's incoherent.

I thought that was just tremendous. I've diverted again.

AD It's very helpful for people to realise that these blemishes aren't the product of mechanical transformations, which can have that effect sometimes, but the result of jazz-like playfulness.

AF That as well. And I think you need to elaborate even that, because the word jazz has a lionesque tension, a line… it's not malign for you and me at this moment, but there are moments where if you said it was jazz it would not do it. There's some improvised music which isn't jazz.

AD What is it then?

AF Derek Bailey. Derek Bailey's not playing jazz.

AD It's not jazz? *[lionesque is wrong but the right word could not be found. line-ess or malignesque?]*

AF So there's that aspect of it, and then it's to do with painting as well. You'd be making marks that you'd planned, and then a drip occurs or a slight mistake occurs, or a lack of skill occurs, a demonstration of your lack of skill occurs, and you make a decision to leave it, because you recognise that it's made a better visual impact than you'd anticipated. And to correct it to the anticipated shape would actually not improve the work but do the contrary. So that kind of activity, it's not quite improvisation, it is, but accepting a mistake because of the improvement that it's provided.

AD Is there a political message here? It always seems to me, society has rules and you generate behaviour by following the rules, to a large extent. But because you're a conscious organism you can also introduce variations, and this seems to be so important about the subjective experience of freedom, and I imagine that what you call damage is actually a metaphor for that.

AF There's no question that terms like damage are… It's very difficult to find a vocabulary that's not metaphorical. So let's just be more elaborate. Let's just say that, Damage is almost metonymic in that sense, because it's much more deliberately used than that, you can deliberately use metaphor. I'm just thinking that it has that potential to stand for a whole range of different aspects of occurrence that when looked at much closer you wouldn't typically call damage. Obviously there's a metaphoric transfer. It's also because you're using a word to stand for it because of its emotional impact. Or its social impact, or its political impact. Damage feels in current society for example as negative, politically. And so what would it mean to start to say that there's a need for damage. The politics of that would be quite hard to deal with, because of the social emotive context of the word.

AD I relate it to Utopia. Utopia is somewhere you can't go because you'd have to behave so perfectly that it would be unbearable. If you can dribble some paint in the wrong direction and improvise on that dribble, then Utopia comes back to life because you could live in it.

AF There's also the other side of it, which is to do with terms like happiness or contentment or something like that, which are the state you wish others to be in rather than yourself. So they're happy, I'm pleased they're really happy but I'm glad I'm not in that situation. It's quite surprising how vocabulary misleads in that way, at times, as if we all wanted happiness, one of the promotional ideas. That's one of these debates that go on, well, I think one of them was dead at the time, between Blanchot and Levinas. I don't know, Blanchot in the 1950s was writing, he's got this sort of continuous interest in darkness and death, but it's as if he's not thinking of it as something he doesn't want, it's something he actually celebrates, and allows society to improve around him, wants it to improve around him, providing he's not part of the improvement. And Levinas comes along, and critiques that in terms of being a spiritual idea of the whole business, so it's quite odd that the two get on at all. I don't think they do, actually. I don't think they ever spoke. Levinas' work on escape is actually earlier. I can't remember the dates. It might be an early work. It might well be contemporary with Blanchot rather than being later. Coming back to mutation let's see where we've gone on that. One of the explicit ways of looking at this would be to look in the book that came out from The Gig recently, *Entanglement*, and in that there's 'Fish Jet', which is second in the book, which came out originally from Peter Middleton's and Tim Woods' press, and called 'Fish Jet', and it brings together three poems, within the context of *Gravity as a Consequence of Shape*. It brings together one called 'Fish' and one called 'Jet' and another called 'Jellyfish', which is just the jelly, I've lost the title, in the middle. It's 'Jersey Bounce'. The way it's printed, you can see stanza by stanza I put them together. That is instead of going through Jersey Bounce 1 2 3 4 5 6 I've done it Jersey Bounce 6 followed by Fish 6 followed by Jet 6. And then what you would do is read those through, and you would recognise that one of them appears to be the earlier of the three, and then another one seems to be the last of the three, because there's a transformation going on, line for line, or word for word, through most of the text. There's you can see that there's some playful changes to what I've just said. But that's really like a, what's the word for it, an illustration of what's happening, in a larger way with the whole work. That is, *Gravity as a Consequence of Shape*. But in the whole work the symmetry of 'Fish Jet', such as it is, has been damaged, deliberately damaged, in such a way that you can't make these explicit, this to this, this to that readings, because that's not what I'm after. So that would undermine what I want, really. I would much rather it happened in a mixture of subversive way, but also in a way that is positive towards increasing the readability, increasing the interest, the energy for the reader. Or the reader's ability to make energy. I think that's only possible… if you provide all the answers it doesn't make it possible, it takes away the possibility. So you're asking the reader to make their own answers. Question and answer makes it sound so straightforward. I mean, as if there were answers to questions. Now, one of the interesting aspects of this also which I've been involved in is narrative, because it seemed to me that in the '70s and subsequently, much earlier but also subsequently, there was a whole debate about the critique of narrative in the whole debate about, quite a deep debate, Ricœur and others, about narrative and whether one should use it or not. Foucault particularly for instance, looking at historical narratives, Hayden White, even, looking at similar things. Now, I have been interested in narratives in a way that is divergent from that, but has flipped in and out of taking an interest in that debate, because I recognised a reading in narrative, that is, there is a certain sequence and order in what one reads, whatever one chooses to read backwards or read forwards, it's a sequence like it or not. And I'll critique what I've just said in a moment, but if we just carry that thought through. One of the ways narrative works best for a reader, quite often, is to find elements of recognition, elements maybe of repetition, maybe of recurrence, of similar characters, similar word sequence, something of those kinds, which help a narrative, it propels the narrative forward, so to speak, historically. So I've allowed that to happen, because I've wanted it to happen, I've recognised that it's already there. Why not therefore include that as part of the compositional discussion. One of the points going on. So there are moments in *Gravity as a Consequence of Shape* where there are quite obvious sequences of events one could almost call based on a story, or based on something that's happened. And there are moments when you can't see that's there at all. Both parts are true I think. Both of them deliberately. It must be my unconscious. And then what I've done is recognised that because of the critique of the grand narrative, because of the critique of the continuity of narrative, there's also the other debate, which I eventually began calling crowd-out, as a method, which is, instead of using collage, which is one way of dealing with overlapping realities, of recognising that continuity is multiple, there's more than one thing going on at the same time while I'm talking to you there's traffic outside, there's a cat screaming down the corridor, someone shouts in the distance, and so forth. That those perceptive indicators can actually become quite obtrusive in terms of the continuity you would, you needn't collage it in the sense that you allow simultaneity or allow transparent overlap. It might actually be quantum, it stops and starts, stops and starts, as I'm talking to you I suddenly turn and starts talking about Giotto's geometry, I suddenly start talking to you about the grass I can see through the window. So the continuity keeps getting broken. So my use of narrative is therefore part of the instrument of composition, because the expectation of continuity gives the license for interruption, increases the effectiveness of the interruption.

[…] So we've been looking at mutation, have we for the moment done a temporary closure on that?

AD Can we just talk about this phrase crowd-out, because it could be… Like, what is being crowded out.

AF OK. I understand from some psychiatric students that there are lots of technical terms for what I'm talking about. What I'm thinking of is a method which is post-collage. Let's just describe what collage does first and it might help us lead on to why I'm thinking about something being post-collage. What I'm quickly recognising as I say this is that it doesn't mean that collage has been removed, there's no new method that replaces collage. It just means that there's been a development from it. As I've understood collage that's been meaningful to me it was first of all proposed by people like Picasso and Braque, in which they recognised the process of making something like a still life as they're standing in front of, it's going through a process of time and change and therefore space-time, because they recognised that they would come back, go off and make a coffee, come back, they seem to be in the same position but they're not, back in exactly the same position, and in any case, 15 minutes later the light might not be exactly the same, and so on. They might not be feeling exactly the same. So their experience of reality shifts, but the end product is as if it's one experience of reality. And so we recognise when we look at a Cubist painting, so-called Cubist painting, we would say well, that's come about because it's multiple reality shown in one space, at one moment, quickly. And that was developed socially, politically, by the different Dada groups. Let's just take Max Ernst as a good example of this. Ernst articulates, when he writes about painting subsequently, he's talking to Breton, Breton then steals the... or rather Breton then takes on board what Ernst says which is that for him collage is putting together two planes of reality into one plane. Surrealism is proposing effectively that one plane of reality, to Breton, is internal, and another plan of reality is external. His surrealism puts the two together. So collage is effectively a form of realism in the sense that, but it's a realism that has understood more than one reality at once. Dream life, the subconscious life and the life of perception. Of course we recognise that as immensely simple, over-simple. That's neither here nor there. What we then subsequently recognise is that with collage you're putting together more than one reality. What happens when you do that is that one reality cuts out part of another reality. So if you put one sheet of paper with blue writing on it over a sheet with red writing on it, it's clear that some of the red writing disappears, because it's being obliterated by the fact that you've put one sheet over the other. So although you're proposing to present two realities, what in fact you're doing is fragmenting either one or both of these realities. So collage technique at that moment becomes a fragmenting technique. It's therefore I suppose metonymic of consciousness, it's metonymic of the experience of consciousness. That's where it starts to develop from. Because I recognise that consciousness is informed from a whole range of different sets of information. Partly to do with direct perception from the eyes, from smelling, from hearing, and so on, and also from a recognition that consciousness has elements which you might put together and call them memory. These things are happening at the same time, that is to say whatever I'm doing, whether I close my eyes or open them, close our ears and open them. And what we recognise then is that the fragmenting that occurs is a kind of crowd-out. As I'm talking to you now, for a split second a car goes by. And I've included that in my hearing, while I'm speaking and hearing my own voice. Now, the elements of that overlap and happen at the same time. You feel like you can hear them both at the same time. But quite often really what happens is your focus of attention momentarily, however briefly, changes. And your consciousness so to speak goes out of the room and then comes back in again. That's a way of saying. That's the way I think it. Then you can start working to become quite deliberate about that. You can plan it almost. And if you think of this developing as a way of composing you'd recognise, or rather, a set of permissions within the compositional process, one recognises that syntax and straightforward sentences, from capital beginning of the sentence to full stop at the end, starts in places to be inadequate. It doesn't fully account for these crowd-outs and these sudden changes. Well, I don't think of them as sudden changes. You could, but I think it's better to just say that consciousness operates in that way, there are quantum jumps and changes, or punctuated changes in a continuum, so that change isn't thought of in a logarithmic way, but it's thought of in a more step-like way. Your perception in other words is step-like. Or potentially can be, and quite often is. And it's just a matter of realising it. So that's where crowd-out is coming around. Coming out, coming about. One sensation, or one perception, crowds out another for a moment, or for a period.

AD So the emphasis definitely isn't on what's lost, it's more on the set of instructions that control the editing?

AF Yes, it leads to different kinds of, permissions isn't quite right, but that's what's used a lot in discussing this word, so let's just use it for a moment. Because permissions makes it sound like there's some authority involved. What happens is you might be making commentary on the way in which some Palaeolithic groups were making drawings in a cave, and in the process of doing so you suddenly start talking about the Levellers in the 17th C. And there's a perversity about that or maybe it's not, actually, Maybe this is a sudden change, a sudden crowd-out. And that can be done accidentally. You could invent a method to accept the accidents for doing it. It could be done through a pair of scissors, would be another accident, if you had a series of texts and you just grouped them together. It might be done in a burroughsesque way, he used to say you'd create columns of text and you'd read across the columns. So the accident of where they join up across columns gets elaborated. And the third way might be, because I think of both of those as collagic, the third way is actually much more deliberately thought through, so that you find juxtapositions that you want, I can't think how I would connect the Levellers to the Palaeolithic drawing, I'm not going to try to, but there are moments when you can make such juxtapositions, such crowd-outs, meaningful and useful. And they sometimes inform each other. When they work well. It might be they inform each other because they're so unalike, and they kind of refresh. But they might do so because they connect. Another old-fashioned word that I use is an anthropological way of talking about consciousness, a pattern of connections. That's also a word I use to describe aesthetics. So if you think of that as being a fairly overall general notion. Disruption to pattern, disruption to connectedness, is part of the debate. We've talked about the debate about pattern earlier. Intrusion into pattern, change of pattern, damage to pattern, and connectedness as part of our discussion. Let's try and move it on from free association, stream of consciousness, to a much more palpable model, that's not the right word. A more palpable experience. That's not quite right either, but that's just not difficult enough, in a sense, it's not important enough. What's important is something else, which it's quite difficult to articulate quickly. And that's to do with… One of the simple ways of saying it is, what we're looking for is understanding. What we're looking for in a model is coherence. What I'm saying is, that's no longer enough. That's far too much of a summarising exclusory activity. This is understood, this is part of a coherent structure. And I'm saying that won't do any more. And that it's not enough to say, this is the best way forward. We have to recognise that there's more than one way forward, quite often. See, philosophically it leads to recognising the fallacy of the idea of coherence. Therefore you're struck with this difficulty, or you have been struck with this difficulty, of being offering alternatives, which is being incoherent. Now we're not in that position. We have been for some while, before the word was rediscovered. Before the ideas of decoherence, you could be in the state of recognising that of course you're not going to find a paradise on earth, why on earth did you think you should. And in any case if you did want it, as we've debated earlier, discussed earlier, and so if that's recognised as the case, if you've come to the stage of saying, We recognise we don't want it, what exactly do we want, if it's as simple as that. That's where we over-simplify as we go forward. Oh, we want this. We want a whole range of things. It's not possible to just

AD We want unpredictability in a steady and predictable supply.

AF That's very good. Yes, that's true. One keeps playing with the vocabulary, you want to almost say that in order for that to work, there would have to be a disruption to the supply. It's very playful to say that, but it's true.

AD This is surely a feature of all really good art already.

AF It is, yeah. There's not a need necessarily to theorise it. I think it's quite useful to do so, because you can then move on, and hopefully we try to do that. I'm kind of sceptical about it really in some ways. Every so often feel that we could be…

AD This might actually be a rule of thumb I could apply to a half-finished poem, to see if it's good and how I should finish it.

AF When Olson plucks that line out of Keats' letter to his brother, about negative capability. It was really very apposite, I think that's really moved us on. That recognition, that that's needed. I'm not a lover of Keats' work, but that particular extract, that's really useful. Then when we apply that in the conversations between Einstein and Heisenberg, and Einstein and Bohr, we elaborate what negative capability is, elaborate what certainty and the lack of it is. It starts to really impinge on very useful recognitions, I think, about a whole range of levels and experiences. Not just straightforward experiences about nutrition through to, which I suppose is comparatively straightforward, to areas where choices are very very difficult. They're so difficult that a single choice wouldn't be a solution. Then you know, once you've understood that that's so, then that negative capability, through negative capability you recognise the need for this complexity. This whole business in the war machine of a solution, and wipe-out or take over, or whatever, is one of the problems that kind of assume this or that. It doesn't take on board the range of choices. Many of the choices need to be available.

AD The war machine… I thought it was a film by Peter Watkins?

AF I meant for instance the political social structure that imposes its will on another social structure without limitation. All the levels of that, that's what…

AD So the Cold War is the nightmare from which we're trying to awake?

AF Describe the Cold War.

AD A world with two systems which both want the maximum and will not be satisfied without destroying the other system. And where a hundred other conscious agents are denied conscious agency because they haven't got the bombs.

AF Is it always a state of impasse or is it a state of one eventually conquering another, wiping out another one?

AD Well, I think the bit which rigidified Western art in a certain period, Western thought for a certain period, was where it was very very stable, but where you always thought disaster was just around the corner, so you were completely scared, you couldn't speculate because speculation in itself was terrifying.

AF When do we recognise that in Britain? is that in the immediate, is that 1950s Britain? and into the '60s probably to some extent?

AD I think people emigrated from it on an individual basis during the 1960s.

AF From it. Yeah. Yeah. So you've got someone like Raworth writing to Dorn all of a sudden in the early '60s. I mean, I didn't know that was happening until I read about it in *Chicago Review*. I was quite rewarded by the early date of that. Quite extraordinary. Dorn hadn't published his first book yet. It was just amazing. It was just about coming out. Astonishing. So fast a turnround. It was quite surprising.

AD He had quite strong motives for looking for something else.

AF The fact that you could come across Dorn so early on without there even being a book out. Even if there had been one he wouldn't have seen it in Britain. So there's that kind of extraordinary… It just must have been so devastatingly poor in Britain in terms of what you had to read. You'd have to be reading pre-war work to find anything interesting, except the occasional accidents. Late Jones or anyone like him.

AD Some people were still reading exclusively uninteresting material in 1980 or even today.

AF Yes quite.

AD On an elective basis.

AF The English at Roehampton, they've just started a Writers at Roehampton series. The first writer they've provided is Matthew Sweeney. When they told me I just laughed. What am I supposed to say? He's a very nice man. Whether his writing is of interest is difficult for me to say.

AD It's probably quite coherent.

AF I'm sure it is. Positive. Still, we've diverted again. Let's think back.

AD Finite machines, the war machines, negative capability, incoherence…

AF Where do you want me to elaborate? Who would ask a question, what would be the question they asked? We've summarised decoherence in the earlier part of the tape, so we needn't come back to it at this stage. We've started to talk about what you and Rob were talking about in terms of mutation. I've allowed the slippage into the word transformation, because I'm worried about the negativity of the word mutation. Though I recognise its [ ]. I have a propensity for that, that is to say for instance the word *traps*, which crops up over the last [ ], is quickly thought of on the surface as a negative word, it's a word that's involved in *I am trapped, I am trapping, I am involved in catching mice or animals* or something. Then all of a sudden if you say a camera is a trap.

AD The printed page is a trap for data.

AF Then you start to build it into understanding what knowledge is, understanding what history is, what a trap is. And so you elaborate the vocabulary to enrich, you don't enrich the vocabulary, because the vocabulary is already available. It's just that you make it more available. You renew its availability. Maybe that would be a way of saying it. And that's very necessary because. I think turning those negative words into words that are much more interesting and complex, you're not just changing them into nice words, but you change them, you complex the context, allows for a recognition that a single choice of context doesn't work, effectively. Come back to that singularity worry. I've often had that worry, I think it. I used it as a sort of metaphor because some mathematicians have used it as a metaphor for a type of sequence of algebraic thought. I mean a sense of singularity which is used to describe the status of a certain sort of ideas you get in Penrose, or Hawking for that matter.

AD I didn't know that.

AF So you get the idea of singularity. Quite a short way of saying it is they're using it metaphorically. They mean it positively. When one hears the word, particularly when one's talking about concepts, political ideas, social ideas, singularity can quite often mean overdetermined, or blinkered, or too straightforward or not elaborate enough. Or simplistic. All those terms. And it needn't do so. It often does for me. I've always had trouble with it. I'm always worried about it as a way forward, really. I think there's likely to be some overview, which says actually you've always had this. One could summarise your views as being singular. It's an overview really.

AD That's a right-wing rhetoric.

AF I think it is.

AD A kind of symbolic violence.

AF There's another issue that crops up in number that's very interesting to me, which is ongoing, which comes I would say out of quantum mechanics and some of the work of John S. Bell, who is an Irish physicist who was one of the people at the CERN laboratory in Geneva, with the particle accelerators, and he talks about the speakable and the unspeakable. That's the title of one of his books. He's not alive any longer. His philosophical stance is quite remarkable. Quite succinct. Quite difficult to read. And he deals with the issue that you can't make a measurement. Which is an issue

I suppose raised by Bohr and Einstein in most of those conversations. But Einstein wouldn't have it, of course. Until later on, anyway. [field came out in the fifties (?)]. and Bell comes back to it. Quite late, '60s '70s. Even '80s, I think he died in the late '80s. And the word that crops up as a consequence of this difficulty with measurement—as measurement interferes with what you're measuring and changes what you're about to measure, and so on and so forth. And because the idea of precision in measurement is a fallacy, it's actually not feasible. It leads on to the philosophical problem, let's just quickly share it, takes on the conceptual problem. If there's a quantum leap, doesn't that imply there's a boundary between one leap and another, or a boundary between one state and another? And therefore, isn't it possible therefore that the measurement can define it? because if you're seeing one box and then another box, there's a wall between the two boxes. Two walls. Anyway, it impinges on that philosophical problem. It doesn't get solved. But what Bell leads on to then is the idea of invariables, and the vocabulary is just so exciting for me, because it just allows—it just sounds a bit too weak really—it improves one's extemporisation is what one might say. At least I can. It makes possible. It leaves open and provides the recognitions that words are complexed and that context shifts change the words. And therefore the building of poems is contexts and therefore shifts or potential shifts of context, and therefore shifts of vocabulary, therefore shifts of ranges of meanings and illnesses and rhetorics and so on. So it's recognise as many of those things at the same time as possible, is what I try to do quite often.

AD Can you give us an example of an invariable?

AF The problem is that it's not to do with that, it's to do with Bell saying that if you found something that was invariable that is really a way of saying you can measure it. So it's recognising that they're unlikely! And yet, you see, what physicists... why that remark is so important in Bell is that atomic weight, for instance, is thought to be a way of defining different elements, and so on and so forth. But if you're saying that actually these things are variable, you really are making something quite difficult, for people's operative chemistries. Of course, the reason why this is possible is because whilst he's taking the precision out of the science to some extent. He's saying, It's not as precise as you're pretending, it's not actually as concise as that. He's not throwing it all out, saying that there's nothing. He's saying that it's actually much more complex and difficult to recognise. And of course as a macro-person looking at a pile of atoms that you call a bowl of water, of course you can recognise that they're all collectively, as an average, H^2O. It's only when you get very intimate with them, when you get below the level of oxygen atoms, you recognise they're not all the same. All these molecules H^2O aren't the same. They do vary very slightly, comparatively tinily, in very very small ways, they vary. And I've just been interested in that whole business. Always been interested in the way colour is partly defined by crystalline form, and not by its chemical content. So that as a painter you know that if you're mixing cadmium red in oil you get a certain red, you get a certain kind of red, and if you're mixing cadmium orange you get orange, but actually if you ask a chemist to tell you the difference, he'll say there's no difference. They're the same atoms. The same quantity of atoms. So what's the difference? Well, they're configured differently. Different shapes inside. It's made, brought about a different reflection of light. So when you look the colours are different. So that's like a macro example of, applying a macro example to Bell, that's unfair on Bell. Saying Bell is. I'm just recognising, that's my poetic license if you like. I'm able to jump around in that way, able to use those vocabularies to increase my and therefore the reader's I hope, capacity to experience. So, sounds a bit inflated really. I didn't mean it to. I can't presume what it does for the reader's. You just have to hope that that's what. I don't think of, this is what I'll do for the reader. It's not thought of in that way, is what I mean. It can't possibly be as pompous as that. When one reflects upon it, one might think, that was what I was involved in doing. You're involved in doing it in the sense that you want, i.e. disrupt sometimes, so that would be a different ploy. Think of Albert Ayler playing a very straightforward Victorian spiritual, that he's picked up from some Southern city. All of a sudden the honking ends the sweetness of it. That sort of jump.

AD I'm just wondering if I should footnote Albert Ayler.

AF In what way?

AD There is a famous paradox, which is that if you set out to explain your poetry by explaining bits, you rapidly end up with 80 pages of prose to one page of poem. And you realise, This was not the right way to go at all! A lot of people reading this have got no idea who Albert Ayler was.

AF No, I know. Except, you know there's a new box set coming out? In November. And it, I think it's about 8 CDs, it's the whole of his work. It's the whole lot. It has replicas of some of the notes you used to get on albums. And it has a plant in it, a squashed plant in a bag, I haven't worked out what that's for. An encyclopaedia of his life. Which also describes these CDs. Two of which are mainly interviews anyway. Along with 'Spirits Rejoice' and so on. It's in a facsimile of a wooden African chest. About this size. It's made of plastic actually. It's as if it's carved black mahogany. And you open it up, and the CDs are all rested in a well in the middle with these literature on top of them. It's almost like a sacred object. He's obviously come back in vogue all of a sudden for some reason. I saw the review about a year ago. So it must have been before November, actually. It didn't get to Britain, there and then, I don't suppose.

AD If I put in, "Albert Ayler, jazz musician, 1920-66", or whatever, it's useless. If I try to describe the way he played in words, it just explodes.

AF It wouldn't work.

AD Yeah, it wouldn't work anyway.

AF The only way you could do it really would be to put a CD out!

AD I'll mention it to Chris (Emery)!

AF Let's talk about, before we close this, make quite sure we've mentioned some things you might like me to research before I talk to you. Research in the sense of broad thinking about. So that there's more readily available… so that I don't wander too much. We don't become too diverse.

AD I'd like us to talk through one poem line by line. I think a lot of people would find that helpful.

AF If one thinks about it there is another range of discussion, a number of channels of discussion. One would be music, and the different ways in which one talks about music. As being a set of shapes or whether one thinks of it as a set of impacts, like sounds. And then there's another parallel discussion about painting, or visuality, the influence of visuality on what you read. You know, the sense in which Williams' work is looking like a Greek vase, or something. Olson's movement across the page compared with Clark Coolidge's *American Ones*, or something. And so the difference between them, what is the difference between them. There's a visual difference. So I'm interested in both those things. There's a third level which is to do with vocabulary choice. Beyond the conversational, beyond the everyday. That is to say, specialist or refined vocabularies. What's the word—restricted vocabulary. I've obviously been interested in those for quite a while, particularly in terms of the debate about how you fit them to an audience (??), for about seven or eight years. About the difference between science and poetry. Which actually I have returned to, and so revisited something which affected me while I was at school, which I'd heard C.P. Snow talking about the *Two Cultures*, 1959. I went back to it this year. So I started to write something about that, about science and art, the intellectual cultures, the difference between them, and what Leavis said.

AD Do you read Judith Field?

AF [...] can't get into it because it's boarded up at the moment because it's unsafe. It was built for Clive of India's brother.

(Omitted discussion of Roehampton site. how William Harvey used to be a tutor on the estate. John Seed is interested in the history of the estate.)

AD One of Eric's poems uses Harvey's *De motu cordis*.

AF It does, yeah. *Local Movement*. It's one of the better books actually. More successful in terms of. I found his collage style sort of dragging. It does very little for me, that's the trouble. In the sense that it pulls it through a lot of undergrowth which clings on to it all the way. Sometimes you want it to shed some. But that's quite an interesting set of poems that.

AD I'm always glad when I can retrieve something of Eric's. It does work out a lot better than some of his things.

AF One of the useful areas of Eric's work is not so much the poem really, it's his ability to formalise his reading about Harvey on a quite informal basis without making it seem as if he was teaching. So that's quite a facility, quite a treasure really. I learnt a lot about Blake from Eric and he gave me many ideas about him. Most of all he was succinct about the poems I'm less interested in, *Songs of Innocence and Experience*. The stuff on *Prophecies* is always having these grand theories about it. That's what makes the work formidable. Makes it actually almost unreadable. He would just say, I'll get right to this. So he was quite good on that for that reason.

AD There was a boundary around poetry which excluded most kinds of knowledge, and it somehow dissolved in the second half of the Sixties, I suppose.

AF It was made possible before that, by Americans and some others I suppose. But it was just somehow wasn't realised at the time. There's only a few examples, aren't there, of a different sensibility. I mean Bunting's quite a limited example to me.

AD He had this terrible idea about the purity of poetry which means that he didn't explain what was going on. When you read the explanations in Victoria Forde's book, you think Oh! that's what he wasn't saying!

AF I must say it was very very difficult. It's the legacies of Latin, the legacies of all that sort of thing in David Jones. And those aspects of stuff that really. The fact that really… Seeing as God is not really my favourite topic.

AD I think Jones was a genius, but the philosophy he was articulating doesn't have much in common with anybody else I know. It's unfair really. He wasn't written up. He wasn't a pioneer only because nobody followed him. Literally he was a pioneer. He didn't make a break in the wall, he was just seen as someone with psychological problems.

AF It's much easier with his drawing style. To see. It helps a lot with the work. Because of the transparent overlapping you get. So he's drawing a ship with a goddess on it and footsoldiers on it, and you can see through them. Through the soldiers you can see the boat. It's extraordinary. They're lovely things. Who else is there, do you think? MacDiarmid, particularly after the Second and subsequent Hymns to Lenin. Tremendous stuff. Very very good. I don't have the same feeling with Graham. Although he's paralleled with people like Peter Lanyon. I've always preferred Lanyon, strangely enough. It was the coincidence of their friendship rather than their technique.

AD Yes, I think one of the things about that group in St Ives is how different they were. I don't think Graham wrote any poems about flying. It's hard to imagine it. That's what Lanyon's all about really.

AF That and the experience of landscape from walking round it. Have you seen the way he constructed his landscape paintings? In his studio he would spend weeks and weeks and weeks walking around drawing and collecting bits and pieces and making small paintings, really, and then he'd bring them back to his studio and make 3-dimensional objects of the landscape that he'd experienced. And that's what he would paint. The paintings are of the 3-dimensional objects, which he'd collected and produced, via the sketches and drawings and collections of bits. And some of them are now exhibited. Quite extraordinary. 3-dimensional sketchbooks. Although they don't have the same sense of perfection or order, they shouldn't be over-emphasized. It's very laudable, not (?).

AD With Lanyon what I often feel is that there isn't a direct visual equivalent of the geology he's trying to get across, but what seizes you is his excitement about it. It sort of pulls you over into something else.

AF Very much so. His biggest disadvantage was that he was living in an area where the green was gone. It's rather a dirty green, kind of dull. A lot of the work is not very graphic. It's not shown, he's still not credited with trying to deal with this issue. There's this kind of censorship. Every so often there are moments, like 3 articles in *Artscribe*. There are a couple of books. The books are works of dedicatees rather than scholars. So that's a way of talking through some of the things. He influenced my ideas about collecting materials, collaging, he influenced ways in which one could set about making something complete, that sequence and what that implies, and what is the debate about completion. What is the difference between visual. And he set out on a sequence. He showed why would you do that, and what would be the best way of going about it. So in that sense I think you can see the influence of painting in rather a strange indirect way, rather in lots of mini-linguistic ways, which alight on different aspects of different works. Musical, visual art which would help you think, help you conceptualise and plan and compose all those things. Hugh MacDiarmid saw resolved in Ronald Johnson's work. I forget the name, of those Scottish painters.

AD William Johnstone.

AF Johnstone I know is just about known. Others I don't. The way in which they would interact with him. He's an avid reader of scientists as well. It's not a good example is it, it's not so resolved, because it's so massive. Each poem is summed up by how big the *Collected* is, but also how big the poems within the *Collected* are. This 'Hymn to Lenin', that 'Hymn to Lenin'. You know, these aren't small things. On a beach, what's that…

AD 'On a Raised Beach'.

AF So I feel they're the best legacies. The ones I've mentioned. I've never really gone back to some of the first references, I read at school. I still think of Eliot as a positive. I'm not thinking about Eliot's social being, but about the Four Quartets and… actually I mean the 'Four Quartets' and 'The Waste Land', the two of them. One of the people I read very early on, whom I've almost come to dislike, although it's very very very unfair, and not very accurate to say so, is Dylan Thomas. It's not his life, I don't dislike him, it's his work, and the kind of influence of that. I'd almost rather have Edith Sitwell or someone. Any of those people who are pulling off of Symbolism, some parts of Europe. Don't you think?

AD I'm a big fan of Edith. It's hard to see anyone who's actually been influenced by her. Someone else who translated eccentricity into isolation.

AF I've been influenced by the way she rhymes one word on another. Maybe it's not quite true, but she seems to invent words as a consequence of the sound in the line. And I think that would be to do, not necessarily that it's been a big influence, but on reflection I've been influenced by that, because I've always liked that. I've always enjoyed that aspect of Edith Sitwell's work. I've only just realised that, as I'm saying it. It's definitely the case. I can't think who it is, but there's somebody else does that, too, that I've been struck by. It might be Lewis Carroll or Edward Lear, it's that sort of era. Where they muck around with new vocabulary a bit. It was quite a serious in one way, I suppose. And on one level it isn't. By which I mean you wouldn't want to exclude play and devalue it. Strangely we've been pretty lucky in Britain in music for quite a while. Up until, I don't think of it quite as strongly now, but I thought that the new English composers, post-Schoenberg post-Webern post-Stockhausen, '60s '70s, some of the best of my generation, you could almost say that, but by now my generation is quite a bit older than me, have really given me the confidence to make things worth doing. It kind of gives you the confidence to still do something that you feel is important. The reason I say it like that, what I mean is, English poets didn't really provide that confidence much. That's why. So I think that's why I went to other disciplines for the confidence. And then Americans of course were providing it but that wasn't quite enough. Without being nationalistic. But there really is that sense that it's geographically, textually, historically different. It really is. And no-one can understand it translated across.

AD There should be a work on this. Because that's what everyone's found. Andrew Crozier was saying something quite similar. He is so close to his American sources, but when he wrote it down it was just so English.

AF Yes. That's pretty extraordinary.

AD You were talking about being given confidence by English composers. I just wondered who those composers were.

AF I think Maxwell-Davies would be the most conventional end of it. Some of his work was very strong at that period. I think certainly Cornelius Cardew, and Howard Skempton. Brian Ferneyhough has always been very important for me. There was Birtwhistle. His work in that period was always terrific. I think Johnson, what's his name, Robert Sherlaw Johnson, but he moved off into a different mode which interested me less. Just interrupting myself, comedians was another thing Eric was very good on, he had lots of recordings of comedians. I was also and still am an extensive early blues fan, and Eric wasn't. He much preferred jazz.

AD There's a reference to 'Stone Pony' in *Prosyncel*.

AF I used to have Howlin' Wolf's record of that. Howlin' Wolf's first recording. Howlin' Wolf actually knew Charles Patton, so he must have got it from him directly.

In One Side and Out the Other:
Lulham interview 2, 12 May 2005

(Side 1 inaudible, was about improvised music, the improvising group AMM, how a poem is part of a dialogue of many voices. Ken Edwards arrives at some point during the session. Immediate topic is the suggestion that Rubens' "studio" was like the Fluxus group.)

AF But more seriously, what were we talking about?

AD The difficulty of writing the history of Fluxus.

AF Oh, that's right. Because of the ephemeral, and not having the entourage that people like Rubens had, who had this. I mean, he's doing stuff for the king, and he's got 16 people doing the painting for him. What he's saying, you do the cabbages now, you do the landscape. It's a bit of a different situation really. But we were worrying about the problem of collaboration in poetry. It's almost the unusualness of it occurring or working, in the sense of it being a process… when you think of products, what products do you think have worked where more than one poet has been involved in the writing, is the problem. It might be amusing to take part in, it might be an interesting community activity, but really what poems have I read and said, Oh, this is really better than it would have been if it had been by one writer. And it's not very often I can think of one. And if I looked along my bookshelf I could probably go, oh yeah, there's that, but I can't actually think of one for the moment. It's a, New York poets have done some things which are quite amusing. From O'Hara to Berrigan to people. Padgett, and people like that. Because they were collaborating, as we said earlier, with the painters. O'Hara and Rivers, O'Hara and Grace Hartigan. And we talked about John James and Andrew Crozier and Tom Phillips. But that's not their best work, I have to say. I'd rather read John James and then read Andrew Crozier than in combinations. That's a very interesting difficulty. Either my reception's poor, I'm a poor receptionist, or it doesn't produce work as engaging. On the positive side of this collaboration, we were initially talking about how AMM works and when they are working well they are listening to each other as musicians, and it doesn't work if they don't. We argued for instance how Harry Gilonis' argument against somebody like John Tilbury would be, he doesn't listen enough, he's always playing Mozart or Debussy. And in fact then we debated whether or not that's really true, and whether it's just as much the case, that someone like John, because he's playing other things like Mozart or Morton Feldman, is likely to have a whole vocabulary of motor habits and motor references which are based in what he's previously played. And therefore it's not the, Harry may have some insight into Mozart or Debussy that I haven't had, but I wonder, I don't think it always is quotation, I think it's more a mixture of styles, or different ways of touching the piano. It's not necessarily in other words a repeat of some notes that have been laid down by Mozart. Anyway, coming back to the story. I do think that when John Tilbury plays well he's listening to what Rowe is playing on the guitar or what Prevost is playing on the drums. It is true to say they've recently disagreed about that. But that's only a recent history, a very very recent history. They've been together for 40 years—getting on for 40 years, anyway, more than 30. I don't want to put this on tape because I wasn't there, all I've heard is anecdotal. (rest omitted)

I don't think I'm going to solve the problem though of why this is more difficult in poetry, this business of improvising with more than one. It's not to do with the maturity of it, either. It just might be. I don't think it is. Certainly, obviously, poetry's well matured. Whether you think improvised music isn't, it's still in its early stages and able to be more co-operative in that sense, I don't know if that's true. We've earlier distinguished it from jazz, not just a theoretical difference but actually a difference, like a Venn diagram there's a period in the middle when it's jazz and improvised.

AD I think you have to go back one step and argue that poems are based on procedures and these might be shared procedures. Poets don't necessarily like that idea.

AF But I do though as you know. I like it very much. I think it's very true. I think they are based on… if you don't make procedures conscious, that's a different debate, whether you're conscious or overtly conscious or not of your procedures. You don't write good poems out of nothing. They're based on compositional ideas, always. Even if those ideas might be more free-form in some than others. There's no way it would be, one, recognised as a poem, two, readable as a poem, without that, some aspects of that compositional recognition to be in place, which is what the procedures are about. Is that what you meant by…

AD Yes it is. That's why if you lose the surface detail of a poem, get back to something which isn't there in the surface of the poem at all, that thing once you've resolved it might be shared by several people.

AF Part of this discussion has cropped, has bumped into the idea of coteries, or groups of people who recognise what each other are doing.

At certain periods of time that's been continuous, that's happened a lot certainly in the 19th century and the 20th century. And we didn't think of that as innate, as a way of operating. One of the things which happened when Paige picked up, the third time, she picked this book *Place* up was she hadn't noticed before how many poets are referred to all the way through it, like addressed to them or quoting them or, and that obviously wasn't set out as part of the procedure of writing. Except in the sense that it was open to say those things. And then it moves round the idea that you work in a sort of network, a coterie of some sort, however precious or unprecious you may think of it, however changeable it is. And that's to do with reception and that's also therefore a feedback mechanism to your, or a response mechanism you might respond to. It makes some theories of poetry quite interesting. If you laid that, if you were talking about Gerard Manley Hopkins for instance, it would be interesting. No one ever read him when he was alive. Obviously that's an unusual sort of coterie thing.

AD Yes, coterie is it, he corresponded very intensely with two or three friends.

KE Emily Dickinson, as well. Another artist who's generally regarded as being in isolation, but who wasn't really. But that's different from creating work together.

AF It is, yeah.

KE It has something to do with the complexity of those compositional procedures. To complete the analogy with music, if you think about composed music, there's very few instances again of composed music that's written by more than one composer. It's exactly the same as with poetry, you can think of a few instances but it's not those people's best work. So there seems to be something.

AF You've got that interesting context of the librettist or the songwriter. Like Schubert and Goethe. Often that analogy goes wrong because the musician's using a poet who is no longer alive, so it's not quite the same situation. I think it's shifted what we first started talking about. Let's shift it this into a visual one and written. More than once I've been asked how they relate, because sometimes I've been making drawings and paintings as well as making poems. And there are moments when they overlap, when you might say not incorrectly you're illustrating the poem. Or when the poem comes out of a picture that you've made. Those last two things that I've mentioned, they're quite unusual and different, really, different from the situation of different energies and different aspects of conscious attention you have from drawing and attending to a visual surface and writing a poem. What's interesting about the overlap. Let's just start, one of the interesting things about the overlap, is that sometimes quite often when you put a text down there's a visual aspect of the typesetting, of the typing of the writing that is part of how you want the poem presented. So even because you want the visual presentation of the work to take part in the effects the work has when you read it. For instance linebreaks would be one visual aspect. If you kept having long lines and very short lines it would look quite different than if all the lines were roughly the same. And the same if you keep changing your left hand margin so that you've got more than one margin down the page because of tabs, or the margin's random if you want, clearly that not only has a visual effect but a different effect in the way you read it, because it affects the way you read it. One of the examples of that, I spoke to a typesetter many years ago at a conference in Warwick, who maintained that justified type made reading more difficult, and that a good typesetter would never use justified type left and right, you would only have a left hand margin if you were writing in English or a Romance language from the left, and they would complete the word at the end of the right hand side and come back to the left margin. They wouldn't break it in order to make a justification, two straight edges. And he maintained that it was actually generally bad spatial practice to try to justify it. He's not always right, I don't think. But I can see why he says it, because sometimes when you see justified prose it really looks quite poor, it's poorly typeset. Of course it's to do with whether it's well typeset, as well, gets involved in this. But it's to do with not only how you use space between words and whether or not letter-spacing is involved in the organisation of the lines.

AD I'm just looking at this which is clearly right-justified, but it's because the spaces have been automatically adjusted.

AF But I bet they've been adjusted between each word rather than between letters. I don't know, clearly there's been some progress on this, they're probably able to do both. But I mean I'm talking about 1970, computers weren't particularly on the horizon for writing. What I'm coming back to really is something much less categorical, pedantic. What I'm saying is the visuality of the text can affect the reading, the potential speed of it, it affects the way in which you relate one word to another. An exaggerated example would be I was setting a text by Larry Eigner, which I published ages ago in the '70s, I can't remember its title so I'd better leave it, it's probably *What You Hear* or something like that. And he used a typewriter system that Robert Duncan used. Sometimes when a word came under another word he was able to make a new word out of the vertical column of letters. The consequences of that he would, say there were three words and s k and y came, you could read SKY vertically, you could read three words horizontally. You don't really want to think of three words with s k y. But so when I came to set it in letterpress, it doesn't work, it doesn't have the same space for every letter like a typewriter used to have. It was just an absolute nightmare to try and set it, because he wanted me to have horizontal and vertical alignment, which is why Robert Duncan refused to allow typesetting of his work. If you look at the New Directions books, the two large volumes of his work which came out just before his death, *Groundwork* 1 and *Groundwork* 2, they're typewritten. In an age where they needn't be and because he insisted on it. I think he's eccentric in that regard. But that's up to him, isn't it, to be so. It was noted some while ago in a nice article by Tony Baker, whom we mentioned earlier, *[connected to a collaborative poem with Harry Gilonis, on lost side 1]* he was doing some work on William Carlos Williams in Durham, which showed that Williams had organised some of the text in a kind of collagic manner, in the manner that you might understand Juan Gris, or one of the Cubist painters, to have done. And in such a way that it almost explained where the different texts were coming together. So then when you visually saw it, in *Paterson* and some places, there were different texts that had been called the same text on the page. You're looking worried. You can see it in Olson all the time.

AD I'm just thinking of a printed version I might have read which loses that.

AF So it's difficult just to talk about that as visual. But clearly the visual aspect of that is one of the components, the contributors to the text. And I'm looking at *Place* obviously that's an influence on the way that something like that work's laid out. The bigger problem really is, let's just talk about the solution then we'll come back to the problem. One of the solutions about the activity of making visual work and the activity of making written work is that they are different energies, and this first came up very noticeably for me when I was connecting Elaine to dialysis machinery at night. There would always be the alarm, or the blood salts different, or this, or that, and we were rushing down trying to sort it out. I could not write under those conditions, or I could not write well under those conditions. I stopped doing so and I started painting, because it has a different physicality about it. And painting doesn't have to be painting, you can stand at an easel, physically using your arms, making paints, and so on. It was something I could do right through the night when she was on the machine. It's a different energy. A different psychic energy you might say. Different way of engaging consciousness. Anyway, that's a positive aspect of the difference. But one of the other aspects of the difference I think is to do with representation. I think when you write the word badger it's a different kind of representation than when you paint a badger. What a badger looks like. We touched on it earlier on, when we were talking about how quite a lot of literature can use semiology, or semiotic texts, to make an analysis. You can't use semiotic texts alone in making an analysis of a painting. You have to evoke another component. I think that's quite interesting though. We had this business where Saussure says, if you say the word tree it doesn't look like a tree. But if you paint a tree it does actually look like a tree. So there is a sort of interesting, I'm just being simplistic. It is interesting that people have had to return to earlier theories you find in Americans like Pierce, who instead of signifying-signifier they actually have to invoke a third term. Well he doesn't use those terms because he precedes Saussure, he's got icon and index. Works better. And then that's why people like myself still use old texts from the '30s and '40s, like Panofsky on iconology, because it still works for some of the visual texts that aren't figurative.

AD But language might represent a person speaking. Because it imitates the detail of the way they speak. This might be what improvisation stops. It goes somewhere else.

AF Because there's a transformation going on?

AD Because habit's left behind.

AF Habit being? meaning that the speech is conversational or has a cultural naturalism? Why would it… I'm not sure.

AD If you have a poem which sounds like the person who's writing, then it represents them. If you arbitrarily change various features, the changed bits wouldn't represent the person in that way.

AF That touches on where we were earlier talking about the critique of the self, or the critique of the use of pronoun. So like in *Place* there's a dominant feature of we/our, we our, through it. Who is this we? who is this our? So actually it's, we're not talking about the whole world when we say we or our, we're talking about a tangible environment. But then as a critique of that tangibility, if you like, critique of that use of pronoun, in the work that follows, in the next decade. And it deliberately uses he she I in a way that doesn't refer to the writer. Or does, the writer is one of the she's in the poem. Even though it's a male writer. So it's making more complex the idea of the self. It's really a critique of the idea of the single self, or the idea of something you could encapsulate as self.

AD Is that where the figures come from? The Bellman… the badger.

AF Well, I don't know if I can answer it that way round really. I know where they come from in that normal sense. The Bellman on one level exists, or did, if you like. It's sometimes known as the rag and bone man, who's coming through town with a bell asking for old rubbish, really. Now this is very very close and similar to the figure who comes through Blake's London telling everybody that the plague was on its way. The plague has been found at another door, and they would ring a bell, and he's known as the Bellman. It's in Samuel Palmer as well. And Blake and Palmer have painted these people, banging the bell as a way of indicating some pestilence. And in fact ringing the bell for pestilence has been mediaeval at least, probably older, but whenever they started making bells. But it's not the only reason for ringing bells, but it is one of the reasons that bells were rung, a distress call. And then there was the joke, it's true, that Lloyd's ring a bell every time a satellite falls out of the sky. Actually they do. Whenever they lose money they rang a bell in the whole of the chamber. Extraordinary, isn't it. It's a real pestilence for them you see. The Bellman is coming out of something I'd experienced. But then I recognise it for however, I don't know how articulate it is before I do so, but when I've done so I can look back and say one of the things that's going on is, it's being used as a metonym, it's standing in, it's standing for a whole range of somebody giving warning of all sorts of problems that are occurring. In the social situation, in the political situation that we're in. I'm in, you're in, whatever. So it's. How that comes about is therefore many-faceted, depending on where we want to start. The badger crops up because of a particular kind of repression that's been going on in the last, that's still going on. To do with what badgers do, which some people would say they bring disease. In fact they're accused of bringing TB to cattle. And on the borders of Gloucester and Herefordshire over the last few years they've just been *en masse* slaughtered, to see whether that stopped the TB. And in another test case on another border, in Yorkshire or somewhere, they're not going to do it, to see if whether or not, and to see what the difference is. But I also thought of these badgers as being a repressed animal, so to speak, an unwanted animal. And then at the same time I was at Herefordshire College of Art and Design, where a number of the students coming in to do a particular course I was helping to run, called Design Crafts or Small Studio Practice, were travellers. Or young people who were travelling around. And they were using, they were ecotravellers, because they were using scrap metal, scrap glass, they were using rubbish in order to make objects for posh homes really. Like eco-warrior. There were moments when you'd walk through town and the braiding of the hair on some of these guys, the hair and the painting of the hair and the faces, turned a couple of them into badgers, and they were walking on two legs. And there's a moment when they were treated just the same way, they were treated as scum, as the outcasts from, they shouldn't be in town. They smell. Whatever they do. They steal, probably. You know. They don't earn money and the rest of it. So they became part of a whole range of peoples I'd identified as being dispossessed. I was working on a whole series of pictures to do with Dispossession and the cure of dispossession. And as you know, may know, there was a little group of poems under the same name at the same time. There was an overlap of concepts going on. And there is a moment in Ken's edition and mine of, um, in there, where there actually is a picture of a badger, and a picture of a beaver, and so on. And then I went I think I went deliberately to research that sort of business, because people like Jean-Paul Sartre and, who wrote *The Second Sex*? de Beauvoir, were known as beavers, and I got interested in that side of animals, so I looked at bestiaries and how certain animals were carriers of certain ideas really, effectively. Those mediaeval bestiaries. And Joseph Beuys is the other end of that overlap. His use of animals as metonyms for a whole range of ideas. He uses the hare as really an allegory for European religion and culture before Christianity. Eurasia, and so on. So I tried to pull in both ideas, mediaeval and contemporary, to do with animals. And there's a third element here, which is to do with the transformation from use of animals in childhood writing a lot. Obvious, I suppose. Certainly Toad of Toad Hall. *Wind in the Willows*. And so on. And I think it's been quite strong in Britain as a tradition, really, effectively. We were looking earlier this morning at Blake's Dante. The students trying to write something for me on allegory. Looking at these four animals in the sky, she says, They're the Four Zoas. I said, just a minute, who are these people? they're not animals. That's a bearded man. What's the second? These four figures in the sky that Blake has called the Four Zoas are actually the four saints.

AD The Evangelists? Matthew Mark Luke and John?

AF And this is the Byzantine way of showing them, as an eagle, a bovine… Romanesque and Gothic churches use them all the time.

AD The Tetramorphs. They're often carved on bedsteads as well. On bedposts.

AF So it's three animals and Matthew. Because Matthew was then thought of as the first gospel writer, he's shown as an old guy writing a book. Oh, that was just by the by. We've done quite a lot of research into allegory, here, because of what I've been teaching. We've picked up on the fact that Walter Benjamin wrote on it, in the *Tragedy. On German Tragedy*. And the subsequent writers like Paul de Man, Guattari, Paul Ricoeur. A whole range. It's been quite interesting on the whole business of how allegory is no longer just a mediaeval pastime or a conceit from that period. That went out of phase. It did go out of phase with the Baroque period, and with emblems and so on. But it really has come back in the post-war period, I think, for all sorts of reasons, to do with, I could give you a range of reasons. Why it comes back—I could give you a whole range of examples, rather, not reasons. It means eventually that you can really start looking at texts, completed texts, whole texts, whole poems, whole groups of poems, as not just representative of themselves individually, but representative of something much larger conceptually. Which is one of the motives I've got really. You can think of something rather than myself, trying to think of somebody else that does that! So I can't think of somebody for a second, but I will. Quite easily. Eventually.

Oh well. In your experience, the *Sonnets of Orpheus*, Rilke. They could be taken as individual sonnets, and they're together as something else, aren't they. You wouldn't quite do the same to Shakespeare's Sonnets, because they wouldn't be presented individually. Certainly Rilke's. And then subsequently you've got *After Lorca*, by Jack Spicer, is a book of poems, but they've got a larger umbrella, they're held together, and you needn't necessarily read them all through all the time. You can pull them out and read a poem and it would not be damaged. It would just be different. I would have thought a lot of poets have done that. Your own *Good Science* is not just single poems, the poems are all together.

KE Which one are we talking about?

AF *Good Science* brings together individual poems, if you like, but there's an intention behind them working together. You've not included some poems in the book because they don't work in it. It depends, there's different levels of determinism as to how we might go through writing to reach that. Or you might, so to speak, some writers might look at an array of poems and from it make a collection from the array which is smaller than the array, and it might cohere better as a consequence. This is a different procedure. I don't want to make a judgement about that. It wouldn't be a qualitative judgement that you could make about it, you would have to look at the work to see if it was relevant to it.

AD This is something which either I or Charles might write a book about. Clearly it's something which changed quite rapidly in the '70s and probably the later '60s. I think it's something which is hard for people outside the small press immediate audience to understand.

AF You could help them, though. You could take a book like *Crow*, by Ted Hughes, who's done that.

AD It's more animals!

AF But that brings together a certain range of poems. They're deliberately put together, aren't they. Writers have been doing that most of the time, haven't they. Dante doesn't write *The Divine Comedy* in retrospect, does he. Can you imagine that? Neither does Milton. There are poets who write incidental poems, like most of us might, but it's the idea of writing in sequence, or writing a group, or making a larger or different coherence, is quite common isn't it.

AD I think there has been a historical movement.

AF What I'm worrying about, why would you lay that on the '60s and the '70s?

AD I did make a list of long poems, or long poems I liked.

AF Oh, long poems.

AD Perhaps grouped poems would be a better expression. There's this huge take-off in, I've got about 50 in the '70s, in the '60s it's a much much smaller number. I know this is subjective.

AF I can see what you mean. But it's probably like a sine-wave, too. You might if you dipped into the 1920s find. You see what I mean, there's a rise and fall of references, styles. Anyway, that might be true.

KE Having brought out *Place* in its entirety, someone said to me, Oh, I'm looking forward to reading it from start to finish. And I'm just wondering what your reaction to that is.

AF That would be a way of reading it, wouldn't it.

KE It wouldn't be your favourite way of reading it, though, would it?

AF It wouldn't be how I would read it, no. But I wouldn't want to be prescriptive about that. I wouldn't say, that wouldn't be a way to read it. That's a very interesting question. Because, you know very well, some of the pages relate to other pages which come quite a way away from each other, and they feed off each other. This whole business we talked about ages ago on mutation, we wanted to drop the word and move it to transformation, it's effectively this debate, because when we came to republish the work, there was a decision about, do we put new page numbers in, or do we leave the old ones in to show the relationship, because in the old book, *Place* Book I went from 1 to 100, and *Place* Book III went from 100 to 1, and then read backwards. Well, not chronologically written backwards, but in terms of the text it feeds from. And then of course there were distortions of it, *Grampians* and *Lakes* were distortions of the procedure. But that all falls, just to pun on it, out of place when you start to looking at *Unpolished Mirrors* or something like that, which distorts all that idea. But it actually is the beginnings of what happens in *Gravity*. It gets much more complex and much more involved in line by line ideas. So when you ask about the reading order, you might choose, you might just pedantically be going through with a list of numbers and just reading certain pages. Which is how I often read.

AD We could publish a list of numbers.

AF That's right. Like, at the moment I'm researching Orpheus and Eurydice, for reasons which are too obscure to talk about, to do with teaching, but I'm looking in the indexes of books just to see what their different takes on the business of Orpheus turning back in the Underworld, looking at Eurydice, and realising that it kills her as he does so. But I don't want to read all these tomes and tomes and tomes and tomes, so I just look up Orpheus and Eurydice, then I'll read those pages, that refer to it. I've got a list of numbers of the pages I'll read. I think it's a completely interesting, viable way of reading. Produces a different text.

AD Like indexes on a hard disk. Perhaps we could see words as pointers to a body of knowledge that already exists. So a set of words is like an index.

AF No, I won't pun on it. But that's one of the terms that Peirce uses, he wants icon and index to be part of the debate. I think his index is slightly different.

A Tour Through the Resources for *Stane*;
or, a History of Locks and Weirs

Lulham 23/5/05 tape 1

AD There are 3 possibilities we talked about for the interview. One about analogies with the visual arts, which you suggested. One where we go through one poem and talk about its commutatory sources in fine detail. And one where we would go through some resources for one of the books. I brought *Stane* along, I'm interested in that, and talk about what the resources mean for you. They're kind of historic now. Those books are hard to find.

AF That's very interesting. It's an issue raised up… What the resources are? Oh, that's interesting. The issue was raised in a very mild way by Robert Sheppard recently, in a brief reappraisal of the whole Collected [*Place*]. I don't know if this is an answer, I didn't find it anathema, but I was intrigued that he found it something to talk about. It's on his blog site.

AF Shall I look at them? Would that help? Certainly it's a shorthand. It's not even a summary. It might be thought of as synoptic, but that wouldn't be a fair description either. It's more, salient I suppose is the word. It's a list of the salient resources. And I would particularly prefer it, if I'd actually quoted from books, directly, to try and put them in there. But that doesn't mean everything's in there of course. There are. I mean, it hits this, "this brief summary continues the list of many texts from before which were used in this work". That by implication means that there are books which I might have used in this book III, *Stane*, that I'd mentioned in the resources list for Book I, for instance, and therefore weren't repeated. It might just be useful just to be pedantic and to look at the list, because there is a variety of at least two things in this list, and then you can expand on that variety, but two different kinds of reason for putting the item in the list. One is to do with an ambient sense of reading, so one gets a feeling for the kind of books being used in the process of the writing. It might not therefore be thorough, in the whole list of everything that was looked, and the second kind is where there's been direct quotation used, and that particularly occurs, they sort of jump out at me as I see them, going through. So going through here it mentions *New Scientist* magazine 1974, that's obviously explicit, to do with particular articles, though strangely not explicit enough, because it doesn't tell you what. Knuckle newspaper, 1975. *Expanded Cinema*, Gene Youngblood. *RSVP cycles*, Halperin. *Sixpack* magazine. Those kind of things aren't really ambient, they're much more directly used. We can come back in a moment to why I've done that, why they're used, because it might then lead into saying, how could this be any use to the reader or not. Then the ambient list starts at the top here. *The Thames Highway, volumes 1 and 2, General history & Locks and Weirs*, and so forth. It's not proposed here that the reader would pick that book up and look through the whole thing. That's what I mean by ambient, I mean that's the kind of thing I'm looking at, and you would therefore when reading the poem look at it and say, well yes, that's the kind of thing I'm feeling in this poem or not. Unless you were a different kind of scholar from just a reader, you wouldn't need to refer to it beyond this list. I don't think. You might. I've also said elsewhere, one of the reasons for these resources is to thank people. I've also got here *Cities* by Robert Kelly. I think it would be wrong of me if I wanted to use that and hadn't included it. Because of its obscurity, really. It was important to me, in the sense of it was salient at the time of writing that poem. To refer back to what I said about using specific texts, like it says New Scientist magazine 1974, you would find that in later days, for instance in the '80s, they're more detailed, those references, to *Nature* magazine, for instance, which by that time I'd been a subscriber to for a number of years. Which is a weekly magazine like *New Scientist* but it's more detailed. So I've been more inclined to include the information because the article writers for *Nature* are typically the scientists, on their discoveries, or their attempts to make discoveries. Typically, *New Scientist* reports are journalistic articles written by journalists about reports in *Nature* magazine or other technical magazines published in America and Europe. I feel less inclined to just give you a list of the journalists in this list. Cause that kind of makes you go to something which doesn't have any use-value, I think. I nonetheless feel the need to signal it. I need to just flip to 47 to see what that might be. 47 covers a number of different pieces in here, I don't know where it starts, but let's suppose it does start on page 6, here. There's no indication there that New Scientist has been used. I flick through here, on page 10 there's 47 again. What you find here is a potential implication of *New Scientist* because it says *We do not research to reach ignorance /but reach ignorance* as if that's almost a commentary on the inclusion of *New Scientist* there. And this discussion of formula here, a misunderstanding. I think that's come out of a journalistic approach to some of the work in *New Scientist*. Let's see if I can find something else that would help. If I went to 72, these numbers I'm looking at are the face numbers along the top, and they don't necessarily follow a linear sequence. 72 is so explicit that it's evident, because the poem is subtitled *after Cities by Robert Kelly*. So that's so explicit that it's not… It's actually saying to the reader, if you really want to take this further you're going to have to read *Cities* by Robert Kelly, because it's a celebration of it, or a critique of it, or both. Let's try another. Just two examples. 62 says translations from Artaud. This binding holds up better than the other books. You try to flick through *Brixton Fractals*, it's a nightmare, it just falls apart, it cracks, because of the glue used. My bad choice. I used something very very similar to wood-binding glue, and it wasn't bookbinding glue, it was woodbinding glue. It didn't quite work.

AD Not quite woody enough.

AF You're going to have these silences while I glance at these things to see what. So, in 62, which occurs across from page 38 to 41, you've got

> 'Our anxiety this drumming our depression
> counting on miracles to express the forgotten.
> the hidden beating
> or that 'incapable of starting' Artaud talks of

—so, immediately there's a reference to Artaud, he talks of. One line in 5 volumes of work, or whatever, so to be more friendly about it, if you go to this there's only one book you can have to be looking for the reference: *Collected Works of Artaud*, volume 2. So at least you've got a chance of finding what I'm talking about. Now, that isn't to say that you couldn't read the poem without that. You don't need to look up the Artaud to read the poem, I don't think, as a consequence of what I've just done. Because it's an or, in fact, in this case. It's another way of saying something I've just said. One of the indicators here is not simply, what does this mean, the indicator is, I'm not the first person to recognise this, Artaud's already been saying it. So it's like saying, it's offering, well it's not saying it's a convention, but it's continuous with or part of what Artaud was saying.

AD I'm just wondering how this compares with the dialogue between jazz musicians which we talked about 2 weeks ago. There's a conversation in which many individuals have a part without it belonging to any one of them.

AF That's so complex and really interesting. There's two levels of it at least historically, in terms of time. When Charlie Parker is playing 'Summertime', is he referring to the composer of 'Summertime',

Gershwin, or is he referring to, I can't think, Parker may not be a good example because he's the first to have done it, but is he referring to a previous player, of 'Summertime'. Gerry Mulligan, when he plays 'Summertime', is he referring to Charlie Parker's instance of playing, or is he referring to the composition that he pulled off a shelf or he heard somebody singing. So I think that's one level of the relationship between jazz's re-use of a tune, or re-use of a song, and improvisers from a set structure so to speak, and an available set of informations. But then there's another kind of improvisation which isn't quite that at all. There's another kind of improvisation which doesn't rely on you knowing the origin of the structure. And that's the one I would call the ambient or the salient. So for instance you would not need to have read, ever to have read, *The Thames Highway* volumes 1 and 2 (the history of locks and weirs) to understand the improvisation that may have occurred from that text to this one in *Stane*. Do you see what I mean by that? the difference that. So I think there's a difference of referral, of representation, because in the first instance the referral... you'd have a job hearing 'Summertime', if you lived in Britain or America, or France, and not recognising the tune. So therefore on that basis hearing it played by, improvised by, somebody, includes that recall as part of the representation. It includes it as part of the image of the hearing. The sound image. It could be more complex than sound, of course. And yet what you would get, let's just try this, you would get something from this ambient reading. So on page 8,

> I joined the main flow at London Bridge
>   joined in with it
>   rode it from the Temple

—now it might well be that in the text, on the *River Highways* and so forth that I'm using, the salient or ambient texts, it just shows me a map of the flow of the water, and I've just got it in my hand, and I'm walking down beside the water trying to follow, to follow something it's telling me about the underground rivers—which is one of the ways this writing occurs. So I'm trying to follow a map, because the rivers being underground you can't always see them. If you do see them, well there's a bump in the road somewhere actually, like a sewer or something. You suddenly realise why that bump's there. So that kind of improvisation isn't the same kind. But I've just noticed when you move to page 9,

> The kidel becomes effective
>   the smallest fish
>   trapped in a brushwood net

>   across current
>   on Ordnance Survey Map

—what precedes that on the Ordnance Survey map is a shape, and that shape is what a kidel is. A shape across the Thames on the map. Which is catching the fish. I've obviously taken that from the map in the book.

AD Is it a fish-weir? There's the remains of one of those by the boats at Chelsea. It's poles in the mud.

AF I can't actually articulate that, because that's a shape, so I can't actually say that, but there's the shape. Is it in the Thames? That's a direct lift from the book, that shape.

AD That's really interesting, because you'd think it would be more efficient if it were straight, but obviously it's a practical design.

AF I suspect it's a simplification of something with quite small detail. And this might have some other reasons. Does that begin to help with this resources business?

AD Yes it does. From a critic's point of view, if you try to explain the text, I think it might be difficult for someone who has taken in lots of culture, but it's contemporary—academic work, comics, TV, whatever. And someone who actually shares a quite a lot of these resources, for biological reasons, because they were reading books in the 1970s.

AF So by biological reasons you mean the same generation or something?

AD Yes, if they weren't born in the 1970s.

AF I have to tell you that wouldn't be the case. A lot of these books aren't available in the 1970s. I'm having to go to Norwood library specially. *The Thames Highway* volumes 1 and 2 wasn't on the shelf. It wasn't like that, no. Even in one of the greatest libraries I've ever used, which was West Norwood local library, because someone in that library was interested. I mean, I actually ordered both volumes of Stukeley's work, from the 18th century, on Stonehenge and Avebury, and I got the originals. 18th century originals. On ordinary local library loan. And he said, I don't think we'd better let you take these away. I was speechless. I don't think that kind of thing goes on any longer, in quite the same way. So many of these things that are esoteric are here because they're esoteric. But you're right, there is a generational element in here. Obviously the newspapers and magazines fit that bill. *New Scientist*, for example, or *Knuckle*. I don't know if *Knuckle*'s still going. There's other things down here, I suspect. Some of this eccentric stuff, like the work on the divining rod, is very 60s-70s. *Expanded Cinema* is dated 1970. *RSVP Cycles* is dated 1969, it's a very 1970s book. It's about organisation, about biological organisms. *Cancer biopathy*, although as a book it's much older, the English translation is 1971. I remember Andrew Crozier being quite interested in the fact that that's quoted. Because it was a book he'd got at about the same date. Anyone reading Reich before that date couldn't have read what is one of the most interesting books by Reich, *Cancer Biopathy*. As well because it's what follows on from *The Function of the Orgasm* and *The Discovery of the Orgone*. It's volume 2, in a sense. That first one had been translated in the 1940s and then probably reprinted in the 1960s by Noonday or someone. It's important and it's a 70s book in that sense. It's a Compendium book, which is how I would have found out about it. There are some issues here that are very interesting. It's a kind of library interest. The reason *The Eternal Present* turns up here although it was a 1962 book, is because it was remaindered, so I could afford to buy it. It's a very very fat expensive book. I managed to get hold of it. It's a book about Stone Age and prehistoric painting. Siegfried Giedion. The writer on architecture and space. He wrote a book on the Palaeolithic work, in Altamira and Pech Merle and places. For its time, it was an excellent book, well illustrated.

AD It's present because, when you look at it, it's there looking back at you? Is that what he's saying?

AF Say that differently.

AD Well, the moment in which the bison is portrayed, or whatever animal it is, will always be the present moment as far as that surface is concerned.

AF That's right. That's his 'eternal'. Some of the things he's questioned have only been researched and understood in the last ten years. It just wasn't known before. What some of the things he was looking at were. Why they were there. So there were lots of complex, completely misled, ideas about hunting and magic, and in America even crazier ideas I think, about sexuality and dream, that really aren't... you can't explain why people have chosen them except possibly because it's the fashion to be talking about that particular subject at that time. It's that... It might be that new discoveries now, for example, might be thought of in ten years' time as bogus. They feel right now, at the moment they feel appropriate.

AD This is why I'm interested in the history of ideas. He was Swiss, I think. He wrote a…

AF *Mechanisation Takes Command*, fantastic book. Absolutely amazing.

AD He wrote a project describing what monumental art should be, in the '40s, about how to say something in art about the Second World War. About the victims really.

AF That generation are very interesting, I have them in high regard. People like Waddington, Kepes. They're interested in pattern, they're interested in quite large ideas. And I'm still intrigued by people like Carl Schuster and Gregory Bateson, who were interested in the anthropology of pattern and linking it to aesthetics. Simple things like why does somebody make something that shape with a V in it, instead of with a curved shape, like a U. And there are natural reasons for it, sometimes, because of the way a twig bifurcates off the end of a branch, and therefore creates a natural V. But there are also sometimes functional reasons for it. It's just very interesting. The book about natural patterns, patterns of connections repeats something I tried to write about in the 1970s. I can't find it on the shelf at the moment. I found the, I got very intrigued by. In the front of book 1 there's another explanation which I haven't repeated in book III. 'The collection of the books into one volume has provided the opportunity to present the resources in a more or less uniform manner. But this retrospective advantage has not led to rewriting the lists in a more scholarly form. The original intention has been left intact, to acknowledge and thank the originators, and to make open part of the process.' It's almost three things in one, really. And that business of making open part of the process is still with me. I still feel that. I don't know why I prefer that. Why do I prefer that? I liked for instance that Prynne put difficult notes in the back of *Aristeas*.

AD Only that one time. And 'A Note on Metals'.

AF I never really got to a full conversation with him about that, but I have spoken to him about it. And I can see why. It's a kind of almost like an alchemical reason for not saying what the resources are. So that someone can tease them out and get the pleasure of doing that, maybe. But I was reading Keery the other day, writing about Prynne's *White Stones*, a vast text on *The White Stones*, about 60 pages, and what he does, he does an analysis of where the phrase *white stones* comes from in the title, in the Bible. I quite enjoy that investigative reading, but there's an element of me that doesn't want it, in a way.

AD I think we have to dwell on this, because one of the questions that I might have asked was, has there been a movement from roughly regarding Blake as a model to regarding mathematical physics as a model. Is that one of the changes over time that you see, between the early parts of *Place* and, say, *Gravity*?

AF There needs to be other inputs into that. Robert reminded me recently in his review, his commentary on *Place*, the new volume, that Olson still features quite largely in there. He reflects, So also does Pound. And neither of those two—in fact, we benefit from the fact that both of those two have companions to their long poems. Without Terry's two-volume set on the *Cantos*, makes the *Cantos* penetrable to a lot of people who don't have Chinese or a whole range of things. The same with the Butterick *Companion to Maximus Poems*. I think that's less so with the Maximus poems. That might just be a generational difference, I don't know. I found that much easier to read, and I'm not always helped by Butterick's *Companion* insomuch as it sends me somewhere I'm not that interested in. I'm much more interested in the poem than where it's sending me. I think I was responding in some way, this idea of openness is a response to the way Pound and Olson had handled it. It's kind of like saying, I didn't think that was necessarily the only way of handling it. It gave me quite a bit of difficulty. I started reading the *Cantos* when I was at school, and I found that very very very hard. The whole thing wasn't out in the 60s as you know, but it was a big enough chunk for me to find difficult. It wasn't so much reading the Chinese characters and realising, I can't read them. I don't know what they mean. That's all right. It's not realising what you don't know. You look at a Chinese text and realising, That's obviously a Chinese text, I'm going to have to wait until I find out what that text is. The much more difficult things are when there's quotation after quotation after quotation, from a whole range of Renaissance writers, or legal writers in many cases, and there was a moment when I realised, that if I knew the context this is coming from, it actually improves the reading of the poem. That's not the intention of my resources in the same way. I think you can read through without that necessity. There's a sense in which Pound's work loses its impact without some of that information, and I don't, my view is, standing at the second on this, that's not where I feel it in my own work. I argued this process with Mottram quite a bit, I don't know whether it was an argument, it was more just a discussion, and he typically would try to use resources. Like me, he's fairly unscholarly about the way he lists, even in his scholarly articles. I was doing some work on Burroughs recently, looked at *The Algebra of Need*, and the bibliography in that is really quite off the top of the head, it's there's no indication of where the stuff has come from. This would be an easy one, but he would just put a reference like "Sartre, *Being and Nothingness*", and you wouldn't know whether it's been translated, what date it was, where it's from. So it's that kind of reference that makes me feel inadequate.

AD It's boring doing that.

AF So there's that whole business. I did actually reflect on Pound, in parts of *Place*, to do with his intrigue with some writers like Waddell.

AD A complete nutcase.

AF Yes he is! I know why this is. It's because Pound and Olson both use Waddell.

AD And MacDiarmid, actually!

AF But they use different books, because they're after different… I found him completely mistaken. I think I must have booked the stuff in somewhere. I must have referenced Waddell, I don't know, wherever I used it, because it's so eccentric. But there's a whole entourage like that in here, that needs to be listed too. Like *Feng-shui*, by Eitel, 1873.

AD You can still buy that one.

AF Well, it was published in the '70s, you see, that's the ambience, the revival. It was probably published again under another. *Temple and the House*, by Lord Raglan.

AD That's probably very good, actually.

AF Yeah, it is, it is. There's that kind of… And you contrast that with *The Public Inspector's handbook*, and so there's a complete different usage going on here. A different historic account going on. One account is about the ambience, the books around. That's what you're suggesting, isn't it. There's a kind of bibliographical ambience within which this is written, as well as a larger ambience.

AD I was trying to say that what you're doing is like a musician playing in response to what someone else has just played, as in AMM.

AF It's actually very hard to convey, what you've just said. That's quite right though. I've tried to just mention this in the introduction to the new collection. I didn't use the word music though. It's a good analogy. The first line says, "The planning was contemporary with the first development of Fluxus in England." And it's actually indicative, the reason partly is that AMM is much earlier. It's actually a generation before me, or two generations, it depends how you count generations. But certainly it's 1960 rather than 1970.

AD I didn't know they were going back then.

AF I may be wrong. That's how it feels. I was just… by the time I was hearing AMM they were already playing, as it were, they weren't just forming. I suppose I was thinking of The Scratch Orchestra, which had Cornelius Cardew, and so forth, before he was killed. You can see how the debates come up here, because at the bottom of 81 it says "Charles Olson and Ezra Pound, by Charles Olson." That book in which he tells you about his visits to Pound in St Elizabeth's, in the hospital. So I'm interested in Olson's debate with Pound. That then became I think quite sour in the work of Charles Bernstein and Bob Perelman. Perelman's rather good book on, *The Trouble with Genius*. And I forget the articles that Bernstein wrote. And I think Olson was facing the problem in a much more useful way for me, because he was realising that he was getting a very sensitive and sensible energy in Pound's poetry. And very difficult energy from Pound's politics. The fact that they don't reconcile in an obvious way troubled him and me, as it would anybody. Rather than taking the pitch position, which is that if the politics are wrong you don't touch it. Which is eventually is what PC has moved towards. What it's leading to is you wouldn't read Evelyn Waugh as a novelist, even though he's a great novelist, because you didn't agree with his Roman Catholicism. It's just not the right way to make a judgement in literature and aesthetics. I think it leads on to a most difficult question which we can't deal with fully, and that is the relationship between aesthetics and ethics, and the relationship between politics and ethics. And how there's an overlap of ethics there which is almost combative. There's a level at which you could say Pound's aesthetics does lead to some ethical values that you might want to continue valuing, even though the politics that rests on it you might not. Because it doesn't have to be that politics that rests on it. That's so to speak after the fact, after the event of the ethics. The politics is like an ideological decision laid upon the practice of the ethics. I don't know if that's true. I'm just speaking it aloud really at the moment.

AD I think that consciousness happens where there is an unexplained form, which might be explained. If these forms are fairly simple, like an unexpected car comes towards you along the road, you can deal with it in half a second. But if the uncertainty's on a great scale perhaps it might take you a year to make sense of it. Or it might be impossible to assimilate within a human lifetime.

AF That's very well put. It's a debate that's not going to stop. I started a debate with Alan Marshall, at King's, about this, a few years ago. and it was partly because he'd attended a talk I gave on Tom Raworth and ethics, and because I'd said that Raworth's poetry, the kind I was then reading, was ethical and had an ethical base. And I said I could only explain that, or explore that, through the aesthetics, through the art, through the poetry, rather than through anything to do with the meaning of the work, in the sense of what the words meant, the politics of the work. They didn't help me describe what I was going to say at all. And Alan said, in which case you're mystifying—he felt, I think—what ethical is, and so on. He wrote to me, but I never got back to him. Though I do recognise this as a difficulty. I don't think it is significant. I don't think it's mystifying, rather. I do think it's a complex and difficult subject in the first place. I don't think you can say because of that it's therefore mysterious to try to talk about it. It doesn't turn it necessarily into a theology just because you can't explicate it all.

AD I think you have to move your brain towards the areas where there is a great deal that's unexplained or simply lose consciousness. Your brain will refuse to work.

AF I think there are moments when I realise I won't live long enough to try to sort out some of the problems I've been thinking of. For certain I know that. And so you're, I'm sometimes lying in my room in Templeton, which is a second library really, a smaller library, and books are piled there, because it's the only way of getting them in the room. So I've had to categorise them, really, in kind of oddball ways. Not on purpose oddball, but because there's not enough shelf space to be better organised. One of the ways I did it is the way they're piled, on the shelves, is like an idea complex, and it was funny, because there was a whole series of emails to and fro, between Karen MacCormack and myself, in preparation for our joint venture at Philadelphia. There was a sort of semi, what do you call those things, videoconference. And in the process of these emails

Lulham 23/5/05 tape 2

AF It is an interesting problem, yeah. And in the process of these emails it was clear that I'd started to talk about to you at the moment, these emails in that evening or that day or something of that kind. And I realised that a lot of what we were exchanging were notes from books, almost. So it happens during the process of this email that I'd post to her a map of my room, showing her the piles of books and labels on them. Using ready software used for redesigning kitchens or something. Circles and squares all over on the plan. I remember her being quite surprised at receiving such a thing. It's quite a good subject for me, this, isn't it. It does bounce in and out of work and it is a subject that troubles some readers. And it does help to try to talk through some of the issues, because they're not as simple as they're first expected to be. Oversimplified, usually. Either positive or negative.

AD These areas of uncertainty? or, how books work in the writing?

AF Coming back to that improvisation question. Talking about the exchange of emails and the use of texts that you happen to be reading at the moment, or have just read. It's clear that that plays a part in the improvisation, because what it does, it provides some of the energy source or some of the springboard from which you might rethink something or restate something or investigate maybe just a sound, maybe a word, or maybe a thought, or a whole group of ideas. If we glance at the list here, it's got under no. 63 *Gem Therapy*. I'm not really interested in gem therapy. I must have picked that up and thought, What on earth's this about? That really is part of the ambience of the period. And that is a sort of improvised expectation. It isn't the sort of thing that would have been on a research list, put it that way. Books on the rivers running through London, I would have picked up every one I found.

AD John Michell thought that the crystals in megalithic rocks were some kind of energy storage, and gem therapy was based on a similar kind of idea. It might come from Rudolf Steiner.

AF Certainly Steiner's interested in that whole Indian side of things. And if you can see if you on page 43 under '63', there are elements here. Cosmic sprays. And a range of colours listed here, spectrum. That's coming out of some of that reading. Whereas whatever's here isn't. This is something else. I'm just wondering what 74 is in the list. Oh yes, that's why it links. Next to page 43, page 42, it's got like a fraction (63/74). 63 has some implications to do with gem theory, but it's not using it directly.

And 74 is Arcana magazine, and The Listener, and feng shui, and *The Temple and the House* by Lord Raglan. So it is that sort of improvisatory base, you might say, or springboard, it is creating that, stimulating is too big a word, but it's encouraging certain ranges of word orders and thoughts, ideas, isn't it.

AD OK, so it's like the local game rules for that bit of the game.

AF Yeah, that's right. It's another way of putting it. Provided we. I suppose we need both senses of game, really. It's as much fun as it is serious. I was just wondering, is this Game Theory, which is heavy, or is it actually just playing a game, which is not. So it's neither of those things but it's something in between the two. Which is poetry I guess. I think that's true really. Let's try 57. Let's just see what happens there, because I've still got that. I've got that set of volumes. Let's see if I can find it. I'm surprised I don't list it, it must be because I've pre-listed it, but I've used *Ley Hunter Magazine*. It's listed in brackets, that indicates that it comes from thinking about it, it's not directly quotation from it. Here, 57 is used in conjunction with 80. Once again it's the rivers of London, and the bridges over those rivers, and so forth.

> It becomes a question of language, of the substance
> and accidents of the relic.

So it's linking the, um. 57 is a book called *Wonderful London*, 3 volumes. Wonderful old photographs. Brown, sepia, photographs of London. Or maybe they're just dull grey ones. But they're certainly old-fashioned as hell. The book itself is… undated. It says undated, literally.

AD That's so they could go on selling it for years.

AF It's like *Illustrated London News*, only published in the war, or just after the war, or something. That doesn't take us much further than that, but it's just to put up on these recognition that some of these things I've seen in photographs of them rather than the actual things because they don't exist any more in the time of this writing.

AD So it would be very naive to think of London in 1972 as the complete basis, because it's not.

AF So it's a speculation about what London might have looked like, but more often than not speculation about what it did, on the basis because of photographs you've got, and some knowledge you've got when you're standing there, and that bit of broken concrete over there is in fact a tower. There's a marvellous booklet published in Hereford on the Lugg river, by a local woman, a biologist, and she's done research on the weirs, and on the sites with buildings on them, the Lugg. A lot of what she's writing is based on her knowledge of plants, she knows that plant that would or wouldn't have grown there, because of building work, because it would or wouldn't have been unsettled as a consequence. It's the debate about ancient grasslands that you get, which is that you can identify them from the plant life, and that if a field is ploughed it loses that plant life. I walked through a park near Bower Ashton in Bristol where the art college is at the other month, and we came across a field which had anthills more than 12 inches high, and Paige immediately said, This must be ancient meadow or grassland, because there's no way, it would have taken so many hundreds of years for it to grow that high, it just cannot have been ploughed. And then she could immediately see from the grasses, or from the plants in the grass, that it was an undisturbed land. A very small part of the land. Most interesting though. Sometimes when you're with somebody like Paige in the landscape, even from a long distance she can say, That green isn't possible for plants without heavy nitrates, and know it's either been fertilised by run-off or deliberately fertilised, and thereby creating a false green. And those kinds of signs I've often been interested in, actually right way back to *Long Shout to Kernewek*. It's interesting, because Robert calls *Place* the first of the long poems, in fact it's not, it's the second. It came out first, but *Long Shout to Kernewek* was published in 1975 and it was written in the '60s.

AD I'm glad we've actually got a count. I really like that poem, actually.

AF It's romantic and lyrical in many places, and has a sort of Jack Kerouac naivety. Which is probably what I was reading at the time, actually. In fact, I don't think it crops up in the poem, but it was in that time I misread somewhere, or misunderstood from somewhere, that Ed Sanders was a lorry driver and had used Ezra Pound's *Cantos* as a pillow. Complete rubbish, apparently. No mention of it anywhere. I don't know where I got that from. Maybe he said it once. The Fugs were like that apparently. Would say things that were rubbish.

AD I'm sure it's true!

AF Somebody told me it's not true. Maybe they're wrong. It was actually that kind of statement though that led me into thinking it was worth reading. If somebody as important as Ed Sanders thought that Ezra Pound was worth using as a pillow… 56 coming to 59, here. Now that is interesting. I think in fact that all the information is not always here.

I think that's because I've previously referred to it. If you look at page 36, 56 over 59, it would imply that I'm using *London's Natural History*, by Fitter, which is fantastic, 1945, and the natural plants in London, because he deals with the bombsites, over 59, which is *The Uncommercial Traveller*, by Dickens, with an introduction by GK Chesterton, and the *Pickwick Papers*.

So when you get Londinium which is Latin across there, clearly it doesn't come from either of those books.

> by 1851 Greenwich Camberwell Brixton Battersea
> part of the Great Wen

Maybe that's in Fitter. I doubt it. I would think it's come from something else.

AD The Great Wen is a Chestertonian phrase, isn't it. Maybe it's in the Introduction.

AF Ah, yes. I see. That's probably right. And some of it you can see would be from Fitter, I suspect.

> within yards of Westminster
> "shameful instances of neglect; intolerable tolerations

No, no, no. That's Dickens. And this is Fitter

> people still blown into Surrey Canal
> the large houses with gardens
> preceding continuous built up areas.

So he's observing where the plants have been propagated and not propagated and so on. So there is actually some mileage out of using these resources, in a sense. I think one of your early questions or worries was, so what do you do if you were born in the 1960s and see this? do the resources have the same richness or the same value? the same use-value? I've got no idea actually.

AD I think there will have to be a Companion to *Place* at some stage.

AF Would there? is that right?

AD Nothing's compulsory, but I do foresee that as a product. The whole question of how to write down an intellectual ambience is so unresolved. It does seem to me that there's a complete lack of books on British intellectual history, the kind that poets use. The history of philosophy, fine, but that's nothing to do with it.

AF No, it isn't. It might overlap but it's almost an accident.

AD If someone doesn't know Bateson, I just find that so alarming.

AF You'd have to be just deliberately not checking anything, to do that. You can't really write for someone who refuses to check anything. I mean, hang on. You could I suppose. I suppose that would be a difference from the kind of reading I prefer.

AD I think, if you set out with a rule to write nothing that needs to be explained, you end up with a certain kind of poetry. It happens that I can't stand that sort of poetry. I seem to have used it up before I even start. But a lot of people see that as in some way as democratic and open.

AF They almost use it as a value-system. I've noticed that. I think that's one of the BBC's value systems. A whole group of people who work for them think that way. Not necessarily the poetry, but when they talk about poetry on the Today programme in the morning, or something like that, you've got someone quite literate, like Naughtie. Well in the sense that, Leavis, because he's always talking about fiction. They have a sense of poetry which comes out of a different time, is not even Victorian, actually. I can't really figure out. It's very poor poetry of that ilk, it might have been written in the 20th century but it's written in doggerel.

AD So there is a great temptation. It's like a choice you're forced to make. Either you can write poetry which has nothing new in it, or if you're going to write poetry which has ideas in it you've got these tremendous questions of notation and rhythm and the whole idea of what to draw on.

AF Then I suppose you're posing the whole question of the function of poetry. It might have a whole range of functions. Some of them might just be very simply social. That's not what mine are, but I imagine someone might propose that and under social you'd get sub-headings like entertainment, pleasurable, relaxing, and so forth, which aren't particularly interesting to me. I think there's a whole range of functions. You could have a religious function as part of the poetic practice. Gerard Manley Hopkins say. Which doesn't mean you can't read him without it, it doesn't mean you can't read him and find other functions in the work, as I do. I still have a rather old-fashioned feeling, understanding rather, which is that poetry includes an aesthetic function, so that part of the activity is aesthetic. And as that function, or that component, reduces, so does my interest in the poetry. So because it links to what we said earlier, that as its ethical value reduces as its aesthetic value reduces also. You could almost put that on the same conveyor. I think where's there no interest in the aesthetic activity, the interest in—that component of consciousness, then there's a problem. Let's just be tangential for a moment, just in case it's completely weird. Because I've got quite developed ideas on consciousness which are, that's not boasting, they might be completely eccentric to me, that's what I need to say. And that is that three of the biggest books I've got on my shelf in my bed at the moment are researches into Cognition. And that's because that's where the main interest has been in the last 40 years, in brain research. And if you look at all the conferences, they happen at least once a year in Santa Fe, for instance, at the university there, where there are also physicists. The books are on cognition, and they want to talk about emotions, our abilities to appreciate beauty, rather than aesthetic, you'll find them under the word cognition. More recently, and I might be wrong, but I think in the last 20 years, in fact in the last decade, there have been more books, and more research done on the relationship between the brain and the emotions. And the brain and physiology. It's almost a reappraisal, of the kind of thinking that was going on in the 1950s, and much earlier. Well certainly in the '40s, with Reich. What I've never been able to understand is why there's no real deep analysis of aesthetics. If that's not a component of consciousness, I don't know what is, really. And yet they said it isn't cognitive, and it doesn't have an emotional base in the simple sense, or rather the explicit sense used by the scientists that are making these pronouncements on their discoveries and their explorations. So my eccentricity is likely to be that I think all consciousness by definition has a component called aesthetic. And when that component dominates in the practice, in the function, then that work usually becomes articulated as art in one way or another, poetry or music or. Although it's not measurable in the normal sense of the term, although I'll come back to it if you want to ideas of measurement, let's just say it now. Although it's quite clear that that's not measurable, it's actually been made false to say that cognition is measurable. It's a falsehood. In fact it's quite interesting that some of the best practitioners and writers in quantum mechanics, for example, have recognised that measurement is an artificial truth that's been put in place in order to continue, to continue research. But actually if you wanted to be explicit about, you'd have to say there are moments when the size of what you're talking about, large or small, when measurement is impossible. Immeasurable, in other words. Wheeler, yes. And John S Bell, who was the manager of CERN laboratories in

Geneva, and his wife. Irish. Died less than years ago. He wrote a book called *Speakable and Unspeakable*. He wrote articles on immeasurability and the unmeasurable. In his particular case he's talking about very very minute measurements to do with subatomic structures, but it applies to very very large structures, which are just too large to measure with, you have to use instruments, you can't rely on your experience. In any case, what would it mean to rely on experience to measure. When I say, literally, if you want to be that tangible, you put this *[ruler]* down here, and you said this is 18 inches across. Everybody knows about minutes, everybody knows the parallax that would occur. Just by the fact that that line *(notch)* itself is a measurement, is a quantity. There are all kinds of problems with measurement. So when I come back to talk about the brain, when cognitive scientists and so forth are having these discussions, they have a false sense of exactness, a false sense of, this is the story. It's actually only part of the story. So that's why I diverted. In order to say that. It's an interesting and difficult issue. And now the problem with this aesthetic function discussion, one of the difficulties with it, is that it's quite convenient to raise Aristotle's categories, because it helps you understand what could be meant by the content of an aesthetic function. Because it's clear that if you just split it up in the way Pound did, for instance, between didactic, delight, and persuasion, so that there would be rhetoric, and delight or pleasure, and information, all three of which could be part of the aesthetic component. And in different poetry and in a different part there would be an emphasis on one rather than the other two and some would put more stress on the other one. So some work like *Place* for instance has quite a large information component, and a reduced measure of the last two components. It may—depends who's reading this—have a reduced rhetorical element to it, whereas you may pick up *Long Shout to Kernewek* which may well have more interest in being pleasurable, or it might have more interest in rhetoric. So it—you can't measure these things in a normal sense, but there are clearly things which takes over as emphases in some of the works in one way or another. But those things are rather old-fashioned, those terms, early Renaissance at least, that makes those distinctions.

AD It might even be Aristotle in his treatise on Rhetoric.

AF I'm not even sure if it's there or not. I got them from Pound's, Pound no doubt didn't invent it. It might even have been Agricola. Is that how you pronounce it?

AD I'm not sure who he was. It means "farmer", so he might be some German called "Bauer". Those Latin names are frequent.

AF I only know it because he quotes it a couple of times, in, let's guess, in *ABC of Reading* and *How to Read*, that sort of thing. Certainly *ABC of Reading* was a big influence on me at school. I tried to read everything in it. I couldn't but I tried. I remember buying what is it, the translation of the Aeneid, Gawaine…

AD Douglas.

AF I've still got it. I've never got through it. It's too arcane.

AD It's very good, actually.

AF Pound was very good for that. I read 'The Seafarer' because of Pound. Amazing, actually. I put it back on my reading list. I'm running a course on poetry at the moment. For the bigger course, which runs from Homer to the present day, I put *ABC of Reading*. I put one of the chapters in *Literary Essays*, which is to do with (??). We had—this might sound tangential but it's not eventually—one of these course meetings the other day, which was to ratify and make and allow to happen a degree in the main in creative and professional writing. So we were sitting round the board table, and the two advisers who'd been brought in, one was Robert Sheppard and one was Ric Allsopp and there was a load of other people there, and I was walked in to be asked questions about the modules of the degree that we were contributing to it. I said something rather shocking in the meeting room. It sort of went cold at one moment and then Robert picked it up and thought it was absolutely a good idea, fortunately. What I said was, I didn't think a part of my module was about teaching people to write at all, it was about teaching them to read. Because until they could do that I didn't see how they could write anything. It was one of those moments and it crops up and they realise I do mean this and they're going to have to accept it as part of the reason they've taken me on. Also I think there's been a culture of reading that's been quite important to me in the '70s and in the '80s. It was very strong among a small group of us all, a small group of poets, mainly poets, and I was reminded of it last night because I got an email from Pierre Joris, who's got hold of the new *Place* and wasn't travelling with it, too big, and he said in there on the same site, his new blog site, he's commemorating the death of Paul Ricoeur, his anecdote of amongst other things was to remind me, and perhaps Ric Allsopp, that I'd persuaded him to read, we were together reading *The Rule of Metaphor*, and we were both very interested by his whole idea of it. We'd come across this. There's a range of ways of talking about rhetoric, metaphor, metonyms, in terms of the word, the single line, the paragraph, the single stanza, or the whole poem. You could apply it to the whole or the parts. The book could be allegorical for a whole idea, say. And the poem could be an allegorical for a different thing, smaller. It's this discussion of the permutation of rhetoric. You're looking worried.

AD Yes. I've never actually read Ricoeur. I think he was Swiss?

AF I think he was actually. He wrote in French.

AD He may have come from Geneva; they speak French.

AF He was a Freudian, he was a humanist. Both of those elements make him awkward at times, awkward for me, but I did find him on rhetoric very strong. On narrative he's good as well. I haven't read all the three volumes, but the *Time and Narrative* book is very. But when I was referring to it I was not just namedropping Ricœur, but the whole ambience that *Place* was written in, and also not just the ambience but the people reading things for the first time and trying to grasp the whole complexity of the history of ideas, and new ideas. That's I think how people like myself used Eric Mottram, because he was quite useful because he had a generation of knowledge that preceded mine on the history of ideas, which was actually much more current to his generation than mine, in many ways. What was that guy that wrote *The Great Chain of Being*?

AD Lovejoy.

AF All those people went out of fashion. All those books dated from the 50s, and weren't available in the 60s and 70s except second hand. They may now be back in fashion. The whole way they dealt with the debates on evolution and civilisation. I've lost track. You still see them on the shelf sometimes, you still see Burckhardt on civilisation, or Vasari on 16th century art, because he's… It's not to do with what they say, or whether you agree with what they say, it's because they're intelligent about what they say. It helps considerably, because there's just so much poor journalism that's written and textbooks that seem on the surface to be about fairly important subjects, well they are, but inside them is nothing but (???).

AD I think there's a category of the aesthetics of ideas. Not that some ideas are boring and some aren't, but the whole game around ideas can be either a good one or a bad one. It seems to me that some poets have looked at Pound and Olson and decided that one had to write like that, but they weren't actually intellectuals, so there was no life of ideas to feed the poems. It went incredibly badly.

AF That's very true. Yes, I've often been disappointed by that trend, because what it does is, it gives the mentors bad names. For false reasons, in many ways. I don't know, it's very hard this, but sometimes there are writers who've been influenced by both of those people who other people read and who I don't really care to. I was struck the other day by a difference, I don't think Glenn Storhaug would mind me mentioning, although I haven't talked it through with him very much. Glenn Storhaug lives in Hereford as I do sometimes. He amongst other things is an avid reader, a very powerful reader, of many books of poetry. More than anyone else I've ever met, I think, he can quote Ezra Pound very very clearly. He lent me a tape of Gary Snyder's work, reading for a videotape, and halfway through the discussion with Snyder and what he was saying my whole nerves went on edge, because I just thought the whole intellectual rigour of what he was saying was so absent that I therefore worried about anything else he'd said, really. It was to do with his understanding of ecology in relationship to the planet, really. Maybe it was being over-simplified for the videotape, so there is that potential licence. But I must say that I did stop reading his work at one time. I enjoyed *A Range of Poems*, *Earth Household* was an interesting book, something happened halfway through the '70s into the '80s that stopped me reading him. I think some of that kind of element that I pulled away from and found unproductive in terms of the human value from reading it.

Lulham 24/5/05 tape 3

AD I'm terribly interested in this question of the musicality of the intellect. How someone can present a sequence of ideas and it's just hopelessly flawed and corrupt, it's just a wrong shape, in the way that some mountain is a wrong shape. There's nothing reasonable about that, but some mountains just are. It's a faculty. This is a bit like criticising the beauty of someone's nose, in that they're going to get very insulted very quickly. It's quite central to modern poetry, and I mean really modern poetry, something of significance in the last 40 years which was much less significant in previous periods.

AF Come back through that again. What's become more focused?

AD The need to be, not just clever with ideas, but aesthetic with ideas.

AF I'm not sure that's true. It probably is, but there are instances of exception. Wouldn't Horace be a difference, or some of Spenser?

AD Well, yes, because having written about this I then read *In Memoriam*, and the intellectual focus is just so good. He really understood evolution.

AF Tennyson's actually standing in Weymouth or wherever it is, I think it's in Weymouth, looking at the strata. Absolutely extraordinary. It's quite explicit there. That is actually a moment of change in his work, about that time. I think the poetry gets better after that. But that's my bias, because I don't have the same religious interest he has, I suspect. I'm not a deep reader of Tennyson's work, I prefer the later work. I haven't come through the full struggle of King Arthur.

AD I don't think the ideas level of that is very good.

AF There is the case to teach it through a whole strand of things from *Beowulf*, through that to T.H. White or somebody, right through from what amounts to a Roman-Byzantine story. I once went to a lecture by an anthropologist, whose name escapes me for the moment, at Oxford, because I used to go to the lectures and they were given at the Ashmolean, at other places in Oxford. He talked about shamanism in the Horn of Africa, south of Egypt, and within that culture you could see the origins of, or associations with, the story of King Arthur and the Grail. An extraordinary thing. Not with the same names, of course.

AD Was it I.M. Lewis?

AF Yes, I think it was. He wrote *The Deep Well*, things like that.

AD He wrote some fantastic books.

AF He didn't write *The Deep Well*, that was Nylander. Lewis has written some really good things. That's why I went. He was a sexist, too, which I thought was terribly interesting. In the audience there were people cringing at the things he said. He was very old-fashioned about things like that. In a humbling, silly, way, to make it easier. Sherratt too, he used to be very good. Sherratt used to be one of the curators of the Ashmolean. He's very good on Mesopotamia. There was a moment when you were linking the facts that if aesthetics includes information, therefore has a component which is information, then it's clear that the history of ideas and the history of aesthetics have a parallel existence, an overlapping existence. That would be an interesting study. I'm not quite sure how you do it.

AD I'm still trying to work out what the history of ideas in this country in the last 50 years has been.

AF I can see that. When *Place* comes to an end, in 1980, there's a decision to change the way I used texts and vocabularies, quite explicitly. I went though a couple of experiments to see what should be done. By which I mean small pieces of work. *Bending Window* was one, *Defamiliarising* was another. And it led to a new kind of use of existing texts and vocabularies by starting to insist on transformation, which meant that there was an emphasis more on the transformation than there had been previously. It would be silly to say there was no transformation from the text that precedes *Stane* to the text *Stane* becomes, but it would also be fairly evident that there's a more strident attention to the transformation in *Brixton Fractals* and subsequent works. Now I think that has to do with engagement with the history of ideas in a way that almost makes the history of ideas too loose, really. But it's to do with very specific groups of ideas and clusters of ideas, really, to do with particular vocabularies, particular areas of vocabulary. By vocabulary I mean descriptions which have been made, so I suppose I mean use of language. I made choices then, at that moment, which I suppose I'd previously done, I made almost categorical choices in the sense that I was reading through *Nature* and there were some elements of it that were more important to me than others. One of the areas was biotechnology and one of the areas was quantum mechanics. It was because of the discoveries being made in those two fields. And the kind of implications that some of those discoveries were leading me to understand, or believe I understood, all that about. I'm summarising maybe through a faulty memory, if I went back it would be maybe three or four areas I'd alighted on, I'm sure there are, I don't remember exactly. There have been pervading interests which are threads in a lot of the poetry that comes right through and doesn't cease, really. I've always had an interest in boundaries, or how one thing moves to another, or how one crosses from one era to another, and how that's made possible. I'm therefore interested in routes as well, roads, passages. And that of course links idea clusters as well. So you might find in one cluster comparable words, or the same words being used, but in different meanings. And there are other threads that you will find, that are like boundary threads, like perception, I've had an interest in perception, that is, that debate between what is outside you, or what is inside you but you can't see, but understand in other ways, proprioceptively and so on. There is a thread of interest in, therefore, you'll find I have heightened interest in synaesthesia because of the apparent breakdown of perceptive boundaries when that applies. And I'm pretty sure but in the first place

I know that's been one of my concerns. On reflection, without doubt that's one of everybody's concerns, whether they like it or not. But that would be to make it too simple. I'm much more specific about what I mean, in terms of perception, much more directed. Well I suppose partly because I'm teaching it. Some perceptual practices, I'm teaching, theory of colour and aspects of construction, visual construction of shape, and containment of shape, which comes back to this boundary business. In drawing practice boundary's very very important, because it can make or break the aesthetic potential of the drawing, how one deals with the boundary, edge of the paper, or the frame within the paper, or whatever it happens to be. This has been known for a very very long time. In mediaeval churches, in stained glass windows, in sculpture, you'll see the figure of Christ inside a mandorla, with a foot just over the edge, just to break the sequence, it makes him three-dimensional, because it brings him forward in the space of this kind of egg, and what it does also is it alerts your eye, it causes an interference in your eye's movement around a clean circle, a clean curve. Some of them aren't circles, they're much more oval, aren't they. That excitement that the eye gathers from that is useful because it makes the art more attractive and the eye more attentive, and interested and so on, and the eye is therefore standing in that sense, really, the eye is metonymic for a larger idea of consciousness. It's standing for a whole range of demands that you're making on your experience. The eye is simply dealing with information. And that idea is coming right through to some very advanced draftspeople in the 1970s, like Harry Thubron for example, could recognise, he gets it partly from Paul Klee, he's understood a rectangular piece of paper, and he recognises that, if you push a line to that edge, the eye automatically understands that as meaning it could be going beyond the edge, and because of the edge you can't see if it does or not. Whereas if you push the line up and don't touch the edge, you've made a completely different statement about the gravity of it. This line here could be leaning on the edge and therefore relying on the edge for its stability, and this line clearly isn't. So this whole business of edge is so important in drawing for no more difficult reason than that it's important for our physicality, it's important for our knowledge of spatial experience. It stops us falling over. It stops us walking through walls. Because we recognise the difference between vertical and horizontal, we recognise the existence of gravity, not simply by the fact of that gravity is pulling us on the earth, but by visual signs. Architecture provides a lot of those visual signs for us, as I suppose at one time the forest did. It's so fast that you can pick it out that you don't even have to be told. It's extraordinary, this whole orientation in space is based on it. This whole business of orientation can be explicated or understood, or has been, partly on the basis of what the boundaries are, the edges are. So that's why I have quite an elaborate interest in boundaries. So if I just go like that you know that some of the weight isn't on my foot at all, it's on my hand. Just because of the angle of that activity. So it's all kinds of activities that you relate to your experience of the earth.

AD So the eye can actually see thrust?

AF It gets much more complex and interesting in some ways with Paul Klee. He wrote a couple of big chunky books on the nature of design and so on. In one of them he wrote this very strange line, which was explicated to me by August Wiedmann, who's a philosopher, when I was at Goldsmith's. He used to teach history of art there. Two of the things Klee was saying in this diagram were, my experience on the earth is, light generally being above, the earth generally being below, or the experience of life generally, is the same experience as this tree is having, it has the same forces working on it, even if they are articulated differently. So he has a relationship to this tree which is much more interesting and complex than you would at first expect. Then he also had a sense, which was a different boundary situation, of being able to draw the tree knowing what it looked like from behind the tree. Blake also had this information. It was not the idea that you see through, but the idea that you have knowledge of that, and you include that knowledge in your expression. Why does that get so interesting? The person I got most interested in doing that was Peter Lanyon, cause he's a landscape painter amongst other things, in Cornwall, died in the '60s quite young.

AD In a glider accident.

AF Yeah. Friend of [W.S.] Graham's. He understood that fully, and what he did, in order to make a painting of a landscape, was to, he would investigate it, know it from all the sides that he could get to. From inside it, in the mines. From out to sea, looking in, and of course eventually from up above, in a glider. Then what he would do is more often than not, he would construct in his studio a three-dimensional model of what he'd been looking at, using collaged materials. I don't know whether he went as far as Rauschenberg, using only materials he'd come across in his travels while he was doing the investigation. I don't know, he could have done. But what he painted, what his paintings are of, are those models in the studio from the one point of view he's looking at, like still-lifes. But, of course with the knowledge of how he'd constructed them. How the landscapes he saw had accrued in construction.

AD But he didn't invent landscapes? the models are of things which are already there?

AF That's right. And it's very strange to think of it, but I realised after *Place* that I was interested in moving to Lanyon's position. So *Brixton*, I am in Brixton, it was to actually be described differently in a way, articulated differently. I don't mean I use language to make the articulation. But I mean he was like somebody informing me about a practice that comes from Constructivism, effectively. That he was talking about. And I've never really lost it. Franz Kline's work is so deeply constructed in that way, it's so unexpected when you first look at it. It seems so quickly made, or brashly made, but it's not, it's just not, not at all. Kline's interest is much more in industrial steel, structures like bridges, steam engines, things like that. That is why you get a lot of girder type stuff in his work. He recognises those things breaking frames. So then I get interested in breaking frames. It occurs on the back [jacket] of *Entanglement*. The interest of breakage. This is about the boundary that there is broken through, you can see it gradually tipping here. That's the kind of transformation I'm interested in investigating, looking at. You can eyesight straight through there. It's been broken. It still hasn't been destroyed. It's still physically there, not just a palimpsest, although it is that. It's more than a palimpsest, it's seeing one thing through another. Almost in some David Jones drawings it happens that the background is in the foreground, it's come through it as if the foreground's transparent. And that's what Paul Klee was talking about, and that's what Blake's talking about as well. About the ability to convey that. That was a long cycle, wasn't it.

AD The thing about knowledge is it's there before the poem. That's why you can see the side of the tree that you can't see. But this is the key to liberating the information in a poem.

AF But it's not like a box that opens. Knowledge is an activity. In that sense it, knowledge of the other side of the tree, changes. It may not change very much. Is there knowledge that never changes? because that would be a debate, wouldn't it, that would be a question.

AD It might be more procedures that repeat.

AF In my lifetime it's unlikely that some aspects of the granite that I walk by in some of the buildings is going to change very much. But it doesn't mean that an earthquake doesn't hit this place. Or something ridiculous like that. I was sitting here the other week, did I tell you, and there was a car crash outside. It just hit the wall. Of course I can't see a thing. Neither can I climb the wall to look over it, and it's a long way around. I knew there'd been a bad accident, so I phoned somebody. But it's just that suddenness, that realisation that there is always that element.

AD So there was an acoustic stimulus? Everything else was supplied from knowledge of how the world is constructed?

AF An uninterrupted car alarm going off, a car horn. So it was as if a body had slumped on the horn. Judging by how many ambulances turned up, and how long they were there, I should judge it was quite nasty. About four hours. There was really a massive impact, everybody in the building wondered what was going on. That's quite interesting, I'm worried about, I can see what you're saying, I'm just worried about the concept of knowledge as such. You might take a book off the shelf and say this is knowledge of a certain kind. Of course the context for the reading of that is that people change continually, so that reading continually transforms what's being read.

AD What I'm thinking of is actually the expiry of knowledge. You know what the outline of a tree is going to be like, because it's roughly the completion of a circle of which you can see 150°.

AF But that's a production. You're in the process of producing knowledge.

AD If you read the *Collected Poems* of R.S. Thomas, which I had to do for professional reasons, the level of predictability gradually goes up through the entire book to the point where you can't even read a poem, because you know exactly where it's going to go. You pass out, perhaps. There is this basic difference between people who want to repeat a module and people who accept that you've learnt certain expectations and start to mutate the expectations, mutate the structures, and regard the new element as the most important thing.

AF Isn't there a moment when, for instance R.S. Thomas in that case, wouldn't that be where the aesthetic component is reducing considerably, as almost in proportion to the amount of pleasure, information, and even figurative language that you're getting from it? It's not simply knowledge as such, is it? It's not Aristotelian. Haven't we come to understand it much more as a fluid process?

AD Clearly if you start on page 200 the poem on that page seems much more new than if you'd read pages 1 to 199 already.

AF It depends what you mean by knowledge. What I'm suggesting is you might have a whole set of paradigms which set you up as having knowledge about something, and then those paradigms get shifted, as we know they do. At least that's one of the ways of talking about the shift, in Thomas Kuhn's terms. And isn't it therefore indicative of the fact that knowledge has a space-time, really, and therefore has a potential for change. There was a riveting programme on the tsunamis off the north-west coast of America or Canada, on the Pacific. They were looking at it again very closely for the obvious reasons, and it's not a matter of whether it will happen, but of where and when. Because it's on that fault line.

AD There's no tradition of this. They're quite common in Japan.

AF Those tsunami waves… *Brixton Fractals* was published by Tsunami, the press, in Vancouver. They obviously have large waves quite a lot. But they're not I suppose normally attributable to earthquakes. They must be attributable to something like plate movements.

AD Obviously if the adjustment between the plates were continuous, you wouldn't have discontinuous events like tsunamis. So the information field of a poem might be influenced by information derived from thousands of other poems, not just by that poet but by a lot of poets.

AF We touched on that business of the community of poets the other day, didn't we. When Ken came by. It is something that I hadn't articulated before. When I was proofreading this book (*Place*) I was quite struck by it, and so were a couple of other readers I mentioned. I don't think there's a fault there, I think that's quite right. In fact, there might be a reduced number rather than the full number of readers, if one thinks of all the people taking part in debating poetry and the history of ideas generally.

AD We need a name here, in fact a group name, to be founded. A brand name. I keep saying the '70s, but it's pretty weak, isn't it. To say how things happen.

AF I mentioned Peter Barry's book. On Earl's Court.

AD I can't remember what the book was.

AF I think it's going to be *The Battle of Earl's Court*.

AD Oh yeah, sure. I met someone in Leicester, just after I'd interviewed you, who was very much on the other side. He's called Brian Fewster. Quite fierce and formal. I was going to interview him.

Mirrors for Waste Heat

Lulham Building, 22 August 2005

AF This is just me explaining what I've done to prepare us for something that you proposed the other week, which was to find relationships that I was making through patterns of connection between different poems, or pieces of writing. The way I've done this, is rather than picking the more difficult example which would require me to do an exegesis of my own work, which is a bit crazy to do retrospectively, I've picked poems that do it internally, from one stanza to the next, so that it's quite explicit in how the transformations are occurring. It comes back to the question that you raised that Rob Holloway raised, to do with metamorphosis, or distortion or transformation, I forget the terminologies we were talking at that time. Transformation's a good one, one that I find acceptable. So "Ballin' the Jack" 's the one I first picked, which is in the current *Gravity as a Consequence of Shape*. These are all in *Gravity as a Consequence of Shape*, and some of the ideas that crop up in *Gravity as a Consequence of Shape* to do with transformation, find simpler and earlier versions of ways of approaching poetry like this in both *Place* and—explicitly in *Place*—and also in *Art of Flight*. So in fact it's the poetry that precedes the 1970s and that hasn't been published. Hasn't been republished, anyway. Part of the thinking behind this, I'll just say it while I'm flicking through, has to do with recognizing poetry, that I have time for and admire, plans itself and works out of long structures that you don't necessarily have to be fully cognizant of, but which during reading short sections you find that the work is resonant with work you've already read by the same artist, by the same poet, at a previous time. What you don't necessarily need to articulate for yourself initially is where that transformation is occurring from, or where that resonance of a pattern is connecting. It's just that resonance itself is enough to make you feel as if you're developing in the reading of the work, and it's enhancing your engagement with the work. Engagement could be a whole range of levels, of course, from entertainment through to serious pondering. So many artists in the past have used very simple devices to do this. And the most simple device would be one line followed by the next line as a rhyming couplet—it's very clear that one relates to the other. There's a relationship of a musical arithmetical nature between each line and each word, phrase and so forth. So if you're building that up on a larger structure, if you start using it at the level of, let's say, Milton, or some of Shakespeare's longer works, longer than the *Sonnets*, like 'Venus and Adonis', or some of Sidney's work, clearly the artist, the maker has to conceptualise in quite detail arithmetically, musically. As a reader you don't necessarily have to understand all of that, because the intricacy itself is just carrying you, lifting you. It's not something you have to necessarily analyse, although some people would enjoy the process of analysis. In 'Ballin' the Jack' there's a simple case of this. The poem's set out on four pages, numbered 1 to 4 in terms of stanzas. And I'm almost embarrassed about the simplicity of the arrangement here, but if I say it that makes it clear. So line one of the first stanza starts 'Compassion fatigue' and the last line of the second stanza starts 'A tiredness from exposure'. And then when we get to stanzas 3 and 4, that's made more complex, and so I won't get into exegesis. I'll just pick another example. At the end of the first stanza it says "painted green" at the beginning of the second it says "painted blue". So we can see there's a kind of reversal of the line order going on here. During the poem, during the process of the poem, there are obvious links across between stanzas, and links which aren't at all obvious, and which are to do with quotations from particular artists or quotations from a particular narrative, particular process. I recognise in going through these four stanzas that there's a use of a description from a photographer who's clambering around on wires across water to try and make the photographs possible. Rigging up lighting to make the unusual shots that he does make. Embarrassingly enough I've just lost the name of the photographer. So I think I'll just make sure that I've got that in. Winston Olenk. So Winston Olenk is a photographer who produces huge set-ups. You see a railway station, you see a train passing, you see passengers doing particular things, all in very bright light. You wonder how on earth it's all been possible, and it's because he set it up. So you'll get that occurring, that narrative so to speak, across all four, at particular places in the stanza. But also quite eccentrically in this stanza there are lines beginning with a comma, which in the first stanza reads—

, bulbs spots 60 watts, olive oil, honey

In the second stanza the relationship is—

, work light, ironing-board, oligotoil, laundry

In the third stanza—

, light work, bored ironing, olitory oil, money,

Then in the fourth stanza... I've lost it. I wonder actually whether the comma's been missed by mistake in this printing, and I haven't double-checked that one back, but it would be this one here

scrub pavement, paint railing, polish steps

—is likely to be the last one. Also through this sequence there are extracts from the government's literature on what to do in the case of a nuclear explosion, which were issued by the Thatcher government. To do with air coming through a building, and the light. And that rhymes across all 4 stanzas as well, at particular places arithmetically. There's one here that's another obvious thing, which are recommendations for diet—

a sucrose intake of less than 12 spoons a day

in the second stanza:

three dessert spoons of fibre, offered as minimum breakfast

Another way of thinking about what's going on here, in these particular four stanzas, is that—I almost want to show it visually, but that's not much use if we're on tape. I was going to open five fingers of my hand, open five fingers of my next hand, put them into each other so it's clear that there's an interlocking going on, like a jigsaw, would be a way of saying it. That's what happens in 'Ballin' the Jack'. In 'Wobble', which occurs in *Entanglement*, there's a similar sequence going on, which is why I picked it, because it's very easy to show the relationship, and by the time I'd got to writing 'Wobble', this was done on an accountant's Excel spreadsheet, so I could actually get the alignments right across the page. It wasn't published in that way, it was first published in Salzburg, by that...

AD Wolfgang Görtschacher.

AF I thought it would be a bit much to ask him to do any of that. So they were printed as if they were a straightforward sequence, and that republication is how it's presented in *Entanglement*. So there we have it again, One Two Three Four. And here the instructions to me are quite explicit after writing across. And there's a lot of writing across is going on using quotations usually from Coleridge and Gerard Manley Hopkins.

And probably someone else whose name I haven't got in my head for a second. Not just those people, but those are the significant poets that are involved. William Langland, Chaucer, as well. Now here it's been made more complex, it's very difficult to understand if one wanted to how this relationship's occurring. But what I'm telling you about is a compositional device, not a reading device, so it's not necessarily relevant to know this as a reader. But what's relevant to me as a composer is that I'm setting it up to make the reading more engaging. And so as a reader you get to the next stanza and the next stanza and the next stanza, and so you can feel the relationship even though it might not be entirely tangible. It might not be entirely explicit. And it might just be a feeling you have, there's a rhyming going on even though you don't quite pick it up. In fact I've found people do pick it up, and you'll find that Rob Holloway did a live exegesis in public of one of the poems, around the 'Wobble' period. I think it was called, I think it's in the next sequence, called the "Waddle', it's the one I used in Philadelphia. So let's just glance at this one. It's quite clear that some of this... This one works not in reversal but works across the top lines. But what's occurring also of course because it's poetry, there are other relationships between stanzas, between lines, which haven't been set up beforehand, but occur as a consequence of the process of writing. So that kind of complexes it for the reader if they were trying to do an analysis, because some of the time the relationship seems to be there and sometimes it doesn't at other times. They might find a relationship between 1 and 3, and not find it for 4 and 2. And it's because the relationship is more incidental than composing. So for instance through this particular sequence there's descriptions of the consequences of torture on a body, the flesh, and which are carried across at the same place. There's some analysis derived from some RNA protein experimentation, biotechnology, which comes across, and there are some raw information about being in a city, like

    Helicopter streetscreech lawnrain

almost as one word there. Now how that relates across is not as explicit as it had been in 'Ballin' the Jack', in other words it's a compositional method rather than a method which would be completely open to analysis all the time. But I was just seeing if I could see it reading across. At the end of the first stanza it says

    even now the body is blind

—then there's something unusual at the end of the second stanza. It says

> Above figure of the Amitabh Buddha sound of drillvibration

—that's the Buddha at the foot of the stairs in the British Museum. Bottom of the third—

> Descried notation estimates trauma

The fourth reads

> a small moth hits the light bulb descends vertically

And they're really, one could relate them epistemologically to do with the condition of oblivion or death, really. They relate from the middle section when I was looking at work on torture being done by the Medical Foundation, people like Helen Bamber. I was reading her biography. She was the woman that walked into the camps in 1945 as a young medical nurse, and set up, as a consequence of that, an organisation that would help people who had suffered torture. It's still going. And she retired last year. And some of her descriptions and some of the descriptions in the biography I've used, because it was clear that some of that description was still being relevant to, well, it was Rwanda at the time I think. I was looking at this this morning. The biography of Helen Bamber is about her life, in the treatment of people who were tortured, but it contained descriptions which were relevant, and this was contemporary with the news of what was going on in Rwanda and places like that. How one tribe was treating another and so on. It's an issue that's cropped up quite a bit in the work of John Wilkinson and J.H. Prynne and others. I might be wrong, but things like *Wound Response* and such writing relates to that kind of research as well. Not necessarily Bamber. The idea of the welt. Recently, in the last year, I split my thumb open. It's gone now, but I could feel a thick lump on the side of the thumb as I was healing. That welt is described by some people who've undergone torture all over their body, places round their necks and so on, and in some cases the body doesn't recover, it just produces an anomaly in the cosmetic condition you might say. So that's those two. There's a much more explicit example right in the middle of this work, and although it cropped up chronologically in *Gravity* it's published in *Entanglement*, and it's called 'Fish Jet'. And somebody picked up on this quite early, and that was Adrian Clarke. I don't recall whether he published his exegesis or not. I think he did.

He certainly sent it to me. What happens in 'Fish Jet' is that there are three poems from *Gravity*, one called 'Fish' one called 'Jersey Bounce' and one called 'Jet'. The first stanza of each poem relates to each other, the second relates to each other, right the way through to the twelfth stanza. So there's twelve stanzas in each poem. The same number of lines in each poem for each section. So that, let's not count 1, 1 seems to take two pages, stanza 2 here is 8 lines for each poem, see what I mean. So it's the same number. Let's just read across and see how it works, and then I'll double back and see whether it has or not. By the way this isn't necessarily the order in which they're written, or the order in which the transformation occurs. The order that they're put in the book might be eccentrically out of order in that respect. Deliberately eccentric. So stanza two begins

> Wisdom arrangements permeated with order

—'Fish' 2—

> Receiveth four degrees of impulse the

'Jet' reads:

> Weather formulates permafrost insulated stillness

It's almost opaque in terms of how that links across. So let's just pick a better example which would just help us be more confident about it. The last line, second stanza, reads

> The effects of civil world

in 'Jersey Bounce'. End of 'Fish'—

> Subduplicate to powers all times

Then in 'Jet'—

> Beneath skin enriches civil times.

Now you've got *times* in two of those poems, you've got *civil* in two of them. It's quite clear that in fact what's going on I would think is that 'Jet' is first and then 'Jersey Bounce' follows and then 'Fish' is third, but

I'm not sure. There's a relationship of literally the words here. Sometimes I do that by sound alone. And that happens a lot in *Gravity*. It's not to do with meaning in the normal sense. It's not to do with syntax, where the words are derived from, it simply derives from what they sound. And so I haven't double checked where this occurs. Certainly there's an—*el* cropping up here that's cutting across:

> Shower gels thrive across invest
>
> Power impels drives attracts impresses
>
> Thorough immediacy quells any question.

That's the sixth stanza in each. So what I mean by transformation here is almost elusive, but it's almost there also. Because *shower gels* and *power impels* is quite clearly is straightforward rhyme. *(I)nvest* and *impress*. And then we've got to in the third one, bringing in *quells*, with a kind of questioning of the method, implicitly, in the same line. *Quells any question*. So is that enough really?

AD (assent)

AF Let's try this then. Beginning of 7 —

> Demands hurt by confidence want
>
> in 'Jersey Bounce',
>
> Fronds spurt sky fence wand

is almost accidentally syntactical, if at all. It's clearly coming from the rhyme. Because in 'Jet' [*Responds pervert descry wax code*] starts *responds*, which is where *fronds* is coming from, *pervert* is where *spurt* is coming from, *descry* is where *sky* is coming from, and so on. And then instead of picking up on *wax code* it flips back on *want*, there, as *wand* here. So there's a movement going on between the first lines. So you could imagine a kind of grid structure when composing it, and a playfulness occurring, and moving one line to another place, and juxtaposing it with the place. One line in one poem being pulled out and replacing it with a line from another poem. Which then the displaced line goes back to the gap. So they're the three I picked. There are actually more interesting examples, in terms of, when you're reading through the work, you find that there are lines or narrative elements that recur, and you don't necessarily need to know where they've recurred from, it's just that they help you realise that there's an elusive narrative, a thread that is broken, you're getting elements of. Indicating that there was once potentially at least, a thread there, whether that thread is narrative or some sort of other construction. And I think that helps engagement with the work, and I think it improves enjoyment of the work. That's all I've done in terms of what you asked me to do. What I haven't been able to do, because I haven't got them handy lying around, is pick up old notebooks, so you could see more obviously. That would just become kind of encyclopaedic really.

AD When you speak of an elusive narrative, I'm thinking of something that goes underground and emerges again, I'm thinking of London rivers.

AF It's not just elusive for the reader, it's also elusive for the writer. Cause I think the narrative experience is like that in the contemporary world, at least the one I'm living in, it might not be the same if I was living in Delhi. But certainly in the urban world it's like that. Our narrative experience is complexed by walking the streets. Now whether you could extrapolate that further and say that's part of our condition now, it's part of our consciousness, I don't know. Probably you could. My hesitation in saying it is that I wonder whether that's always been the case. Really narrative structures have been artefacts rather than realities, if that's the alternative category. It is artifice that we're talking about. What's his name wrote rather a clever book on it, *Poetic Artifice*. I can't remember his name. One of the early writers for Ferry.

AD Veronica Forrest-Thomson.

AF No no. He's become quite famous writing books on Dickens and London.

AD Oh, Ackroyd. It wasn't *Notes for a New Culture*?

AF I thought his work then was more interesting than it's now become *(omission)*

AD There are one or two things I was curious about. For example works other than *Gravity* and *Place*. For example *Long Shout to Kernewek* and *Blood Bone Brain*, which, it would be quite easy for someone not to be aware of their existence.

AF *Long Shout to Kernewek* got rewritten during the process of writing *Place*. When I began writing *Place*, *Long Shout to Kernewek* got rewritten, and there are elements of it therefore which date later than the sixties. It got much reduced I think, so far as I remember. It didn't actually get published until 1975, in its entirety, I think that's right. Which is a year after *Place* Book I. *Blood Bone Brain* has a much more complex publishing history, because it got, although the first four books got, published in small editions in the early 70s. The entire work was mainly experienced through performances and installations, so it ends up as a set of microfiches. Microfiche readers are probably becoming antique items I should think.

AD It's in the British Library. Or at least the catalogue says it is.

AF Oh good. That should be the case, but it doesn't mean it always is. I got a note from them about six months ago saying I'd been using the wrong ISSN number for a long time, and my magazine had been confused with another magazine called *Spanner* which was selling engineering products. They were irritated by the inquiries they were getting for poetry.

AD I love the sound association!

AF It was the intention at one time that the British Library received all the *Spanners* and so on, and they certainly did, but whether it got them is another issue. It used to go through somebody called Smail.

AD He's still there. A.T. Smail.

AF Whether or not he, or she or they, did the work properly, I don't quite know. Never mention distribute it to Wales, the Bodleian, the British Museum, and somebody else.

AD Probably Edinburgh.

AF *Blood Bone Brain* is difficult to talk about in terms exclusively of poetry, because it's not. Or it's not ostensibly poetry, it's got poetry inside it. But it's about process and processives visually and performatively, and documentation of performance, and documentation of installations. So it's that sort of biz, really. One of the things I still think of as important about it is that it's a sort of support mechanism for *Place*, really, in the sense that it occurred contemporary with it. It's a conceptual apparatus which you wouldn't see by reading *Place*, really, but which provided a, more experimentation of conception, ideas of conceptualisation and process than the poetry does, on the surface. By which I mean for instance you wouldn't particularly get engaged, unless you were led to, in the way in which *Place* got published in rather ephemeral almost unfinished publications, as if they were almost handwritten at some points. There were moments when you pick up a copy of some of the early *Place* and it feels like you were picking up a manuscript rather than a book. And that comes out of that experience of *Blood Bone Brain*. Very much immediate, very much made for the audience on that day or week. It was contemporary also with using the thermography technique which was very cheap. You could copy anything you had in your hand. So because it responded to colour. So you could make a drawing or you could write or you could use a photograph and it would pick up on a stencil.

AD I was thinking of the pattern of rick-burning in south-east England when you said thermography!

AF No no no! It's a drum which is burning a stencil. So that it can be used for printing. It was a technique I'd developed from one which was being used by Beau Geste Press. Felipe Ehrenberg. Using a Gestetner. There was some other work which has probably sunk, in many ways. But which will probably partly surface because I know that Robert Sheppard's recently written something on *Apocalyptic Sonnets*, a small book which Pig Press put out in the late 70s. And there was *Poetry for Schools* which I'm still quite fond of as a set of works. I forget how many sets of these. But it had poems in there like 'Black Light' and suchlike. *Imbrications* was another set which came out of *Business Verse*, which is pretty much the only publication of that business verse. That is to say, verse written from the experience of being a salesman, a technical rep, in a car running around different small manufacturers. I suppose one of the significant features for me that comes out when I reflect on it is that not very much is incidental poetry. There is not—no, apparently not a lot of poetry being made just from the instant, from the occasion. But that's only an apparency, it's because that momentary experience, of particular sensations or heightened interest, or dulled interest, whatever one would want to draw from, is used explicitly in *Gravity* as a source, in the same way that some of the written sources are used. I'd find them in notebooks and they'd come across in particular places, and you could pick them up out of *Gravity* as elements that appear random, or appear less constructed in the construction sense. But actually I don't like occasional poetry in the old-fashioned sense of it, or rather, the conventional sense of it. And that's a deliberate decision. And that's not to say I never have, I've just never published it. I wouldn't do so either. If I was putting together a Collected, it wouldn't appear. It would just be thought of as material in preparation for work. So that makes me slightly different from a lot of people's writing, I would say, particularly, certainly in English, and even more particularly in French and American. And that's as I think, I would say, there's too much incidental, or poetry of that conventional kind, occasional. I wouldn't write like that because that's not what I'm doing.

AD If I got these microfiches from the sixth floor down in the earth of Euston, what would I see?

AF I'll post you a set. I might get the numeracy wrong here. I think there are nine microfiches, and they're all postcard size. And on each postcard size microfiche I think there are 98 images. Anyway, whatever numerically works. There are so many rows and so on. We can check that. And what they are are literally reproductions from 35 mm slides. Some of them are portrait, some of them landscape format. The person making the microfiche literally takes that set of 90+ images and reduces them down photographically to the size of a fingernail, a small fingernail. So when you hold the postcard you've got a piece of transparent film with lots of small squares on, and quite clearly, when you hold it up to the light, you can see they're photographs. Sometimes photographs of text, sometimes of places, sometimes of jars, materials, and so on and so forth. In fact the three main things are photographs of probably places that connect with *Creek in the Ceiling Beam*, which are mainly cemeteries. Photographs of cemeteries that are connected round South London. And photos of the jars and objects like jars, memory jars, literally memory objects, memory theatre. And the third thing is the photographs from the books, much of which are textual, like *Sicily* and so on. There are exceptions to that. The first book is *FACEC*, is a set of faces. It starts off with a face of a Mexican revolutionary and at the other end has a drawing of a face. And they come together and overlap. And so the photograph becomes the drawing. And they were laid out on a table. Which is in the Tate Gallery. I don't know if they ever show it. They probably don't quite know what it is any more. But they bought a whole chunk of stuff. And so what you'd need to do. Well, there are two ways of doing it. First the microfiche needs to go into the microfiche viewer and you'd just see them one after the other. But I've provided little maps with each one, so that you can understand what it is that this one or two microfiches is. I produced a set of A5 booklets, very cheaply, photocopied, which are explicit about what's in them. The best photographs that are out were made not by me at all but were made following my instructions by Jude Walker, an American photographer who at that time was living in Brighton. Maybe her name's put down as Judith Walker. That tells you it, doesn't it, really. That's *Blood Bone Brain*. I've recently toyed with the idea of putting one element from these four books, *Creek in the Ceiling Beam*, out of the series ABCD it's number C, onto the Web. I was trying to scan it in, it doesn't scan at all well. Which is one of the ironies of it. The book was made using very early photocopiers. And by early I mean it precedes the Kodak photographic method, the dry photocopiers. And I damaged, the three machines just collapsed with me trying to make photographs of the beams in my room which were creaking. The beams were covered with white polystyrene tiles, and so the photographs were of white tiles. So if you try to photocopy white tiles on these very unsophisticated machines which were copying them in sort of brown oily colours, they just burnt out everything that was in the machines. It's very interesting that now when I'm trying to reproduce the stuff I've still got the same problem. Everything just whites out. All the scanners I've tried just don't do a good job. In fact I've given the job to someone who thinks it's simply because I wasn't using a good enough scanner. They're doing something about it. Maybe they'll just come up with it and I'll just put it up. It's quite a fun book. Produced as a consequence. Rather a mechanical poem. Lots of the devices used in *Creek in the Ceiling Beam* crop up, are Ur-examples of later works. *Creek in the Ceiling Beam* is first of all a recording in time in one place in the room I was sleeping in and whenever the beam creaked I would record its time. And then I'd map this out on a graph. And the shape that the graph made I used as a device for selecting from the books that were lying by the bed at the time of the creaking. Mainly a series of poets, in the books. And so that was how the creaking seemed. And I conjected different reasons for the creak, to do with plumbing, and pigeons in the loft, and to do with ley-lines, and the idea that maybe there was a ley-line coming through the bedroom. Which obviously was more than tongue-in-cheek. And then I realised that the beam running through the bedroom was potentially on a ley-line which connected all the cemeteries in South London. So that's what the book's about. So we went round all the cemeteries photographing all the sites. So John Michell, eat your heart out! Clearly it must have been after reading John Michell, I should have thought. Or somebody of that ilk. You know who I mean?

AD Yes, I've got that book in a pile on my floor.

AF I haven't got that book any more. What's it called?

AD *The View over Atlantis*.

AF And there were various related things like a magazine called *The Ley-Hunter*. It's strange that I moved to Hereford where Alfred Watkins used to live. He was the guy who wrote *The Old Straight Track*. Did you know that his archive was put together by Bill Griffiths? he was independently asked, as an archivist, if he could come to Hereford and put the archive together. It's a whole complex of things, it's not just ley-lines. He was an inventor of an early light-meter for cameras, called the bee-meter. He was a bee-keeper. Which is why he used the word bee-meter. So his archive is full of early scientific instruments in that regard. And also lots of tomes and notes about bee-keeping. There's a whole range of different things.

AD Archivist doesn't quite rhyme with Griffiths, but there is an acoustic link.

AF *Sicily* has another aspect to it which feeds in and out of *Place*, in that it was decided at the start of writing *Sicily* that, which is a poem written using very complex mechanisms, mainly mechanical, was that it wouldn't allow any waste. So the words that are being engineered and brought about had to be used. As the process involved a whole range of photocopying, I ended up producing a whole book of waste. Waste products from the writing of *Sicily*. It's almost unreadable. And that's been made evident by the fact that it's green ink printed on green paper, and yellow ink on yellow paper and so on. That business of waste, and letting the waste stay, and making use of the use of waste in some way or other, has a kind of, there's an ambience of the period, in the 70s, to do with the early ecologists, to do with *Ecologist* magazine, the *Ecology Blueprint* magazine which was published in the period. And it's to do with this other business that I derived from Olson, which was letting the dirt stay on the roots. It's another way of indicating source. Rather than cleaning up the work to such an extent that it's difficult to know, or impossible to know, the source of the information, is to leave some of it intact. And of course it becomes eventually, in the backs of some of these notebooks, a list of resources. But in *Place* it's not just a *list* of resources, you get it on the page.

AD Is that why they're called resources? because you can't waste them?

AF Yeah, it's a rhyming on that. Another way of doing it would be to include it in the text somehow, so we read across here, fortuitously (picks up copy of *Place* Book 1 which AD brought along, it falls open at VIII)

> The veins of the countryside standing out
> across the plains and hills—Watkins

So that's without any interest in Jung's synchronicity! That business of waste has always interested me and I did work in waste management, for a short period. The company I was working for were running out of new ideas, and they started to develop ideas to do with waste management. I got very intrigued and interested. They for instance, produced a chimney, a concrete chimney made from the ash of volcanoes and suchlike, and it was very good for very hot chimneys, when you were trying to burn haystacks for instance, hay bales, and hay burning has a very high thermal capacity. It burns very slowly, very hot. So most chimneys you put it in would just fall apart. So you have to produce a special chimney for that kind of burning. There was a time, more in Scandinavia than in Britain, where an interest in burning waste in warehouses that would then heat the warehouse. So you would use compacted cardboards and things like that. So I got interested in that. There's been a lot of that transfer across from industrial experience. I think I told you, I used to get a newspaper every month called *Adhesive News* which was all about glue. I used to really enjoy the vocabulary of that whole business.

AD *Spanner*'s a very difficult magazine. It's covered a wider set of fields and a wider theoretical extent than any other British magazine.

AF That might be true. It hasn't fulfilled all the intentions we had. Partly out of a consequence of people's response to a request for material—i.e. lack of response. And partly out of the circumstances of that time, really. It's responded to people's need, to some extent. But "people" is the wrong term to use. One or two coteries, I would say. It's set out in, Richard "Dick" Miller and myself proposed the idea of a magazine called Wooden Shoe. So, he and I had already started to accumulate manuscripts. I was left with the decision to get on with publishing them or not. In the meantime, I changed the name to Spanner. As clogging the works is where the wooden shoe idea came from, so Spanner in the works is a better English equivalent anyway.

AD Sabot to sabotage.

AF Yes, indeed. And so the initial *Spanners*, well the first one was an interview with John Cage. The second or third was an interview with Dick Higgins. They were already in place for the newspaper. The original idea was that the newspaper would be funded by music bands, who had explicitly agreed to put money into this. But through a third person whose name I've lost. It never happened, anyway. This third person went to jail for some reason I've forgotten. I was left with no money, also, to publish this, it wasn't going to be a newspaper, it was going to be something much more ephemeral. I'd got a small litho press, a table litho press, and I printed it myself. Some of the time. And also contemporary with all this was my participation with Fluxus—or, Fluxshoe England West, as it was. David Mayor, the Ehrenbergs, Chris Welch, people like that. Some of the proceedings or some of the people in the early Fluxus period, flipped in and out of *Spanner*. But it was also overlapping with my interest in poetry, which wasn't Fluxus poetry at all, so for instance Peter Riley edited an edition of *Spanner* at my request. Although he's always preferred to remain anonymous about it. Martin Thom must have been the second edition of *Spanner*. It was an early example of the poetry I was interested in at the time. He was running a magazine from Oxford then.

AD *Turpin*.

AF That's right. Martin then eventually moved off into writing history, rather than poetry. Rather intense history books, or at least one of the ones I've been trying to read is very intense. On the history of Fascism in Italy. So *Spanner*'s always had that ephemeral feel about it, printed using the method available to me rather than anything else. There's an interesting factor that creeps in, about this, which is to do with the subscriptions and sales. Because during the Fluxus period, for whatever reason, *Spanner* was published in an edition of 500, and I would sell most of them. I suppose I'd sell three quarters of them, at least. Some would sell right out, and some, like the John Cage or the Dick Higgins, wouldn't. For obvious reasons, for the reason that one's more well-known than the other. And today the edition is 150, so there's been a shift of subscription interest in the magazine. But I'm very very poor at marketing and promoting sales. But *Spanner* continues today. And a Bill Sherman *Spanner* came out two months ago. So there's a manuscript on my desk at the moment from Scott Thurston. What else is there on the stocks? cris cheek is someone who keeps promising to send something and never has. So there's been a range of people in and out of different coteries. By which I mean literally what was meant in Manet's time, really. Groups of people that bumped into each other quite a bit, at occasions like concerts or venues or readings of some kind or other. And became acquainted with each other's work, and had some affinities for it, quite often. And not necessarily explicitly, but often by something less tangible really. Bill Sherman's an example. I don't write anything like him. My work, if you put it inside the same coterie with him, you'd say, well that's a bit strange, I wonder what the connection is. The connections are much more social, sometimes. And in Pierre Joris' case for instance, it was someone who was running the modern equivalent of a salon, in Tooting, where there were readings every week and it was a way of meeting lots of poets every week. I found that useful in the 1970s. And the consequences of those coteries are some of what Spanner produces. It overlaps with some of what was already going on. Edible magazine started in the 60s. New London Pride was an explicit series of poetry books that came out contemporary with it. And Aloes Books were also contemporary. Aloes was run by three people and ended up being run by two, mainly Jim Pennington and myself, and in the early days Dick Miller. Dick and I also ran I Beheld books, for an edition of three books. And it's been very much like that, very ephemerally occasioned. The different names have to do with different owners really. I started Edible magazine. Aloes Books was three people. Dick and I started Spanner, in a sense. He produced three American Spanners, eventually, Spanner NYC. New London Pride was Elaine and myself. Elaine Fisher, Elaine Harmsworth as was then. So that experience flips in and out of the Spanner experience. It's a kind of social situation. In terms of the content it's very difficult to be more elaborate than I have. I've mentioned so to speak a mixture of coteries, overlapping coteries, clearly not linked always, sometimes they link quite incidentally, and so on. So there was the Fluxus link and the two, maybe three coteries of poetry which overlapped. One around Pierre Joris and a sort of international group, that Eric was involved in as well. People who were doing things in London. One was a group of people that I had affinity for, in poetry, like Martin Thom or more recently Lissa Wolsak, so that sort of range. There was another premiss underneath Spanner, which is that everything is thought of as a working document, something you would produce, this gives you an example of how far this poet's got with this particular work. Eventually, of course, some poets never give you that, they give you something much more finished than the original intention encouraged, but still, that's just one of those things. That's how some poets prefer to work.

AD It was a radical concept, but people were scared of it when it comes to it.

AF There was an idea of samizdat. Not with the pretention of samizdat, not that we're eastern Europe, but the idea it would be something which you could get cheaply. That you would get something and it would be alive, it wouldn't be something completed. So *Place* was very much part of that, in that sense, philosophically, aesthetically, incomplete. In the process of being made. The work is abandoned, the work is not finished. It stops and starts but it doesn't come to a conclusion. Some would say it does. Not intended as such. A Spanner.

AD We talked briefly about Eric Mottram last time. I wonder if you could talk about Eric's poetry. I find it very difficult to deal with. Its surface is too complicated.

AF I think that there are moments when it's free-flowing, and moments when it feels congested. I think sometimes when he's writing, I can't remember the title properly, but I think it's *Life of a Private* or something like that, which has to do with the First World War and Georges Braque, it's very clear and much more poignant and works much better. *Local Movement* works quite well because he's using explicitly William Harvey's work on movement and other muscles, and when he's being that explicit and that out of a project it works better for me. He sometimes moves into a deliberate congealment, so that *Interrogation Rooms* that I published is intentionally difficult in places, it's intentionally congealed, he felt it was part of a political stand he wanted to make. That meant that the work's almost unreadable, quite often. How and or what the eventual judgement on that should be is not really for me to get into. Eric was a catalyst for me and useful as an educator, and helped me a lot in regard to, incidentally or otherwise, helped me with an education I didn't get prior to meeting him. And our conversations more often than not, when they weren't pedagogic, from him to me mainly, were to do with music. That's mainly where our discussions were. Although he would demand from me ideas about composition, ideas about presentation, ideas about formatting. So I did, it wasn't just a one way traffic, it was two way in that regard. He had a very strong library in some regards, particularly, obviously on American studies, particularly good on music, particularly good on some aspects of American painting. So that was very useful for me. To be more explicit about the poetry is very hard. He had interests in some work that I had less interest in. He had a lot of interest in Rilke. He tried to translate, and used to read, some of the French poets, I'm trying to remember the one he used a lot. He also read Hungarian work that was being translated for him, and had quite a strong relationship with [New] *Hungarian Quarterly*, and the people running that. So there are some aspects of his work I have an interest for, an interest in the subject, interested in materials. I've got less interest in his forms, in his compositional ways, less interest in his verse as such. I think his strengths are, I think I've partly stated what they are. I don't want to keep stating what they aren't, which is a bit negative. But Eric's strengths are to do with his knowledge, his commitment, his loyalty towards his commitment and those comparably committed, and therefore his responsibility. All of those things are very strong in the work. All of those things at one time or other come through in some of the poetry. And that's where the poetry's strongest, or where the essays are strongest. And that's where I've had the most benefit. *1922 Earth Raids,* that's right. He's very keen on the idea that, Wittgenstein, just after the *Tractatus* got published, 'Waste Land' 1922, something from Rilke 1922, it stacks up. So it's a kind of finger in the air. He's very keen on time-lines. Many teachers are, I am too. I find it quite fun to play with.

AD You can underrate list structures. You assemble lots of data mechanically and then when you look at it you can see patterns. Sometimes, anyway.

AF You can, yeah. There's an element which is almost Spenglerian, or, even worse, of something like Vico, which Joyce likes. This sort of Hindu idea that you're going to get a cycle repeating itself all the time, which I'm explicitly against. I mean, linear time's one thing and circular time's even worse! Eric's use values are to do with that business of his engagement and commitment to epistemology, and the history of ideas, and he was very clear about that, and very useful. He's somebody who put me onto Lovejoy, who's someone who's interested in that field, 40s-50s, although very old-fashioned. And Lewis Mumford would be another of his interests, Buckminster Fuller. A whole range of old-fashioned writers on Shakespeare and the Renaissance. He was very useful for me. He knew them and had read them and so on. I think I must have heard about Frances Yates from Eric, probably. People whose names I've now even lost. Like it was Eric who recommended a particular edition of the Sonnets because of the way in which it had been organised, and he's still right about that. He's someone who quite late in his life set up lunchtime workshops. He would get the workshop group of about ten people or less to explicitly read one chapter of Foucault or Bataille or something like that. We would literally sit around talking, about what is this about. That's very useful, to have that sort of energy. To some extent that's what we tried to do at the salon. It was a big influence on Pierre's salon idea. Sometimes it backfired and sometimes it collapsed. I remember it backfired rather badly once when John Digby, neo-surrealist poet, and Eric confronted each other on the Freudian content of Breton's work. They disagreed. It was a nightmare. Some of these occasions are just never going to go right. Cause they're both dogmatic. What Surrealism is or isn't. Eric was very useful in the best sense also because he knew some of the American poets quite directly because he'd been to the States. So Ginsberg would come by or Neal Cassady's wife would come by. They could be good people to meet. So I met some of the Americans. But the bottom line is, when Eric and I did our talking it was mainly about politics and music. And we disagreed a lot about poetry. And eventually didn't talk about the subject at all. Because he would not find favour with some of the people I was reading at all. It was quite interesting. I suppose we'd have agreements as well. We both read Barry MacSweeney.

AD I'm curious about this modern music now. It's something I know very little about.

AF The simple answer is that we were both interested in what was happening on the contemporary front in music. That had just been broadcast or that had just been published on record. He or I would buy something. And we would sit down and explicitly do nothing else but listen to it. And then maybe discuss it, maybe not. But what was interesting about it was we would use the fact of each other's presence to just do nothing but concentrate on listening to the music. And it was very helpful to do that, because it's something very difficult to do on your own. I suppose it's very personal, but that's how I find it. I now find it easier to do, as a consequence of that experience. In fact there are many amusing stories I could tell you about it. You'd go to a concert with Eric and he'd fall asleep. Just at the moment when everything came to an end he'd wake up while everyone was applauding and say, excellent, wasn't it, excellent! And you'd go, You were snoring for some of it! But he might say the same about me, I don't know. We did learn a lot from each other. I learnt a lot about Ferneyhough with him. He would pick up on people I was less interested in. But there would be meeting points. I think I liked Albert Ayler more than he did and I think he liked The Doors more than I did. At the two extremes. We both liked Hendrix!

Author Statements on *Place*

Intuitions and Interactions
from *Prosyncel*: page 9

Because of the nature of this work, still in the making (March 1975), I have chosen to be wide-eyed, both tired and generalising, in describing it. I would hope that any work should stand on itself—as itself.

Having noted that I have here commissioned a selection of *place* Book I [the one in *Prosyncel* pp. 44-55, ed.] and regret have been unable to find room for the current work being done in Books I and II.

The work started in 1971 and was projected for abandonment in 1980. I note two books in my library which I feel must have played a large part towards the thinking behind the work: Charles Olson's *A Special View of History*, (dated inside 1971), & Raoul Vaneigem's *The Revolution of Everyday Life*, (dated 1972).

What might also be of interest is how its arrangement structurally (as yet unpublished) has been conceived.

It appears now that the concept was to write a work primarily as an address that came out of my reading concerns at the time of writing, that would reflect upon each other in such a way as to make, as Keats, then Heisenberg and later Olson noted, Uncertainty. Or better, in Keats' terms, a balance by way of "negative capability".

In my terms then, a statement or fact laid on page five of Book I would find SHADING on page 95 of Book III. This reflecting nature brought about the structure. It is generally thematic from *place* I thru to XXXVII in Book I, and from LXXXI to XXXV in Book III. In the meanwhile parts of Books II & IV were getting content by way of 'excursionary reflection' from XXXVIII to XXXX and from XXXIV to XXXXII.

place XXXI then forms Book V (in the centre of that structure) but does not end the writing—merely the structure, so that new reading might instruct me to add further SHADING to any other part, indicated wherever it was placed by the place number, which becomes not chronologic nor hierarchical. The diagrammic showing of this would be a rotating sphere, say, receiving energies and giving off energies as the earth or body might from many parts that in the receiving or despatching caused change (not Doubt) in the sphere itself—in the parts that came to and went from it.

Having given that I would hope reading of *place* could be of the same 'energy-quantity' wherever entered and that all it would come down to for the attentive reader is response to and from the reading—what takes (or does not fully take) his eye/ear at the point at which he/she received the page and by accumulative shading, uncertainty and kinesis, reaches a view of the whole that might give some degree of use—light into what it's all for.
In theme, the not too attentive reader will have noticed from the title (as yet unfixed) place of living, locality, house borough city country planet. Place of being, body, breath, brain. place of receipt and despatch. So it wouldn't just be a matter of the local but a type-up of the position **estrangled** from it.

**

Unpolished Mirrors serial 'H' includes a note called 'a map of approaches' (reprinted below) which describes the design of *Place*.

a map of approaches: one describes how the numbered parts 1-102 are distributed across the 5 books.

a map of approaches: two

reading through the books following the 'place' numbers indicated at the page tops of *Place Book One* and *Stane*, in the contents list of *Becoming*, and by subtitle in other works.

the initial schema read *place* 1-37 as the first movement, *place* 45-81 as the second, 38-40 as the third, 42-44 as the fourth, and *place* 41 as the fifth.

after interweaving and cutting movements gradually completed making this reading a difficult undertaking.
this is made plain by two examples in the published work:—

the place number for the first part of *Fire-place* was 76, later interweaved by place 50 and 78 completing the place number to:

76
----
50 & 78

Unpolished Mirrors in its initial state was *Place* 38, however, publication was deliberately withheld after the first few showings, and was later transformed by being informed by 'place' 41, thus an interweave of movements two and five.

the coding was of more use to the author than the reader as place showings were being made during the course of its making.

the numbers were author-codes concerned with particular attention-areas. they also refer to resources.

a map of approaches: three
sketches showing some of the notions involved in book and 'place' patterning are shown on page 100.A.

they show how a move from book one to three and four, interferes with book two, and how book five eventually informs book two.

another sketch briefly shows a visual clip of the *place* number pattern.

a map of approaches: four (considered void)

simply reading place through from page one in book one to the last page in *Becoming*, or in *Unpolished Mirrors*, dropping out to "cut-in" material like *Grampians, Lakes, Eclipse, William Rufus* or *Birds Locked in the Roof* en route.

one of the purposes of the 'cut-ins' was to ensure breakage of chronologic or developmental apparency offered in works of process; as well as to suggest to the reader a different set of simultaneous activities that were impinging on and leading from Place.

a map of approaches: five
reading the sets as entities.

these sets, like approach two, have complexed.

it is possible to get a reading of place Book One as one set interweaved by *Lakes*. but *Becoming*, for instance, carries four sets broken up and juxtaposed, interfering with each other and emphasising the discontinuous intentions in the process of the work. reading the sets as entities thus misreads the work.

a map of approaches: six

readers have asked whether I consider the work as including single poems as well as less worked material. they have asked whether an arbitrary page selection would offer sufficient readability.

these matters of genre will be left for another occasion.

* *

The last page of serial H also includes a list of parts of *Place*, given in modified form below:

I *Place* Book One
Hooks
II/ *Eros: Father: Pattern*
III *Stane*
IIII Becoming
V *Becoming*
Fire-Place
Docking
Convergences, in Place, of the Play
William Rufus is still in progress with the work *Faust Undamned*.

—as well as, of course, *Unpolished Mirrors*.

Notes from Inside Published Books

Unpolished Mirrors
(note from the 1985 book, partly paraphrased)
In 1979 the first serial of *Unpolished Mirrors* was published carrying the subtitle 'being *Place* book II informed by *Place* book V'. The *Place* project, started in 1971, culminates with *Unpolished Mirrors*.

The title derives from a printing error in Frances A. Yates' *Shakespeare's Last Plays: a New Approach*, published in 1975. She quotes Ben Jonson's preface 'To the reader' to *The Alchemist*, which, in the correct version, includes "For it is only the disease of the unskilful to think rude works greater than polished; and scattered more numerous than composed."

The 1985 Reality Studios book does not include serials F, G and H, which were published separately, also by Reality Studios.

[For "serial" read "serial instalment". There is no *Place* Book II apart from this version re-mixed with Book V; and from *Eros Father Pattern*, which is credited in *UM* as Book II, containing *Place* 1-5. "Numerous" in that text actually means 'in metre'.]

Eros Father Pattern
Place, Book II. Place 38 39 40 has been separated into three sets. (*Unpolished Mirrors*=38, *Convergences*=40, *Eros Father Pattern*=39).

Becoming
Becoming includes four sets, being most of '*Place* Book IIII: the fourth movement' and much of 'Book V: the fifth movement'. The sets include work already moving out in a new voice, as well as having cut-in new work. It is unclear from this typescript that part of the fifth movement in the last sets of this symphony takes place *with* the third movement to be published in typescript during 1979. [i.e. *Stane*, ed.]

[[William Rufus lost?
Splashed Ponds leading from *Unpolished Mirrors*, lost?]]

Movements	*Book*
First *Place* 1-37	One
Second *Stane* 45-81	Three
Third *Unpolished Mirrors* 38	}
Convergence 40	} Two
Eros Father Pattern 39	}
Fourth *Utter* 42	}
Logos Mother Matter 43	} Four
METE 44	}
Fifth *Gait*	Five

Move
(to be published with *Unpolished Mirrors*)

from *Long Shout to Kernewek*

Part 4
August 1965

St.John the homeless sea gulls are turning to
the methodist chapels
"The word of God is preached on the Lord's Day at 3 p.m., God willing"
   the Western National's losing business

Please return   your attraction is needed i saw a
badger dead on the cliff today   time is not immaterial
i can see the badger flowing from a sewage pipe into
your starving body   i can see sinking match-boxes with
your name   i can see hooded capes without bodies
i can see brown copper blood turning beaches black and
green

Can I hear St.John?   are you re-assembling off the coast
of Brazil?   Brazil doesn't need you they're hungry
here too because of your ascension   the bed &
breakfast VACANCY signs   queues on the wharves
they're thinking of pouring burning tin down their desolate mines
i'm tired of eating stale bridge rolls are you hungry
St.John?   we've got you Penwith grouse for Christmas
they're rebuilding Mousehole's pagan hall on the quay
they needed a clock Sinjun, that's all they wanted

You're back St.John! i know you are   the lamp posts
are sparkling   the petrol signs are lit but take care
the vultures are with you   i can see them disguised
on the rooftops   walking the cobbles of sidewalks
concealed in cloth caps and rain coats   some have cameras
careful St.John   your disciples are joining Wren's
churches in Pennsylvania   your monks left you decades
past   they are not monks that ring your bells
that lament in your grounds   i smell money and
victorian feet   or grass after rain   but it's not grass
John   it's a suspicious smell

Sinjun. the other saints have fallen   the monks of
St.Just bathe in folk songs of wine   the monks of
St.Ives shark and surf   their pottery St.John it's
not labelled in latin   they're selling St.Austell's
beer to the tourists and me

Sinjun   you're stubborn   they don't want
a religious settlement   they want careful reminders
of the past   chains of authentic museums   oh boy
i'm excited   please be a museum St.John   i want to
be your attendant

Part 5
August 1965

this is the middle moon
out from this place the head expands
inside this place are the convergences felt

cooking-house fat   cigar smoke   a new mist-hang
not so different   'til i touched it

smelt its   density

villages painted with lies
this is not the first & last place
garage tea-shop gift-shop
and San Francisco isn't the last bay

sailors crossed the world back to here

                        bird hanging from the wind's fast cloak
               Elake   you'd be there   if you were bird
                        carrying the mist in the bag
                                of your body
in London tins of fog and spring rain for sale
the rhythm of the trains controlling the evening's tiredness

between Mount's Bay & the Scilly Isles

                woods, meadows, arable land & 140 parish churches
                            SUNKEN

at the five fathom line   Gear Rock
              half-a-mile off-coast   between Pensans and Mousehole

Mount's Bay's stone-axe factories   supplier to
                    Salisbury and Okehampton
                            BURIED

Cornwall 2000 bc   supplier to Britain
the axes to Wessex
at Stonehenge 2 specimens from Marazion
at Bridlington, Yorks. another

Cornwall main supplier greenstone axes
the outcrops of St.Ives   and from Trenow nr. Marazion

the land inbetween the Duchy of Cornwall & the Scillies
Lyonesse   lost or never was

4000 years ago   Scilly Isles double their present size
                            SINKING

And on the shore at the Red Sea   The Red men   Canaanites
The Phoenicians   the first men-of-war
the first alphabet
                            the first giants
striding onto the Cassiterides of Greece and Phoenicia
the Scillies and Cornwall
                            onto these half-fabulous
                tin islands in the mists and tides of northern seas

to this kingdom of Vortigerns the viking   446 ad

7000 years ago   "Syrian" communities
the phoenicians   a dark-white stock
spreading round the shores of the Mediterranean
                                    to Britain

from 4000 bc an access to copper and tin
                       from the pockets of Cornwall
in 1965, 2000 mines abandoned and 2 working

first Phoenicia   then the Black Death   now London
                                   CORNWALL RAVAGED

through the integration of anima
the sharing of wives
vision the foursquare castle
and from gold produce copper

alchemists John Dee & Edward Kelley 1593-7 ad.

Synopsis

ICA interview   Theory of performance art. Fluxshoe.
Dr Kiss interview   conceptual art in the early 70s
Prosyncel excerpts information on other works (*Blood Bone Brain, The Art of Flight, ABCD*); on controlled permutation with reference to Jackson Mac Low; statements on *Place*
Alembic talk   Random permutation as a mimic of intuition. vocabulary as a conceptual map (of permutable parts); Renaissance Neoplatonism; Egyptian source of 'blood bone brain'. mathematical form in Renaissance poetry. Feedback. Conscious intervention.
Alembic interview   John Michell and occultist archaeology. processual and procedural. Mirroring in *Place*.
Angel Exhaust interview   school experiences; Tree Birst; mirroring in *Place*
Victoria Sheppard interview performance practice; relations with the audience
Scott Thurston interview 'mirroring' in *Place*; on method; on setting up a situation in which a poem may occur; on boxes and their names; Blake, Beuys
Shape Geometrical schemas mirrored in poetry; symbolic space; Neoplatonism; serpent forces; artificial landscapes; on growth and form
Lulham 01 On Mutabilitie controlled permutation in *Gravity*; mirroring
Lulham 02 improvisation in music; improvised dialogue; shared ideas of poetry; Badgers and the Bellman
Lulham 03 *Stane*; the use of resources in *Stane*; poetry and the history of ideas; drawing practice; constructivism; Peter Lanyon
Lulham 04 Mirrors for Waste Heat 'mirroring' in *Gravity*; information on other works (*Blood Bone Brain, Creek in the Ceiling Beam, ABCD*); *Spanner*; Eric Mottram

Long Shout to Kernewek   Britain as the periphery of a mediterranean world-system; accelerated development on partly colonised coasts
Kernewek is an adjective meaning 'Cornish'; as a substantive it must mean "the Cornish language". Cornish, a dead P-Celtic language, is very similar to Breton and similar to Welsh.

Thomas Bushell (b.1594) was a servant of Francis Bacon who on Bacon's death became a hermit, out on Lundy Island in the Bristol Channel, for three years. Between 1628 and 1635, he constructed a magic garden known as the Enstone Marvels. A visitor to Enstone described him as "A mad gim-crack yet hereditary to these hermeticall and proiecticall Undertakers." His involvement with a Utopian settlement in the Lambeth Marsh was during the 1650s. The combination of 'gim-crack' (i.e. inventor) and Hermeticall (i.e. practicer of Neoplatonist magic) amounts to "avant-gardiste" in the terms of the 17th century.

Cross-references

procedural and processual
mirroring
Neoplatonism
Kernewek
Spenser
John Michell
Blood Bone Brain

Sources

Prosyncel preface
Statements on 'Place' either from *Prosyncel* or from notes inside the original volumes
Fluxshoe interview transcribed from tape
Interview with Dr RAC Kiss, 1974: from *Prosyncel*
Interview with editors of *Alembic* was published in *Alembic*
talk for Alembic transcribed from tape
Interview with Adrian Clarke was published in *Angel Exhaust*
Interview with Scott Thurston: transcript supplied by S Thurston
Interview with Victoria Sheppard: transcript supplied by V Sheppard.

The Interviewers

Scott Thurston's most recent books are *Internal Rhyme* (Shearsman, 2010), and *Talking Poetics* (Shearsman, 2011). He edits *The Radiator*, a journal of poetics, edited *The Salt Companion to Geraldine Monk*, and lectures at the University of Salford. He has published widely on innovative poetry. This interview first appeared in *Poetry Salzburg Review* 3 (Autumn 2002), pp. 10-39. Many thanks are due to Wolfgang Görtschacher for his kind permission to reprint it here.

Eric Mottram (1924-94) was professor of American Studies at King's College, London and an organiser of the alternative poetry. He published many volumes of poetry.

R.A.C. Kiss could not be contacted at the time of publication.

Peter Barry is professor of English at the University of Wales, Aberystwyth and author of *Contemporary British Poetry and the City* (2000) and *Poetry Wars* (2006).

Ken Edwards is a poet, a former editor of *Reality Studios* magazine, and is publisher of Reality Street Editions.

Adrian Clarke is a poet and former editor of *Angel Exhaust*.

Victoria Sheppard contributed to a research project on UK poetry performance at the University of Southampton, where she also completed a PhD on contemporary poetry.

Andrew Duncan is a student of speech phenomena.

Sir Aylmer Firebrace is a textual artefact of the 1970s.

www.ingramcontent.com/pod-product-compliance
Lightning Source LLC
Chambersburg PA
CBHW022009160426
43197CB00007B/348